# Joseph and Potiphar's Wife

# Joseph and Potiphar's Wife

## in World Literature

*An Anthology of the Story of
the Chaste Youth and the Lustful Stepmother*

Translated by Various Hands
and Edited with Commentary by

## John D. Yohannan

*A New Directions Book*

## ACKNOWLEDGMENTS

In a project that cuts across so many specialized disciplines as this one, it is difficult to make adequate acknowledgment of one's indebtedness; but I have tried in the Bibliographical Notes to credit my main sources and at the same time to provide leads for further study by those who wish to pursue the subject.

I wish to express my gratitude to the Comparative Literature Society of Waseda University in Tokyo for allowing me to try out some of the material of this book in lecture form during my Fulbright year there in 1963-64. A lecture delivered at The City College in the spring of 1965 and one at Alfred University in the spring of 1966 gave me the benefit of criticism of other portions of the material of this book. I thank the editors of *East-West Review,* published at Doshisha University in Kyoto, for the re-use of material from an article entitled "Joseph in Egypt—and Elsewhere" which I contributed to their Winter 1965 issue. I thank in particular my friend Professor Sakae Morioka of Kyushu University in Japan for making available to me his own translations of several of the Buddhist versions of the Kunala story at a time when I could not otherwise obtain English translations. My former student, Thea Brodsky Amr, at my instigation several years ago anticipated a portion of this study in a paper written for a classics course, and in the process unearthed two bibliographical items for which I am grateful.

I thank the New York State Department of Education, in particular its Foreign Area Studies section, for a grant during the summer of 1963 that made some time available for initiat-

iv

ing work on this project. My gratitude also goes to the librarians everywhere who have helped me, especially to those at The City College, at Columbia University, and in the Oriental Division of the New York Public Library; to Mr. Jerome Fried, formerly of New Directions, and to Mr. Fred Martin, my present editor, for constructive direction; and finally to my wife for constant advice and for assistance with the manuscript.

For permission to reprint copyrighted material in this volume the editor and publishers are grateful to the following:

for approximately the first half of W. M. F. Petrie's "Anpu and Bata" reprinted from his *Egyptian Tales* by permission of Methuen and Co., Ltd., London, 1913. All Rights Reserved.

for the Ian Fletcher and D. S. Carne-Ross adaptation of Euripides' *Hippolytus,* reprinted from a typescript made for broadcast by the "BBC Third Programme," April 27, 1958. All Rights Reserved.

for William Packard's translation of Racine's *Phèdre,* reprinted with the author's permission from *Racine: Phèdre,* Samuel French, Inc., New York, 1966, Copyright © 1966, by William Packard.

for Kenneth Rexroth's *Phaedra,* Copyright 1951 by Kenneth Rexroth. Reprinted from his *Beyond the Mountains,* New Directions, Norfolk, Conn., 1951 by permission of the author and of City Lights Books of San Francisco.

for Winifred Stephens' translation of "The Eyes of Kunala" reprinted, by permission of the publishers, from *Legends of Indian Buddhism,* Wisdom of the East Series, John Murray, London, 1911. All Rights Reserved.

for Faubion Bowers' translation of *Gappo and His Daughter Tsuji,* reprinted by permission of the translator from his *Japanese Theatre,* Hermitage House, New York, 1952, Copyright by Faubion Bowers, 1952.

for "Siyawush and Sudaba," reprinted by permission of Routledge and Kegan Paul, Ltd., from *The Shahnama of Firdausi,* Done into English by Arthur George Warner and Edmond Warner, Vol. II, published by Kegan Paul, Trench, Trübner & Co., Ltd., London, 1906. All Rights Reserved.

for John E. Keller's translation of *The Book of the Wiles of Women,* M.L.A. Translation Series No. 2, Copyright © University of North Carolina Press, Chapel Hill, N.C., 1956.

Reprinted by permission of the University of North Carolina Press.

for excerpts quoted from Thomas Mann's *Joseph in Egypt,* published by Alfred A. Knopf, Inc., New York, 1938, and *Joseph the Provider,* published by Alfred A. Knopf, Inc., New York, 1944. Reprinted by permission of Alfred A. Knopf, Inc., Copyright 1938, 1944, and of Secker and Warburg, Ltd. All Rights Reserved.

for quotations from Howard E. Hugo's translation of Racine's Preface to *Phèdre* in *World Masterpieces,* Vol. II, edited by Maynard Mack and others, published by W. W. Norton, Inc., New York, 1956. Copyright © 1965, 1956 by W. W. Norton & Company, Inc. Reprinted by permission of the publishers.

John D. Yohannan
The City College
New York, N.Y.
March 1968

For Caye and Tim and Tom

## Casts of Characters

| SELECTION | CHASTE YOUTH | LUSTFUL STEPMOTHER | PUNISHING FATHER |
|---|---|---|---|
| 1. "Anpu and Bata" | Bata | Anpu's wife | Anpu (Bata's brother) |
| 2. Genesis 39 | Joseph | Potiphar's wife | Potiphar |
| * 3. Euripides' *Hippolytus* | Hippolytus | Phaedra | Theseus |
| *† 4. Racine's *Phèdre* | Hippolytus | Phèdre | Theseus |
| 5. Rexroth's *Phaedra* | Hippolytus | Phaedra | Theseus |
| 6. *Koran* | Yusuf | Prince's wife | Prince |
| * 7. Jami's *Yusuf and Zulaikha* | Yusuf | Zulaikha | Vizier |
| 8. Arnold's "Potiphar's Wife" | Yusuf | Asenath | Itfir |
| † 9. "The Eyes of Kunala" | Kunala | Tishya-rakshita | Asoka |
| † 10. *Gappo and His Daughter Tsuji* | Shuntokumaru | Lady Tamate | Gappo (Lady Tamate's father) |
| * 11. "Siyawush and Sudaba" | Siyawush | Sudaba | Kai Kaus |
| 12. *Book of the Wiles of Women* | Unnamed boy | Queen | King Alcos of Judea |
| * Mann's "Joseph" Novels | Osarsiph | Mut-em-enet | Petepre |
| Gibbon's *Decline and Fall* | Crispus | Fausta | Constantine |

\* Also has the character of the nurse attendant upon the Lustful Stepmother

† Also has the character of a fiancee of the Chaste Youth

# TABLE OF CONTENTS

# Diagram Showing
## Partial Distribution in World Literature
## of the Story of Joseph and Potiphar's Wife

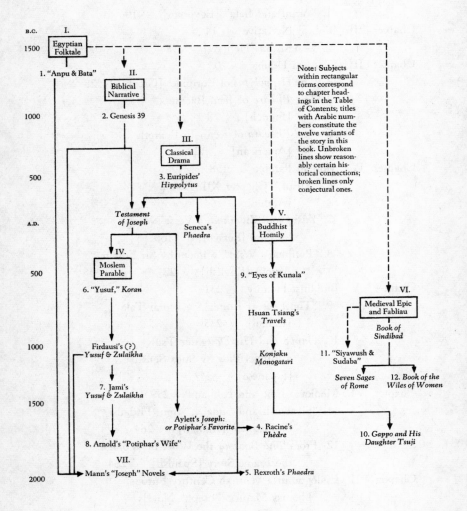

B.C.

**I.**
Egyptian Folktale

1500

1. "Anpu & Bata"

**II.**
Biblical Narrative

2. Genesis 39

1000

**III.**
Classical Drama

3. Euripides' *Hippolytus*

500

*Testament of Joseph*

Seneca's *Phaedra*

A.D.

**V.**
Buddhist Homily

**IV.**
Moslem Parable

500

6. "Yusuf," *Koran*

9. "Eyes of Kunala"

Hsuan Tsiang's *Travels*

**VI.**
Medieval Epic and Fabliau

*Book of Sindibad*

Firdausi's (?) *Yusuf & Zulaikha*

1000

11. "Siyawush & Sudaba"

*Konjaku Monogatari*

7. Jami's *Yusuf & Zulaikha*

*Seven Sages of Rome*

12. *Book of the Wiles of Women*

1500

Aylett's *Joseph: or Potiphar's Favorite*

4. Racine's *Phèdre*

10. *Gappo and His Daughter Tsuji*

8. Arnold's "Potiphar's Wife"

**VII.**

Mann's "Joseph" Novels

5. Rexroth's *Phaedra*

2000

Note: Subjects within rectangular forms correspond to chapter headings in the Table of Contents; titles with Arabic numbers constitute the twelve variants of the story in this book. Unbroken lines show reasonably certain historical connections; broken lines only conjectural ones.

x

## ✠ Chapter I ✠
## Prologue in the Ancient Near East:
## The Archetypal Folktale

A handsome young man of unusually chaste character is accosted one day in his home by his slightly older stepmother. She entreats him to lie with her. From this proposal he recoils with horror, indignantly asserting his loyalty to his father and his dedication to God. Enraged at his rejection of her offered love, she accuses him to her husband of attempted rape. Although disposed to believe in the youth's innocence, the husband submits him to trial and punishment. When his innocence is later established, he is restored to a new and greater fortune and the lustful stepmother is given her just deserts.

This brief plot sketches the familiar lineaments of the story of Joseph and Potiphar's wife, so called after the episode in the Biblical narrative of the sons of Jacob as it is related in Genesis 39. Essentially the same story, although with different casts of characters and with minor variations in the plot, is frequently told elsewhere in world literature. The analogues brought together in this volume range over thirty-three centuries of human history and fairly encircle the globe. The oldest recorded of these is the Egyptian folktale of the two brothers, Anpu and Bata, and the former's unnamed wife. From the classical world we have the legend (embodied in drama) of Hippolytus and Phaedra and the latter's husband, Theseus. The Moslems give us a variation of the Joseph story which they elevate into a full-length verse-novel about Yusuf and Zulaikha, as the main characters are called. The Buddhists tell about Kunala, youthful son of the emperor Asoka, and about Tishya-rakshita, the latter's scheming wife. From the Zoroastrian tradition, as sieved through the Iranian epic *Shah-nama*, we get the episode of the attempted seduction of the knight Siyawush by Sudaba, the concubine of his father, King Kai Kaus. The tone of these and other variations on the theme ranges from the didactically moral through the somberly tragic, the lyrically mystical and the humorously ironic to the flippantly diverting. One would be hard put to find a story that has had a wider circulation among more varied audiences over a longer period of time than this one.

Inevitably a question arises regarding the relationship of these similar stories, but philology does not have a complete answer. The problem is complex, and it should not be over-simplified even in a study like the present one, which is more concerned with resemblances and differences among the stories than with their historical relationship. It would be safe to say that the resemblances are sometimes of the sort that one finds among siblings and close relatives within the human species, and at other times merely the sort that exists between any one person and his so-called "double." That is to say, some people look alike because of a common parentage, and others merely by chance. To put it in literary terms, some stories resemble each other *because* they were diffused from a common source, and others *despite* the fact that they were independently created.

A century or so ago, when comparative studies in language, literature, and religion were in their infancy, it was a favorite notion that most of the stories current in the West had originated in India, whence they had been distributed westward by Crusaders, navigators, commercial travelers, and itinerant Moslem narrators. If perchance a Chinese or other Far Eastern variant of a story turned up, it could be accounted for by supposing a similar eastward movement out of India, of which the chief vehicle would be the Buddhist religion. This theory is not so popular today as it formerly was, because many stories have been found in areas where it was not possible to account for them by historical transmission. When, as in the case of our present story, an Egyptian analogue was discovered that was older than any known Indian variant, one could better argue for an African than an Indian origin. Andrew Lang indeed said of the tale of the two brothers:

> We ask no more than this one *Maerchen* of ancient Egypt to upset the whole theory that India was the original home of the *Contes*. . . .

More acceptable today is the theory of the independent multiple creation of tales, or "polygenesis." This theory makes it unnecessary to trace, for example, an Irish folktale about a Chaste Youth and a Lustful Stepmother to an Indian, an Egyptian, or any other source; it is sufficient to attribute its appearance in Ireland to a familial experience common to all mankind. As Sir Richard Burton said in noting an Arabian Nights analogue to the present story, "Such things happen in everyday life, and the situation has recommended itself to the folklore of all peoples."

This is not to deny that literature can as well borrow from other literature as from life. For example, Lord Byron, noticing that his hero Don Juan is about to be tempted by the harem beauty Gulbeyaz, immediately recalls literary analogies, citing not only the familiar parallels from antiquity, but also one from a recent novel, Henry Fielding's *Joseph Andrews*:

> Remember, or (if you can not) imagine,
>    Ye! who have kept your chastity when young,
> While some more desperate dowager has been waging
>    Love with you, and been in the dog-days stung
> By your refusal, recollect her raging!
>    Or recollect all that was said or sung
> On such a subject; then suppose the face
> Of a young downright beauty in this case!
>
> Suppose,—but you already have supposed,
>    The spouse of Potiphar, the Lady Booby,
> Phaedra, and all which story has disclosed
>    Of good examples; pity that so few by
> Poets and private tutors are exposed,
>    To educate—ye youths of Europe—you by!
> But when you have supposed the few we know,
> You can't suppose Gulbeyaz' angry brow.
>
>                   (*Don Juan*, V, 130-131)

Indeed, not only literature, but even life, will on occasion imitate art. Edward Gibbon reports the Emperor Constantine's murder of his son Crispus at the instigation of his wife Fausta as a renewal, "in the palace of Constantine [of] the ancient tragedy of Hippolytus and of Phaedra." Impressed with the analogy, Gibbon adds:

> Like the daughter of Minos, the daughter of Maximian accused her son-in-law of an incestuous attempt of the chastity of his father's wife, and easily obtained, from the jealousy of the emperor, a sentence of death against a young prince whom she considered with reason as the most formidable rival of her own children. . . .

It is sufficient to say here that, among some of the analogues of this story, there is a demonstrable historical connection, and that among others one can only *conjecture* a connection. The accompanying diagram attempts to show this.
(See page x.) Since the Egyptian folktale is the oldest recorded analogue, it may—hypothetically, at least—be regarded
as the Adam of the lineage. It *might* have begotten the Genesis
story, the classical legend, the Buddhist homily, and, for that
matter, all of the other variants included in this volume. But
it has only one *provable* historical connection, and that is with
the most recent analogue, Thomas Mann's "Joseph" novels,
which consciously and directly borrow from it. However, within the several major categories into which the analogues have
here been grouped, it is easy to see direct lines of historical
descent; for example, from Euripides to Racine to Rexroth,
or from the *Koran* to Jami to Sir Edwin Arnold. Furthermore,
since both the Biblical and the classical stories were known
to the Moslems, there is almost no doubt that these contributed
to the formation of the Moslem variants. Finally, as there is
a natural affinity among all similar stories, it can fairly safely
be assumed that, as the various analogues moved about in the
course of history, they did not fail to affect one another by
that inevitable literary cross-fertilization which keeps stories
as "impure" as human races.

✠

What, we may ask, are the basic elements of the universal
story we know best as that of Joseph and Potiphar's wife? Several attempts have been made to get at the genus without the
bias of any one of the species, but they have not been very
successful. Maurice Bloomfield the Sanskritist sought to reduce
the various analogues to an abstraction, calling it the tale of
the Fortunate Youth and the Would-be-adulterous Stepmother.
The article in which he used this appellation, however (addressed as it was to Western readers), acknowledged the best-
known analogue in its very title: "Joseph and Potiphar in
Hindu Fiction." For the same reason, in the subtitle of the
present volume, "The Chaste Youth and the Lustful Stepmother" is not quite adequate. For there are always analogues
which do not fit into the pattern of the abstraction. Either the
youth is not entirely fortunate (Hippolytus can hardly be so

regarded), or the lustful woman is not really a stepmother (as in both the Egyptian tale and the Biblical narrative), and so on. Donald Keene's treatment of the subject avoids some difficulties but gets into others; his essay "The Hippolytus Triangle, East and West" omits almost entirely the Biblical and the Moslem accounts.

Perhaps the only scientific mode of classification is that employed by Stith Thompson in his *Motif-Index of Folk-Literature,* which reduces stories to their dominant motifs. He defines "motif" as the smallest element in a tale having power to persist in tradition. Thus, instances of the Joseph and Potiphar's wife motif from various stories are listed under the general heading of "Deceptions" and in a subsection on "False Accusations." From this there is a cross reference to instances of the Hippolytus legend, which, however, are classified under "Lustful Stepmother" in a subsection on "Illicit Sexual Relations." Unfortunately, this separation of the two best-known analogues of the universal story flies in the face of all tradition, which has been inclined to bring them together. Thompson's system of classification, being analytic rather than synthetic, thus does not make for a proper definition of the basic story that we are here discussing.

It is even difficult to see why Thompson himself elsewhere denotes one of his *Tales of the North American Indian* ("The Jealous Father") as a Potiphar's wife motif. The reader may judge for himself:

> Once there was an old man named Aioswe who had two wives. When his son by one of these women began to grow up, Aioswe became jealous of him. One day he went off to hunt and when he came back, found marks on one of the women (the co-wife of his son's mother) which proved to him that his son had been on terms of intimacy with her.

The story proceeds to report how the father thereafter sought unsuccessfully to get rid of his son, the boy's *presumed* innocence always saving him. Now in this story, as in no other analogue, it is the father and not the stepmother who makes the accusation. Moreover, it is not a demonstrably false accusation. The father's jealousy remains the dominant motif rather than the stepmother's passion, which in this case is not even evident.

Any attempt to define the character of the story of the Chaste Youth and the Lustful Stepmother must avoid blurring it with any merely triangular or Oedipal family situation. Donald Keene momentarily considers as an analogue but then properly rejects the famous episode in the Japanese novel *The Tale of Genji* which relates the seduction by Genji of his father's favorite concubine, Fujitsubo. In a true Potiphar's wife story (as in the Hippolytus legend, with which Keene is making the comparison), there must of course be no seduction but only an attempt—and by the youth not even an attempt! For this reason, too, it would seem a mistake to regard Eugene O'Neill's *Desire Under the Elms* as a true analogue, as has recently been done in a book on the Hippolytus legend. In O'Neill's play the young stepmother, Abbie, does not make a false accusation to her husband, Ephraim Cabot, for in fact his son Eben *has* seduced her and *is* the father of her child. In only one analogue in this volume is there a sexual union between the Chaste Youth and the Lustful Stepmother, and that is in Kenneth Rexroth's *Phaedra*. It would be rather difficult, however, to deny to any form of the Hippolytus legend its proper status as a variant on the Joseph and Potiphar's wife theme.

In a comment on Near Eastern and Far Eastern analogues of the story, N. M. Penzer approximates a satisfactory definition. He cites three proposed forms of the plot:

1. the woman tempts and the man rejects
2. the woman falsely accuses the man of having made overtures
3. the woman tempts and the man succumbs

The last of these is patently wrong and Penzer correctly rejects it later. The two "forms" left, however, are not alternate forms of the story but only portions of it. Moreover, a third element would be required to complete it; namely: "the man is unfairly punished but finally vindicated." The three elements together, in fact, give us the basic motifs of the story of Joseph and Potiphar's wife.

The universal story, although frequently denoted by the name of only one or two main characters, obviously needs a third major character to effect the youth's punishment. In some of the important variants, this third person has the highest social position: Potiphar is Pharaoh's captain of the guard, Theseus is a great Athenian hero, Asoka is a famous Indian monarch, Kai Kaus is the Iranian King of Kings, etc. This punishing father figure, however, must be free to punish either his son or his wife or both. Some of the analogues add a fourth character, a nurse attendant upon the stepmother and her accomplice in crime, and even a fifth character, a fiancée of the Chaste Youth.

The motive of the temptation may be pure lust, as in most of the cases, or genuine love, as in a few, or a concern for the succession of the stepmother's own children to the high office of the father. The relative importance assigned to these motives, which are sometimes combined, produces considerably different effects in the various analogues, as will be demonstrated.

The chastity of the youth is an essential factor in most of the variants, even though it is not always identically motivated or equally compelling. In most instances it is not inspired exclusively by asceticism, but results from a fear of either the earthly or the heavenly father, or from a concern for social morality. So far is the youth from being a permanent devotee of chastity that he on occasion marries not only one other woman but even two.

The incest phobia plays a part, although not a major part, in the story. The youth is likely to apply the mother tabu to his stepmother, but she seldom shares his moral anxiety. More often, a generalized sense of the sinfulness of the relationship replaces the strict tabu against incest. Consequently, the father may move to his dispensing of justice with equal fervor whether it is the sinful wife he is punishing or the supposedly sinful son. In the Japanese puppet play, it is the father of Lady Tamate and not of her stepson who takes on the role of the punishing father.

Finally, the youth must somehow survive the punishment, the ordeal, or the exile in order to vindicate his status as what Bloomfield calls the Fortunatus type. Only in the classical analogue is the youth killed, and even there one variant of the legend reports him subsequently transported to an immortal life.

Beyond these basic elements and these few dramatis personae common to all the analogues, the authors of our several stories improvise with a loving regard for the variations of local

color and local point of view, as the discussion of the several
categories will show.

✠

The truly archetypal story in the genus here under consideration—if "archetypal" is indeed to mean the oldest—is the
Egyptian folktale of "Anpu and Bata," first discovered in the
mid-nineteenth century in a papyrus now in the British
Museum. The manuscript once belonged to Seti II, a monarch
of the XIXth Dynasty who reigned in Egypt just before 1200
B.C. The earlier portions of the story it tells, however, are said to
date from the XVIIIth Dynasty, which would take them back
in time to the historical Joseph's sojourn in the land of the
Nile. This would permit speculation (but only speculation)
that the Hebrew account took its Potiphar's wife motif from
the simple Egyptian tale then current. It has also been conversely reasoned that the historical Joseph's encounter with
Potiphar's wife—duly recorded by Egyptian scribes—could have
provided the materials for the subsequent Egyptian folktale,
as well as for the Bible story when it came to be written. In
the present state of our knowledge, it is important to be hypothetical about this relationship.

The entire story of "Anpu and Bata" has numerous motifs
that make it a veritable mine of folklore, such as, for example,
the talking cattle in the portion here given. If, as has been
suggested, these motifs were for the most part added as an
embroidery upon the simple domestic tale at a later time, then
indeed this analogue differs from all others in its lack of sophistication and literary polish. For these qualities it substitutes
the merits of vigor and natural charm. Its pious moralizing is
ingratiatingly simple; mainly it tells a tale of swift action.

And yet it provides us with the basic motifs and the essential characters for the universal story. Bata, the Chaste Youth,
does not have the sharp intelligence of Joseph, but he has a
strong sense of duty. He is without the aristocratic lineage of
the Greek Hippolytus, but like the latter he is devoted to his
patron deity, the sun god Ra Harakhti. Not so handsome as
Kunala in the Buddhist homily, he has greater physical
strength, which is just as capable of getting him into trouble
with the lustful stepmother (in this case, sister-in-law). In his
low-class origin (the English translator warms with enthusiasm

for his solid fellaheen virtues), he is unlike most of his counterparts in this volume, who are either royalty or aristocracy.

Bata's older brother Anpu, who is given the father role, behaves with the same outraged dignity as Theseus in the Greek legend, and he repents as readily when he discovers his error. Also, with the same speed as King Asoka or the King of Judea in later variants, he turns his wrath against the woman. She, in turn, is the hussy of the Old Testament story or of the medieval fabliau, and is unnamed here as in the Bible. When her evil deed is uncovered, she gets her deserved punishment without much ceremony.

Until then, however, she speaks her lines with the authority established by numerous repetitions of the episode in dozens of later variants. "There is great strength in thee, for I see thy might every day," she says provocatively to Bata. The perceptive author adds: "And her heart knew him with the knowledge of youth." Thus we are immediately made aware of the closer affinity in age between these two than between husband and wife—an important factor in the basic story. Her invitation to the youth anticipates the more famous "Lie with me!" of the Bible. Her words are: "Come, stay with me, and it shall be well for thee, and I will make for thee beautiful garments." This amusing ploy is to appear again nearly three millennia later in Jami's fifteenth-century Persian poem, and still later in Thomas Mann's *Joseph in Egypt*. Bata's reply also takes the classically simple form of raising the mother tabu: "Behold, thou art to me as a mother, thy husband is to me as a father, for he, who is older than I, has brought me up. What is this wickedness that thou hast said to me?"

We thus have the temptation and its rejection; later, the false accusation, the threatened punishment, and the flight into exile; and, finally, on the heels of Bata's prophecy of his own ultimate restoration to his rights, the execution of the wife. The story of Bata's vindication is long and involved, and, because it contains story motifs that fall outside the present theme, it is here omitted. It is fair to reveal, nevertheless, that, as do the majority of his counterparts—most significantly Joseph—Bata ultimately marries a royal princess. But first, like the Hippolytus of Greek legend—or perhaps more like the Egyptian god Osiris with whom he has been associated—he must die and then rise from the dead.

# 1. "Anpu and Bata" (about 14th century B.C.)

## Translated by W. M. F. Petrie (1853–1942)

(Approximately the first half of the story as translated
is here given. *Ed.*)

Once there were two brethren, of one mother and one father;
Anpu was the name of the elder, and Bata was the name of
the younger. Now, as for Anpu he had a house, and he had a
wife. But his little brother was to him as it were a son; he it
was who made for him his clothes; he it was who followed
behind his oxen to the fields; he it was who did the ploughing;
he it was who harvested the corn; he it was who did for him
all the matters that were in the field. Behold, his younger
brother grew to be an excellent worker, there was not his
equal in the whole land; behold, the spirit of a god was in him.

Now after this the younger brother followed his oxen in
his daily manner; and every evening he turned again to the
house, laden with all the herbs of the field, with milk and with
wood, and with all things of the field. And he put them down
before his elder brother, who was sitting with his wife; and
he drank and ate, and he lay down in his stable with the cattle.
And at the dawn of day he took bread which he had baked,
and laid it before his elder brother; and he took with him his
bread to the field, and he drave his cattle to pasture in the
fields. And as he walked behind his cattle, they said to him,
"Good is the herbage which is in that place;" and he listened
to all that they said, and he took them to the good place which
they desired. And the cattle which were before him became
exceeding excellent, and they multiplied greatly.

Now at the time of ploughing his elder brother said unto
him, "Let us make ready for ourselves a goodly yoke of oxen
for ploughing, for the land has come out from the water, it is
fit for ploughing. Moreover, do thou come to the field with
corn, for we will begin the ploughing in the morrow morning."
Thus said he to him; and his younger brother did all things as
his elder brother had spoken unto him to do them.

And when the morn was come, they went to the fields
with their things; and their hearts were pleased exceedingly
with their task in the beginning of their work. And it came
to pass after this that as they were in the field they stopped for

10

corn, and he sent his younger brother, saying, "Haste thou, bring to us corn from the farm." And the younger brother found the wife of his elder brother, as she was sitting 'tiring her hair. He said to her, "Get up, and give to me corn, that I may run to the field, for my elder brother hastened me; do not delay." She said to him, "Go, open the bin, and thou shalt take to thyself according to thy will, that I may not drop my locks of hair while I dress them."

The youth went into the stable; he took a large measure, for he desired to take much corn; he loaded it with wheat and barley; and he went out carrying it. She said to him, "How much of the corn that is wanted, is that which is on thy shoulder?" He said to her, "Three bushels of barley, and two of wheat, in all five; these are what are upon my shoulder:" thus said he to her. And she conversed with him, saying, "There is great strength in thee, for I see thy might every day." And her heart knew him with the knowledge of youth. And she arose and came to him, and conversed with him, saying, "Come, stay with me, and it shall be well for thee, and I will make for thee beautiful garments." Then the youth became like a panther of the south with fury at the evil speech which she had made to him; and she feared greatly. And he spake unto her, saying, "Behold thou art to me as a mother, thy husband is to me as a father, for he, who is elder than I, has brought me up. What is this wickedness that thou hast said to me? Say it not to me again. For I will not tell it to any man, for I will not let it be uttered by the mouth of any man." He lifted up his burden, and he went to the field and came to his elder brother; and they took up their work, to labour at their task.

Now afterward, at eventime, his elder brother was returning to his house; and the younger brother was following after his oxen, and he loaded himself with all the things of the field; and he brought his oxen before him, to make them lie down in their stable which was in the farm. And behold the wife of the elder brother was afraid for the words which she had said. She took a parcel of fat, she became like one who is evilly beaten, desiring to say to her husband, "It is thy younger brother who has done this wrong." Her husband returned in the even, as was his wont of every day; he came unto his house; he found his wife ill of violence; she did not give him

water upon his hands as he used to have, she did not make a
light before him, his house was in darkness, and she was lying
very sick. Her husband said to her, "Who has spoken with
thee?" Behold she said, "No one has spoken with me except
thy younger brother. When he came to take for thee corn he
found me sitting alone; he said to me, 'Come, let us stay
together, tie up thy hair:' thus spake he to me. I did not
listen to him, but thus spake I to him: 'Behold, am I not thy
mother, is not thy elder brother to thee as a father?' And he
feared, and he beat me to stop me from making report to thee,
and if thou lettest him live I shall die. Now behold he is coming in the evening; and I complain of these wicked words, for
he would have done this even in daylight."

And the elder brother became as a panther of the south;
he sharpened his knife; he took it in his hand; he stood behind
the door of his stable to slay his younger brother as he came in
the evening to bring his cattle into the stable.

Now the sun went down, and he loaded himself with
herbs in his daily manner. He came, and his foremost cow
entered the stable, and she said to her keeper, "Behold thou
thy elder brother standing before thee with his knife to slay
thee; flee from before him." He heard what his first cow had
said; and the next entering, she also said likewise. He looked
beneath the door of the stable; he saw the feet of his elder
brother; he was standing behind the door, and his knife was
in his hand. He cast down his load to the ground, and betook
himself to flee swiftly; and his elder brother pursued after
him with his knife. Then the younger brother cried out unto
Ra Harakhti, saying, "My good Lord! Thou art he who divides
the evil from the good." And Ra stood and heard all his cry;
and Ra made a wide water between him and his elder brother,
and it was full of crocodiles; and the one brother was on one
bank, and the other on the other bank; and the elder brother
smote twice on his hands at not slaying him. Thus did he. And
the younger brother called to the elder on the bank, saying,
"Stand still until the dawn of day; and when Ra ariseth, I
shall judge with thee before Him, and He discerneth between
the good and the evil. For I shall not be with thee any more
for ever; I shall not be in the place in which thou art; I shall
go to the valley of the acacia."

Now when the land was lightened, and the next day ap-

peared, Ra Harakhti arose, and one looked unto the other.
And the youth spake with his elder brother, saying, "Wherefore camest thou after me to slay me in craftiness, when thou
didst not hear the words of my mouth? For I am thy brother
in truth, and thou art to me as a father, and thy wife even as
a mother: is it not so? Verily, when I was sent to bring for us
corn, thy wife said to me, 'Come, stay with me;' for behold
this has been turned over unto thee into another wise." And
he caused him to understand of all that happened with him
and his wife. And he swore an oath by Ra Harakhti, saying,
"Thy coming to slay me by deceit with thy knife was an
abomination." Then the youth took a knife, and cut off of his
flesh, and cast it into the water, and the fish swallowed it.
He failed; he became faint; and his elder brother cursed his
own heart greatly; he stood weeping for him afar off; he knew
not how to pass over to where his younger brother was, because
of the crocodiles. And the younger brother called unto him,
saying, "Whereas thou hast devised an evil thing, wilt thou
not also devise a good thing, even like that which I would do
unto thee? When thou goest to thy house thou must look to
thy cattle, for I shall not stay in the place where thou art; I am
going to the valley of the acacia. And now as to what thou shalt
do for me; it is even that thou shalt come to seek after me, if
thou perceivest a matter, namely, that there are things happening unto me. And this is what shall come to pass, that I
shall draw out my soul, and I shall put it upon the top of the
flowers of the acacia, and when the acacia is cut down, and it
falls to the ground, and thou comest to seek for it, if thou
searchest for it seven years do not let thy heart be wearied.
For thou wilt find it, and thou must put it in a cup of cold
water, and expect that I shall live again, that I may make
answer to what has been done wrong. And thou shalt know of
this, that is to say, that things are happening to me, when one
shall give to thee a cup of beer in thy hand, and it shall be
troubled; stay not then, for verily it shall come to pass with
thee."

And the youth went to the valley of the acacia; and his
elder brother went unto his house; his hand was laid on his
head, and he cast dust on his head; he came to his house, and
he slew his wife, he cast her to the dogs, and he sat in mourning for his younger brother.

# ✠ CHAPTER II ✠

## Biblical Narrative

Whether the Biblical story of Joseph and Potiphar's wife was adapted from the Egyptian tale of the two brothers or vice versa, Genesis 39 has its own unmistakable character, stamped upon it by the didactic purpose it serves in the larger narrative of the patriarchs of Israel. The hero represents the Chosen Seed; he is destined by God to carry out a divine mission. In this great undertaking, his encounter with the wife of Potiphar, his master, is but one more obstacle on the road to ultimate fulfillment of the promise.

Even in its subsequent history in the Christian world, the story retains this Hebraistic bias, to use that word in Matthew Arnold's sense of a desire to make the will of God prevail. If it sometimes loses its strict ethnic meaning, it is never without the ethical intention imparted to it by Judaism. The woman, as Potiphar's wife is contemptuously referred to, is a threat not only to Joseph's manhood but also to his faith. She is, as her sister in the Egyptian folktale was, a hussy; but she is something more—a pagan seductress who can undermine both the man and his mission. Joseph, of course, must resist her, be unjustly punished, later be vindicated, and finally become elevated to the high office for which he is marked. This process includes his later marriage to Asenath, daughter of Potiphera, priest of On. About his status as the Fortunate Youth, there hangs the aura of a religious teleology.

Potiphar, Pharaoh's captain, adopts the Hebrew servant into his home, and thus assumes the role of the punishing father. A shadowy figure in this account, he nevertheless exhibits the two necessary traits of being both trustful and wrathful. The extraordinarily sketchy narrative does not give him an opportunity to discover how he has been misled by his scheming wife; consequently, she remains unpunished except by the ignominy which may be presumed to have overtaken her after Joseph's vindication. The interest of the Bible story lies elsewhere.

Thomas Mann's elaboration of these twenty-three verses of Genesis into nearly two full-length novels well demonstrates how pregnant with meaning (though occasionally cryptic and in need of being eked out) the brief narrative is. This explication it has, of course, received at more authorized hands than the mere retellers of the tale. Talmudic, or more precisely Midrashic, scholarship was brought to bear liberally upon it in the centuries after its composition. A further modifying influence upon it was its contact with the analogous pagan story of Hippolytus and Phaedra. The result was that a secondary or apocryphal version of the Hebrew story was formed. And since out of this Hebrew-Greek amalgam there eventually issued the wide-ranging Moslem story of Yusuf and Zulaikha, we can with justification regard the Genesis account as the very story of Joseph and Potiphar's wife, and as deserving of supplying the name for the universal story of the Chaste Youth and the Lustful Stepmother.

Inevitably a certain amount of rationalization would enter into the Midrashic speculations, growing out of some doubt regarding the credibility of portions of the story. (A latter-day illustration of this persistent skepticism is Mark Twain's comment that Joseph "got into trouble with Potiphar's wife at last, and both gave in their version of the affair, but the lady's was plausible and Joseph's was most outrageously shaky.") The Midrash scholars came up with a set of suppositions about the characters and events of Genesis 39 that were designed to support its intended meaning. They proposed that Potiphar had in the first place purchased Joseph for the express purpose of sodomy, and that the Lord had punished Pharaoh's captain by making him a eunuch. This tradition was full of possibilities for future narrators, especially the Moslem, who were to see in it some mitigation of the wife's waywardness. This was clearly not the intent of the Rabbis, whose attitude toward Potiphar's wife was uncompromisingly harsh. She is compared by them to a she-bear decked out in jewels. They describe her in the attire of a harlot haunting the streets in search of Joseph, saying, like an animal, "Lie with me!"—not at all like Ruth, who so much more becomingly urged her cousin Boaz to "spread therefore thy skirt over thy handmaid."

The Midrash is aware, on the other hand, that Joseph's temptation must have been a sore one. ("It required strong moral steadfastness to flee from such alluring temptation.") The Rabbis were necessarily driven to undertake an explanation of Joseph's incredible power of chastity. According to one

Rabbi, the youth's susceptibilty to the charms of the temptress reached an ultimate test, for we are told that "his bow was drawn but it relaxed." Further, that "his seed was scattered and issued through his fingernails." The Rabbi Jose was once asked by a young matron: "Is it possible that Joseph, at seventeen years of age, with the hot blood of youth, could act thus?" [i.e., reject the offer of the wife of his master]. Hard put to it, the Rabbi shrewdly answered that since the Torah had not scrupled to report the whole truth about sinners like Reuben and Judah, why should it have hesitated to tell it about Joseph —if, in fact, he had succumbed.

✠

Even before the Midrash authors had fully annotated the Genesis story, it had been subjected to some modification by its encounter with the classical legend of Hippolytus, devotee of the virgin goddess, Artemis (or Diana). The Hellenized Jews of Alexandria, we are told by Moses Hadas, were very susceptible to the appeal of the Hippolytus story because its hero was so much like their own Joseph. Inevitably, the stories began to blend for them, the strong tone of preachment in the Hebrew account being softened by the pagan tolerance for the goddess of love. In the first century A.D., the Hellenized Jew Josephus retold the story in his *History of the Jews,* embellishing it with many "modern" touches. But several centuries earlier, the new version had already received full-dress treatment in *The Testament of Joseph,* a Hebrew work belonging to the class called Pseudepigrapha.

In this version, Martin Braun says, the author's soul was torn between his loyalty to the ethical purpose of the Hebrew narrative and his attraction to the Greek force of Eros. As a result, elements crept in from Hellenistic romances on the Hippolytus theme. Joseph is now offered mastership of the house by his would-be mistress, who also agrees to take instruction from him in his faith, if he will but have her. In the manner of heroines of the Greek romances, she proposes to poison her husband, and she sends magically treated food to Joseph as an aphrodisiac. She bares her legs and breasts to entice him. She even threatens suicide, a motif altogether foreign to Judaism. To be sure, *The Testament of Joseph* retains a fundamentally ethical bias, and its didactic tone is not replaced by the tragic tone of the Greek legend; but unavoidably there is a humanizing of the heroine in the light of Greek thought. Erotic love is not seen as simply evil.

This new version of the Hebrew story has had its own subsequent literary history. An amusing English adaptation in verse, made in the early seventeenth century, follows the narrative pattern of *The Testament of Joseph*. That is, the hero tells his father Jacob the story of his recent life, including the Potiphar's wife episode, by a sort of flashback. Robert Aylett, the imputed author of *Joseph: or Pharaoh's Favorite*, draws upon some local Elizabethan color for the climactic robe-snatching scene, by citing an analogy from English tavern life that reverses the roles of the sexes:

> So have I seen some modest country maid,
> With some uncivil usage much dismaid,
> Closely her apron strings, to escape, untie,
> And left it with the clowne, away to flie.

The story of Joseph has of course traveled with Judaism and Christianity to all parts of the world. Its narrative appeal, however, has always assured it a much larger audience than the purely sectarian. It has been treated by both major and minor authors. The young Goethe was fascinated by it and imagined himself a latter-day Joseph. When later in life, however, he came upon the Moslem version of the story, he did not hesitate to appropriate it. Indeed, the whole tradition of Joseph stories in German literature has tended to permit accretions to the Biblical story from its other analogues. Thomas Mann's version, which in his own words "refashioned the story anew for our age," was but the culmination of a long history. Yet Mann realized, to his own pique, that he could do nothing to protect the commercial rights of his work in a film about Joseph, because "the biblical theme is entirely free from copyright." Dramatic presentations in English, too, whether for film or stage, have always assumed the liberty of embroidering what Mann called "the briefest and most prized" version of our story.

# 2. Genesis 39, Verses 1–23

## King James Version, Old Testament

And Joseph was brought down to Egypt; and Potiphar, an officer of Pharaoh, captain of the guard, an Egyptian, bought him of the hands of the Ishmaelites, which had brought him down thither.

2. And the Lord was with Joseph, and he was a prosperous man; and he was in the house of his master the Egyptian.

3. And his master saw that the Lord was with him, and that the Lord made all that he did to prosper in his hand.

4. And Joseph found grace in his sight, and he served him: and he made him overseer over his house, and all that he had he put into his hand.

5. And it came to pass from the time that he had made him overseer in his house, and over all that he had, that the Lord blessed the Egyptian's house for Joseph's sake; and the blessing of the Lord was upon all that he had in the house, and in the field.

6. And he left all that he had in Joseph's hand, save the bread which he did eat. And Joseph was a goodly person, and well favoured.

7. And it came to pass after these things, that his master's wife cast her eyes upon Joseph; and she said, Lie with me.

8. But he refused, and said unto his master's wife, Behold, my master wotteth not what is with me in the house, and he hath committed all that he hath to my hand;

9. There is none greater in this house than I; neither hath he kept back any thing from me but thee, because thou art his wife: how then can I do this great wickedness, and sin against God?

10. And it came to pass, as she spake to Joseph day by day, that he hearkened not unto her, to lie by her, or to be with her.

11. And it came to pass about this time, that Joseph went into the house to do his business; and there was none of the men of the house there within.

12. And she caught him by his garment, saying, Lie with me: and he left his garment in her hand, and fled, and got him out.

13. And it came to pass, when she saw that he had left his garment in her hand, and was fled forth,

14. That she called unto the men of her house, and spake unto them, saying, See, he hath brought in an Hebrew unto us to mock us; he came in unto me to lie with me, and I cried with a loud voice:

15. And it came to pass, when he heard that I lifted up my voice and cried, that he left his garment with me, and fled, and got him out.

16. And she laid up his garment by her, until his lord came home.

17. And she spake unto him according to these words, saying, The Hebrew servant, which thou hast brought unto us, came in unto me to mock me:

18. And it came to pass, as I lifted up my voice and cried, that he left his garment with me, and fled out.

19. And it came to pass, when his master heard the words of his wife, which she spake unto him, saying, After this manner did thy servant to me; that his wrath was kindled.

20. And Joseph's master took him, and put him into the prison, a place where the king's prisoners were bound: and he was there in the prison.

21. But the Lord was with Joseph, and shewed him mercy, and gave him favour in the sight of the keeper of the prison.

22. And the keeper of the prison committed to Joseph's hand all the prisoners that were in the prison; and whatsoever they did there, he was the doer of it.

23. The keeper of the prison looked not to any thing that was under his hand; because the Lord was with him, and that which he did, the Lord made it to prosper.

# ✠ CHAPTER III ✠
## Classical Drama

The ancient Greeks had several legends embodying the theme of the Chaste Youth and the Lustful Stepmother. The oldest of these is about Bellerophon and about the love he inspired in Antia, wife of Proetus, King of Argos. Rejected, she accused him to the king, who reluctantly sent him abroad with instructions that he be killed. However, overcoming all of the obstacles that were placed before him, including the taming of the horse Pegasus, he finally married the local monarch's daughter. The legend sometimes adds that he later had his revenge on Antia by dropping her over a cliff.

This resembles the Anpu and Bata story in the motif of the obstacles, and the Buddhist story of Kunala in placing the punishment of the Chaste Youth in a distant land. Euripides apparently wrote a drama on this subject, but since it has not survived the story of Bellerophon is a less impressive monument of Greek literature than the parallel story of Hippolytus. The latter Euripides told twice over, once apparently to the dissatisfaction of the Athenian audience, perhaps because he had allowed his heroine to make her proposition to Hippolytus directly without the intermediation of the pander-nurse. There is a possibile reference to this play in Aristophanes' *Frogs,* in which Aeschylus speaks of his rival's "shameless Phaedra." The outlines of the earlier *Hippolytus* may have been preserved for us in Seneca's later adaptation and in other allusions in classical literature, such as in Ovid's *Heroides.* In "Hippolytus Veiled," one of his *Greek Studies,* Walter Pater attempted a nineteenth-century reconstruction, in which he took the curious liberty of introducing, from the Biblical analogue, the motif of the robe-snatching.

Moses Hadas conjectures that the earlier play of Euripides must have given greater prominence to the theme of the dynastic struggle between Theseus' son by the Amazon queen (i.e., Hippolytus) and his children by Phaedra. Hadas denotes the shift from this motif to the love interest in the second play as a movement from the heroic to the bourgeois, noting that in the Hellenistic age it was the love interest that prevailed. In apparent contradiction to this, however, it may be pointed out that, during the bourgeois age of the French dramatist Racine, the dynastic motif was replaced prominently alongside the love motif. There are, of course, traces of the dynastic struggle still left in Euripides' extant drama. It is interesting to observe that in the Iranian analogue by Firdausi, in the Japanese puppet play, and in the medieval Sindibad cycle, the struggle for political power remains a considerable factor.

Whatever objections Euripides was meeting in his revised play, it is not without its own problems of interpretation. The use of the goddesses of love and chastity as dramatis personae, for example, has occasioned much argument among critics. Are they persons or powers, actual or symbolical? Aphrodite discharges her functions in a prologue in which she marks Hippolytus for destruction because he has flouted her power, and she designates Phaedra the agent of her stratagem. Artemis is audible to Hippolytus and is clearly his patron goddess (if not, as David Grene believes, the object of his love); yet in the crisis of his life, she shows a remarkable indifference to his fate, being content to promise revenge on Aphrodite through the latter's favorite, Adonis. If these goddesses of sex and abstinence both represent natural powers, why does the author allow the scales to be tipped in favor of one of them? Is Hippolytus guilty of *hybris,* the pride which goeth before a fall in Greek dramaturgy? Has he departed from that *sophrosyne* or moderation which constituted the Athenian concept of virtue? The present translators urge us to see "the whole play as an expression, in mythological terms, of the truth that to reject a stirring and terrible power of life is to court inevitable disaster . . . involving the innocent and the guilty alike."

Hippolytus is certainly a problematical character in his excessive chastity, as translators and adaptors of the play bear testimony. Grene accuses Euripides of being confused in his purpose; Rexroth believes that the two main characters are destroyed by "impurity of purpose"; Warner accepts the theory of *hybris;* Jeffers depicts the hero as a homosexual and throws his support to Phaedra. Hippolytus' inexplicable silence in the face of the accusation is not like Yusuf's awareness (in the *Koran* parable) that "the soul is very urgent to evil," for Hippolytus does not hesitate to launch a diatribe against all women. Bata, in the Egyptian folktale, although silent at first about his innocence, does not hesitate to clear himself at the proper time. Even the youth of the Sindibad cycle, struck dumb by the sage's warning of an ominous event, is finally allowed to testify in his own behalf. One wonders whether Hippolytus' plighted word is sufficient reason for him to maintain his unbroken silence.

There is no question, however, but that the most distinct contribution of the Greeks to the universal story is in the character of Phaedra. She assumes a tragic stature that none of her counterparts, not even the sympathetically projected Zulaikha of Moslem legend, attains. This justifies the later construction of the drama around her person by Seneca, Racine, Jeffers, Rexroth, and others. She is certainly more humanly appealing than the somewhat priggish Hippolytus. She suffers internally more than he does. She has tried to fight off her feelings for him by practicing silence and asceticism, and she is prepared to resort to suicide to prevent shame from attaching to her family. Her accusation of Hippolytus is an act of final desperation, dictated partly by her anger and frustration at her nurse's crafty maneuverings in her behalf, and partly by her wounded sexual pride. She says bitterly:

> I can never forgive him. He despised me
> Knowing nothing of the horror of love.
> Well, let him take his share.
> It may even teach him something of life.

The father figure in this analogue, though perhaps stronger than his counterparts in other analogues, is probably not as sympathetic from the modern reader's point of view. Theseus' sexual arrogance seems as much an excess of the golden mean as Hippolytus' chastity is a deficiency. He was earlier married to Phaedra's sister Ariadne, whom he abandoned on the island of Naxos, and, of course, Hippolytus is his son by the queen of the Amazons. He does not win the kind of sympathy we put out for the emasculated Potiphar of Jewish-Moslem tradition, or even for the somewhat uxorious Kai Kaus of the *Shahnama* story. That his cursing of his son was more than justice required is attested by the persistence of the belief that Hippolytus was later brought back to life by the legendary father of medicine, Asclepius, or that he was made immortal as a heavenly constellation, or that at least his memory was

kept deathless by virgins about to be married, who dropped
locks of their tresses upon his altar at Troezen.

Although the theme of incest does not loom so large in
the Greek play as one might expect, it is nevertheless there.
(In Seneca's Latin version, as William Packard maintains,
Hippolytus actually calls Phaedra "Mother.") When Euripides'
Phaedra falls prey to a passion for her stepson, she most dreads

> . . . that I may play false with my husband
> And disgrace my children.

Hippolytus, when he hears Phaedra's confession of love,
replies:

> Bawd. . . .
> treacherous to your master's bed. . . .

And Theseus, reading Phaedra's suicide note, reacts with a
moral revulsion that betrays the strength of the tabu against
the mother:

> Hippolytus, my son, has dared to force my bed,
> Dishonoring my wife with his mad hands.

Hippolytus himself acknowledges the tabu when he rebuts
Theseus' judgment of exile:

> If you were my son and I your father and you did—what
> you accuse me of, I should kill you, not merely exile you.

Euripides' drama is in the last analysis the tragedy of Hippolytus, not of Phaedra. And it was the story of the wronged
stepson that continued to engage the attention of later classical
narrators, such as Apuleius in his *Metamorphoses* and Heliodorus in his *Ethiopica*. Moreover, some humanization of the
rigid youth was attempted in these versions by assigning him a
fiancee, as the Buddhist legend did for Kunala. Eventually,
however, there grew up a larger sympathy for the unhappy
stepmother who had been the victim of the goddess of love.
And two thousand years after Euripides, in Jean Racine's seven-
teenth-century tragedy, she moved fully to the center of the
stage.

✠

Since the Greek drama had not put the most favorable face on the matter for Phaedra, Racine undertook to make some changes in the story. He assigned to the nurse Oenone the odious tasks not only of carrying the indecent proposal to Hippolyte but also of later making the false accusation against him. Not to denigrate Hippolyte in the process, however, Racine had him accused not of violating his stepmother but of merely planning to. On the other hand, since his moral rectitude approaches a point of fanaticism, Racine sought to impart a weakness to the character of Hippolyte that would "make him slightly culpable in his relations with his father." Thus, he is allowed to love—"in spite of himself," as Racine goes on to say—the girl Aricie, who is of a family inimical to Theseus. Obviously, this also provides Phèdre with the genuinely human motives of sexual jealousy and family rivalry. Finally, Racine's neoclassical bias is revealed in his determination to see that vice and virtue are depicted in their true colors: no doubt is left in the reader's mind of the didactic intent—in the best Horatian tradition which requires literature to teach as well as to entertain. Yet Phèdre becomes a truly tragic heroine because, in Racine's words, "she is neither completely guilty nor completely innocent. She is plunged by her fate, and by the anger of the gods, into an illegitimate passion for which she feels horror from the very start." Her chief venom is directed against Aphrodite, or rather Venus, since Racine prefers the Roman name. After the death of Hippolyte, she confesses to Theseus that his son was innocent and announces that she has taken a poison which will kill her. The drama rightly ends with her death, and not his.

The poet Robert Lowell, who has made a modern adaptation of Racine's drama, frankly regards the French play as superior to the Greek. By way of apology for his own free translation, he expresses regret that neither Dryden nor Pope brought it into the English language in the heroic couplet form so well suited to it. (In the translation selected for this volume, William Packard has gone further, retaining the hexameter couplets, or Alexandrines, in which Racine wrote his play.) Dryden himself apparently did not have the same high regard for Racine's version as does Mr. Lowell. In his "Preface" to *All for Love*, he took occasion to parade some of his John Bull prejudices against the Frenchman's treatment of the hero:

Thus, their [the French] Hippolytus is so scrupulous in point of decency that he will rather expose himself to death than accuse his stepmother to his father, and my critics, I am sure, will commend him for it: but we of grosser apprehensions [i.e., the British] are apt to think that this excess of generosity is not practicable but with fools and madmen. . . . In the meantime we may take notice that where the poet ought to have preserved the character as it was delivered to us by antiquity, when he should have given us the picture of a rough young man of the Amazonian strain, a jolly huntsman, and both by his profession and his early raising a mortal enemy to love, he has chosen to give the turn of gallantry, sent him to travel from Athens to Paris, taught him to make love, and transformed the Hippolytus of Euripides into Monsieur Hippolyte.

It may be noted in passing that John Dryden himself employed the Potiphar's wife motif in his play *Aureng-Zebe*. In the fourth act, when the hero's stepmother Nourmahal hints at her love for him, he refuses to accept her "incestuous meaning." In true Restoration fashion, she urges that "promiscuous love is Nature's general law." As this does not persuade him, she resorts to two contrary devices: offering him a dagger with which to kill her, and then sending him a poisoned goblet to drink.

✠

In subsequent treatments of the classical legend, the heroine has continued to command the deeper emotions of the reader. As has already been noted, Robinson Jeffers' adaptation in *The Cretan Woman* focuses on Phaedra's emotional frustration, which is the result of Hippolytus' involvement, emotionally and psychologically, with his male friends. This inevitable Freudianization of the legend is seen again in a recent surrealistic film by George Markopoulos called *Twice a Man*, though with the focus shifted back upon the youth. Another film, entitled *Phaedra* and produced by Jules Dassin, follows the main outlines of Racine's version but in a modern setting and with contemporary characters. Both the nurse and the youth's fiancee are retained, as is the theme of the dynastic struggle among the children of the several wives—in this case a modern Greek shipbuilding dynasty. Martha Graham's interpretive dance on the Phaedra theme should also be mentioned as a modern instance in which the stepmother is the center of attention.

Of unusual interest is Kenneth Rexroth's adaptation of the play, offered here, since it is the only variant of the Potiphar's wife story here included in which the Chaste Youth is actually seduced by the Lustful Stepmother. (This is true also of the Dassin film.) In contrast to Jeffers' hero, the Hippolytus of this version is said to have been given to deflowering virgins until he had a transforming experience, variously reported as seeing a leper, a corpse, or a former sweetheart of Hercules now gone in the teeth. One is inevitably reminded of the first illumination of Siddhartha Gotama, the Buddha, when he had his introduction to old age, disease, and death. It is, of course, not surprising that Mr. Rexroth, who has elsewhere shown his interest in the poetry and the philosophy of the Far East, should have brought these oriental themes into his adaptation of a classical legend. One wonders whether he knew also of the Buddhist analogue of this very story. The resemblances are perhaps more to the legendary life of the Buddha than to the tale of Kunala. Hippolytus wears a costume like that of a beggar in the chorus, and he is barefooted. He is said to indulge "a saint's gelded wantonry" playing "hermit in the forest." His devotion to Artemis is to one of "pure compassionate heart . . . who hears the world's cry." In a climactic speech to Phaedra, he fairly paraphrases the Buddha's famous sermon that reports all life burning with the fires of passion. It may even be that the Japanese Noh drama, about which Mr. Rexroth has written elsewhere, suggested to him the appropriateness of employing masks and dummies in the staging of his play.

On the other hand, this *Phaedra* is not without its properly Grecian theme. Hippolytus announces to Theseus with sadistic pleasure that he has violated the queen. His father, a man of the modern world, cuts the ground from under Hippolytus' feet by replying that the son was more or less expected to accommodate his stepmother in this fashion and by giving the two lovers his blessing. In the face of the final catastrophe, however, Theseus is at best a sad, uncomprehending man who admits that "everywhere I bring disaster." In an ingenious modification of the legend of Hippolytus' death, Rexroth contrives to bring the denouement about by exposing the hero to the very bull which Pasiphae, Phaedra's Minoan mother, once monstrously loved. Phaedra kills herself with the sword of Hippolytus, made by the "Russian witch" Medea and a symbol of the youth's pride. The final chorus intones:

> Impure intention is damned
> By the act it embodies. . . .
> Each sinned with the other's virtue.

# 3. The *Hippolytus* of Euripides (480–406 B.C.)

## Translated by Ian Fletcher (1920—  ) and
## D. S. Carne-Ross (1921—  )

[The text of this translation is taken from a version prepared for radio transmission by the British Broadcasting Company in 1958. With the exception of some stage directions having to do with sound and musical effects, I have thought it desirable to leave the text unchanged. The translators have taken some liberties with Euripides. Their additions they justify as belonging, if not to the Greek text, at least to the Greek context. *Ed.*]

### CHARACTERS

APHRODITE, *also called Cypris*
CHORUS OF HUNTSMEN *with Hippolytus* (VOICE 5)
                                            (VOICE 6)
HIPPOLYTUS, *bastard son of Theseus by the Amazon Queen*
OLD SERVANT *of Hippolytus*
CHORUS OF WOMEN OF TROZEN (VOICE 1)
                                            (VOICE 2)
                                            (VOICE 3)
                                            (VOICE 4)
NURSE *of Phaedra*
PHAEDRA, *Cretan wife of Theseus*
THESEUS, *King of Athens and Trozen*
ARTEMIS

*The scene is set in Trozen, in the Peloponnesus. The action of the play takes place at the palace of King Theseus.*

[*Music*]

APHRODITE [*Speaking at first over music, the* APHRODITE *theme which heralds her. The first seven lines slowly, formally, with five gong-like beats per line*]:
Great is my power among men: and on high in Heaven:
My name is famous: you know me: Aphrodite.
All those who live and move in this world of light
From the eastern sea to the sandy threshold of Atlas

I honour: *if* they acknowledge the power that is mine:
But the man who thinks to reject me: that man I destroy:
For even we gods take a pleasure in being praised.

[*Music ends.*]

It will not take long to show you where these words tend.
Theseus, the king of this people of Trozen,
has a son—the mother was an Amazon woman—

This boy has insulted me. He holds me
cheapest of all the gods. Alone in this Greek town
Hippolytus refuses the proper motions of love,
mocks at my marriage bed. For the daughter of Zeus,
Artemis the Huntress, queens it in his Heaven.
And day after day with Artemis at his side,
hunter by Huntress, he rides through the bronze shadows
of the dappled woods, his hounds coursing at his heels.
Too close a friendship, you say, of man with goddess?
Perhaps. Why should I trouble? That is not my complaint.
No, it is sin against me, against my divine
nature I punish. I shall have my revenge today.
Not much remains to be done. I have already
cleared my way through the tangle of circumstance.

It began when Hippolytus came first to Athens
to see, and be sealed in, the Great Mysteries.
For there, his father's young wife, the Cretan princess
Phaedra, caught sight of the boy, and by my design
a monstrous desire rooted itself in her heart.
And still in Athens, before her husband Theseus
accepted the people's sentence of a year's exile
in Trozen, purging the blood of kindred murder,
Queen Phaedra raised up a temple for my cult
near Athene's cliff that looks seaward towards Trozen,
for the man she loved had left her. And to this day
they call the shrine she built by Hippolytus's name.

Then Theseus sailed here to Trozen with his wife,
and here, driven crazy by her helpless longing,
not daring to speak out, the poor creature wastes away.
None of her servants guess the growth that eats her.

This fire in her veins must not stifle itself quietly,
it must blaze out sharp, Theseus must learn what is happening.
And this young man who has declared war on me
must die in violence, the victim of his father's curse.
For Poseidon, god of the sea, this clear Aegean,
once granted Theseus three infallible prayers.
Two he has used already. You will see the third
strike at Hippolytus before the day goes down.
I will let poor Phaedra keep her reputation.
She must die, of course. I am sorry for her, but not
so sorry that I rate her death above my rights.
I am asking no more than my due—my enemies
must learn that in me they have a goddess to deal with.

[*Music: Approaching Huntsmen*]

But listen: can you hear Hippolytus coming?
Yes, here he is, back from a morning in the field
with a rowdy throng of huntsmen flush at his heels.
You hear the song they are singing? A song to Artemis.
He does not know a door is opening on to death;
the sun will rise tomorrow, but he will not see it.

[*Fade*]

HIPPOLYTUS [*approaching*]: Come on, men, come on . . .
Here, by her image,
Offer thanks to Artemis . . .
Our lives are in her hands . . .

[*Music*: Artemis Theme]

HUNTSMEN [*singing*]: Artemis,
Incorruptible
Artemis,
Child of Leto,
Child of Zeus,

VOICE 5: Artemis, alive in the hunter,
In the hunted,

VOICE 6: Artemis, lady of the hilltops,
Of the fisherfolk,

HUNTSMEN [*singing*]: Artemis,
Incorruptible,

VOICE 5: Moving
Through the burning element of Heaven,
Through the gold house of the Lightning;

VOICE 6: Friend in the City of Gods,

HUNTSMEN [*singing*]: Incorruptible
Artemis.

[*Music ends.*]

HIPPOLYTUS: Artemis, it is for you, I have threaded these
      flowers
in a gentle crown. The field they grew in was as fresh as a child
where the shepherds never dare to graze their flocks
and no scythe has ever sheared its grasses. Only
the bees go eddying over that innocent earth
all Spring through, and innocent too are the streams
that stroke it into life. Only those pure by nature
can enter, and gather those flowers, but the wicked, never.
Now Artemis, here is the crown: let it capture
your golden head: you have given me this high gift,
I alone am your friend, I answer you when you speak,
hear your voice, though I can not see your face.
Goddess, grant this: as my life began, let me end it,
honouring and serving you . . .

      OLD SERVANT [*approaching*]: Sir, Hippolytus, I am your
            servant
As we are all servants of the Gods.
Would you take an old man's advice?

HIPPOLYTUS: Of course. Say what you like. Only a fool
Refuses advice.

      OLD SERVANT [*slowly, feeling his way*]: You know, Hippoly-
            tus, the way people feel . . .

HIPPOLYTUS [*brusque, but encouraging*]: The way people
      feel?—come on, man, let's have it.

      OLD SERVANT [*plucking up courage*]: The way they feel
            about someone who stands aside

And sneers at things everyone else respects.
They resent it—a man like that isn't liked.

HIPPOLYTUS: No. You have to meet people half-way.

OLD SERVANT: Yes, meet them half-way, that's it, and be pleasant . . .

HIPPOLYTUS [*tolerantly*]: Of course, everyone does. It's the road to success.

OLD SERVANT [*unexpectedly*]: Do you think the Gods look at things in the same light?

HIPPOLYTUS: Surely, if our human pattern is taken from theirs.

OLD SERVANT: Then, sir, forgive me, but look at the way you behave.
Ignoring a great power . . .

HIPPOLYTUS [*sharply*]: What power? Take care what you say, man.
[*sententious*] There are names we may not utter in common speech.

OLD SERVANT: A great power. Her image stands just behind you, sir,
Our Lady Aphrodite.

HIPPOLYTUS [*relieved*]: Oh her. I acknowledge Aphrodite—
But, from a distance. I don't have to worship her.

OLD SERVANT: Aphrodite is a great power, sir, [*piously*] we can't escape her.

HIPPOLYTUS: No doubt. But everyone has his favourites in Heaven.
It's the same on earth—we like one man more than other.

OLD SERVANT: Then, Heaven help you, sir—that's no way to talk.

HIPPOLYTUS [*obstinately*]: I can't honour a God one has to worship in bed.

OLD SERVANT: We must honour all the Gods in their different ways.

HIPPOLYTUS: I'm wasting time.
Inside with you, men, and let's have a meal.
[*moving away*] I'm hungry after a long morning in the field.
Rub down the horses first, though; when we've eaten
I shall be taking them out for a canter . . .
[*calling*] As for that Aphrodite of yours, Servant, a long goodbye to her!

[*Music: Aphrodite Theme*]

OLD SERVANT: Now with humble words, as servants should do
I offer my prayer to your image
Aphrodite . . . Our Lady.
The Prince is young and the young talk wildly . . .
It's their quick blood . . . the spirit of life in them.
Be kind to him, Lady, pretend you cannot hear him.
Heaven ought to be wiser than men! [*Fading*]

[*Gradually fading in, confused chattering noise of women*]

VOICE 2: I'm first, Leucippe, I'm first.

VOICE 3: You cheated, you always cheat, you know you do.

VOICE 2: No, I don't—look, that's my frock in the water.

VOICE 3: I'll be finished long before you are, Myrto.

VOICE 4 [*older voice*]: Quiet, children, remember the Queen
   is ill.

VOICE 2 [*whisper*]: Old Mother Gorgo always knows best.

VOICE 3: Is the Queen still sick?

VOICE 2: Have you heard how she is today?

[*Music: Parodos*]

VOICE 1 [*singing*]: There is a rock of many waters
From whose rifts
A rich spring plunges,
Where the women slant their pails:
And a friend was washing her robes there,
Spreading them out in the sun
On the flat of a sun-drenched rock.
She gave me this news of the Queen:

VOICE 2: Close in the house on a wasting bed
With delicate veils
Shading her bright hair,

VOICE 3: And this the third day of her fasting,
Withholding her mouth
From the holy
Body of the bruised
Mother of Corn:

VOICE 4: Longing in hidden sorrow
For the safety of death.

VOICE 1 [*singing*]: Longing in hidden sorrow
For the safety of death.

VOICE 2: Does your mind wander, my haunted child, is it
    God-possessed
By Pan or by Hecate
Or by the Mountain Mother?

VOICE 3: Do the crested Corybantes
Jangle dissonant cymbals in your ears?

VOICE 4: Did you sin against Dictynna the Huntress,
Are you unholy, child?

VOICE 2: Are your ritual cakes unoffered
That you waste away?

VOICE 3: For Artemis is a harsh pursuer,
Pursuing the guilty
Over and over the waves:
She wanders the oceans to the lands beyond
In the salt eddies of the sea.

VOICE 4: Or is it your husband, King Theseus,
First in Athens?
Does some bed of love that is dark and soft in the house
Lure him away
To another's arms?

VOICE 3: Did some sailor man set sail from Crete
For the gentle harbour here
Bringing sharp news for the Queen?

And she, is her soul in sorrow for this
Imprisoned on her bed?

VOICE 4: Yet woman's wavering nature knows
Such haunting agonies of heart,

VOICE 2: Dark cravings,

VOICE 3: The secret shifts
Of animal desire,

VOICE 4: The crawling
Shadow of child-bearing near.

VOICE 1 [*singing*]: I too have known this pang,
But I cried aloud on her
That watches women in labour,
Artemis, who holds the Bow,
As she walks among the Gods in Heaven,
And ever in my eyes most greatly blessed.

[*Music ends.*]

VOICE 4: Look, at the palace door, there she is,
Her old Nurse is bringing her out into the sun.

VOICE 3: How sick she is, poor girl, just look at her face;
it's clouded with pain—she might be an old woman.

VOICE 2: Shsh, Leucippe, the nurse is talking to her.

[*Fade in*]

NURSE: What a longsome thing this life is, to be sure
And sickness is the worst of all.
What shall I do for you, what shall I not do?
Look, Phaedra, here's the white sunlight you wanted,
And the cool air wrinkling round you.
Now your sick bed is set out of doors.
Your one cry was to bring you here;
Well, now I've brought you, you'll say:
Take me back, take me quickly,
Back to my room in the dark of the palace.
Nothing pleases you, everything makes you fretful.
What you have, you make a poor mouth at,

And what you don't you think would be better.
I'd liefer be sick than be nurse, let me tell you,
All you need do if you're ill is to lie there in bed,
But me, I must work, even if I am dazed with worry.
Still, there's life all over,
There's no rest from trouble and there's no rest for the weary...
Maybe, there's something beyond it all,
But whatever it is
Darkness folds it round with shadows, and our eyes are
    bemisted:
So we are still helplessly in love
With this sharp pulse
That glitters on the ground, this world of light.
For we know nothing of another world,
Nothing of the unseen place,
We are all at sea with stories.

PHAEDRA: Lift me up . . . let me look . . .
My body, cold and lost,
Why does this veil weigh so heavily.
Take it away. Let my hair run where it will.
Along my shoulders.

NURSE: Now, child, be cheerful, don't struggle so,
The pain will be lighter if you don't fret for it.
Be brave, then. Weren't we all born to suffer?

PHAEDRA [in a distant voice]: The water. There. To drink
    narrow water
a mountain stream
cold as the first dew!
to lie down
under the alders
in the deep grass
there . . .
lie down . . . long rest . . .

NURSE: Your words are running wild.
Don't say such things where everyone can hear them.

PHAEDRA: Take me to the hills. Let me go
to the forest, the pine trees, there
where the hounds are coursing hard

on the heels of the flashing stag.
joy . . . joy . . . to shout to the hounds . . . Faster! Faster!
let the lance of Thessaly
sing past my sun-fingered hair, let me clench
the quick spear in my hand . . .

    NURSE: What is it you want now, Phaedra, what are these
        night-wisps?
What have you to do with hunting?
Why drink from a distant stream?
Beyond your palace walls is a hillside veined with springs,
There you can drink as you will.

    PHAEDRA: Artemis, lady of waters, of the fisherfolk,
secret between the cypresses,
you are Queen in Limna,
where the smooth land shudders under wild hooves.
Take me there, Artemis, take me . . . let me ride,
let me tame the Venetian mares.

    NURSE: These mindless words again, child.
First you must set your heart upon the hills
To hunt wild beasts. And next you want to drive horses
On Limna's sands. We need bide for a prophet here
To tell what Power is wrenching you from your course
and driving your wits astray.

    PHAEDRA: I know my pain. What have I done?
How far have I wandered in my mind . . .
wickedly . . . Tell me, have I gone mad?
Some God has maddened me. Yes.
Nanna, hide my head again.
I'm ashamed of what I've been saying.
Cover me. Look, these are tears.
Here in my eyes.
I can see nothing . . . only my disgrace.
It is a terrible thing to come to the surface again,
When you've been mad.
I know what I must do. But to know is agony.
Madness can be sweet.
I wish I had died when I was out of my mind.

NURSE: There, then. Let me cover you.
But when will death cover my old bones?
Live much and learn much.
It is not leal come on earth
To be tangled in friendship with others
So deep, why it startles the soul in us.
The loves of our hearts should be easy,
Easy to throw away, easy to draw close.
When one small soul goes in labour for two,
As I do, for my mistress,
Why, it's a hard burden to bear.
Too sour a course of life I always say
Harms your health more than it helps it.
A little of what you like is better than too much,
Wise men who have seen much of life
Would agree with me.

VOICE 4: Nurse, you are close to Queen Phaedra,
tell us, we can see your mistress is poorly,
what is it that troubles her like this?

VOICE 2: Yes, tell us, do.

NURSE: I've questioned her and found out nothing.
She'll not speak.

VOICE 3:      But how did it begin?

NURSE: You're asking the same question. She'll not speak.

VOICE 4: How wasted her face looks. She's lost all her
strength.

NURSE: And that's not strange. Three days she's had no food.

VOICE 2: Has some God chafed her mind into madness?
Or is she bent on dying?

NURSE: Yes. She is wishing to die.
She's fasting to get rid of life.

VOICE 3: This is strange. But what does the King say?

NURSE: She hides her trouble, won't allow she's ill at all.

VOICE 4: Theseus can guess it surely from her face?

NURSE: It happens he's not here. He has gone
To Apollo's house at Delphi.

VOICE 2: But surely you can force her to speak.
Wring out the secret of her madness.

NURSE: I've tried, of course, tried everything. But all at no
        gait.
Still, I'll not give up.
All of you here will see how I behave
When my betters are in trouble.
But come now, my darling, all that was said before
Let's both forget. Shall we? Put on a likely face,
Smooth out your forehead; don't look so crabbed.
I have been foolish too, I know.
Let's leave all that, and try a better way.
Now, hear me, if you're ill and it's hard to speak of,
We are all women here, to help you to cure it.
But if it can be mentioned to a man,
Then tell us, and we can bring a doctor.
What, still quiet! That quietness is wicked.
Tell me if I have spoken out of place,
Or am I truthful? If I am, then admit it.
Come now, answer me. Say something, do.
Look at me, child. One word, one look this way.
Don't hide. Oh, you frighten me. Friends,
We're troubling our heads for nothing.
We are as far away from her as we ever were;
She wasn't sweetened by my words then
And she takes no notice now.
But, listen, Phaedra, be more feckless than the sea,
Be silent, sick and stubborn if you will,
But if you die and leave your children, do you think
They will sit in King Theseus' palace?
Remember Antiope,
The Queen and horsewoman, gave them a brother,
Her son, born to lord it over your children.
Not pure in blood maybe, but pure in mind,
You know him well, your stepson, Hippolytus.

PHAEDRA [Gives a cry.]: No!

NURSE: At last. That touches you, does it?

PHAEDRA: Nanna, it goes straight to my heart. By every God there is
I beg you: never speak that name again.

NURSE: There, there, you're a wise body now.
But still you won't do what's best for your children,
And still you won't save your own life.

PHAEDRA: Oh, I love my children. It's not there the storm is breaking.

NURSE: Child, you've not . . . killed some one? Are your hands stained?

PHAEDRA: The stain goes deeper than that, it's in my heart.

NURSE: You have an enemy, then? Some one wishes you ill?

PHAEDRA: No, not an enemy. A friend . . . killing me
Against his will and mine . . .

NURSE [knowingly and quickly]: Ah, Theseus has been unfaithful to you.

PHAEDRA: No. And may I never be unfaithful to him.

NURSE: Then what is it, this deadly secret
That's feeding on your life?

PHAEDRA: Let me be alone with my wickedness. It does you no harm.

NURSE: What, leave you? Not even if you push me away.

PHAEDRA: What are you doing, Nurse? Let go my hand.
Let me go, *let me go*.
Do you think you can force me by clinging to my hand?

NURSE: Yes, and to your knees. I will never let you go.

PHAEDRA: My dear, it's ugly, ugly. There's only pain in it.

NURSE: No greater pain than losing you.

PHAEDRA: Why not? Perhaps it is best, that way.
That way, at least, I can keep my good name.

NURSE: Why will you hide the truth then?
I've gone down on these old knees for it.

PHAEDRA: I can't speak, Nanna. Time, with time,
I can tame it and build it into something good.

NURSE: Tell me then. If it's something good, why mayn't I
hear it?

PHAEDRA: Go away, in Heaven's name. *Let go my hand.*

NURSE: Not till I have this little gift you owe me.

PHAEDRA [*a wrenching sigh*]: Oh! Oh, you're too strong for
me. Take it, then,
This gift as you call it. There *is* something holy about your
hand,
The way it closed on me . . . it dandled me once.

NURSE: Now, I will be quiet.
From now on it is you must speak.

PHAEDRA: My mother began it. My mother, Pasiphae . . .
She loved strangely . . .

NURSE [*An excited whisper*]: You mean . . . the Bull . . . ?

PHAEDRA [*In an interior voice*]: And you, Ariadne . . .
sister . . .
Left on Naxos for the claws of seabirds
Till you rested in the arms of Dionysus.

NURSE: They're horrible, those old stories.
Why do they come back now?
It's your own kith and kin you're speaking of.

PHAEDRA: I'm speaking of myself. There will be another
death.
The curse does not sleep.

NURSE: I don't understand. Where are you taking me?

PHAEDRA: There, where my old sorrows first began.
The evil works in my blood. How can I escape it?

NURSE: I'm a blindling. What can be coming next?

PHAEDRA: If only you could speak it for me. Say what I
must say.

NURSE: Well, I'm no prophet
To go unpicking your secrets.

[*Pause*]

PHAEDRA: Tell me . . . what do people mean by . . . Love,
Being in Love?

NURSE: Sweet, my child. The sweetest and most painful
thing there is.

PHAEDRA: Then I have only known the pain.

NURSE: What's this? You're in love, child? Who is it?

PHAEDRA: Someone . . . he is called . . . his mother was an
Amazon.

NURSE [*hoarse whisper*]: You mean . . . Hippolytus.

PHAEDRA [*the last despairing flicker*]: I never used the name.
I said nothing.
It was you.

NURSE: No, no, no, I don't believe it. I won't believe it.
I never thought to hear words like these . . .
Women, you're friends of the house. Did you hear it,
Did you hear what she said?
Ah . . . so good a lady, to think she has come to this.
Oh, I wish I were tucked in my grave, I hate it all.
Hate the sunlight in which such things are spoken.
And as for you, Aphrodite,

[*Music: Aphrodite Theme*]

Love do you call yourself?
You're not the Goddess of Love, but of death,
Feeding on good folk,
Dangering her, dangering me, damnifying the whole house.

[*Music*]

VOICE 1 [*singing*]:
You have heard it, women, you have heard.
No one could live alone

In the hidden world of the Queen.
She cried it aloud in her pain.

SINGING CHORUS: We have heard it and would be dead
Before we had sorrow like hers.

VOICE 1 [*singing*]: Oh daily bread of misery!
How will the long day end for you?

VOICE 3: Bruised stillness, the day falls in storm;

VOICE 4: For over the house the leaning evil
Grows till it stifles the light.

VOICE 2: Aphrodite's shadow sitting in the day.

VOICE 1 [*singing*]: While plain as a star
The luck of your love is waning,
Poor child of Crete!

[*Music ends.*]

PHAEDRA [*with a desperate calm, virtually answering the
nurse, and trying to correct the impression the preceding dia-
logue must have given*]:

Women of Trozen, who live here at this frontier post
In the land of Argos, hear what I have to say:
Often before now
In the slow hours near the still of the night
I have wondered idly what it *is* breaks men's lives.
It is not, I think, through a defect in our judgement
That so many of us choose what is plainly wicked.
No, we can discriminate between good and evil
Well enough, we can recognise the good when we see it;
But why don't we practice it, that's the question?
Not through ignorance, the failure lies in the will.
It may be pure laziness, or is it that we value
Some other pleasure more highly than our duty?
And how many pleasures there are, crowding our lives:
The small talk that women love, in the town square,
Down by the wells, with your baskets in the lemon groves,
Or idling away the warm hours behind the shutters,
Sweet levities—[*changing her tone*]
Once I had seen things as they really are

And that no illusion however sweet can change them
Or change me, or change my purpose ... [*breaks off agitatedly*]
Oh, let me tell you how my mind travelled on.
First, there was love; or rather there was pain. So
I began to wonder how I could bear this sickness,
Still keeping my good name. I began with silence.
Oh there's no trusting the tongue. It knows so well
How to make others smart for their failings,
But brings all kind of trouble on itself.
Then I tried to live with this madness of my senses,
Argue myself out of it,
As if the *will* to virtue could save me.
But however hard I tried I could not stifle Love,
So it seemed best to die.
When I do good let me get the glory of it,
But when I fail, may no one see me.
I know it is as bad to admit to this hunger
As it would be if I were to give it ease,
And what is more I know that being a woman
One false step—and all men's hands are against me.
Oh I curse the wife
Who first soured the marriage bed with strangers.
This famous treachery so many women do began
Among the well-born and in great houses.
When those who are governing in the land
Lose all their sense of decency
The common people will soon catch the habit.
And oh, how I hate women who talk chastity
But in secret hug one soft, dangerous vice,
Caress it with their minds ...
How can they, Aphrodite, Queen of Love,
How can they look their husbands in the face,
Without trembling in case the darkness,
Working with the act
And the very walls of their bedroom, shudder with a voice?
It is this dread, that makes me turn to death.
This dread that I may play false with my husband,
And disgrace my children. I want them to grow up
In Athens, with not a shadow on their lives,
Proud of their mother. It crushes the spirit in a man,
However proud he may be, to learn his parent's shame.

They say that through all the blind happenings of life
One thing alone stays with you: innocence of spirit.
Time holds up a mirror as naturally as a girl
And sooner or later the wicked see themselves as they are.
Oh, I never want to see myself like that!

NURSE: Madame, you quite stole my breath away just now,
I was that frightened. It all came at a blink.
But now I see I was being a foolish old body.
But aren't our second thoughts often for the wiser?
There's nothing eerie or to dread about what's happened
To you. Aphrodite has swept down in a fury—
You're in love. Well, what of it? You're not the only one.
Hundreds of people love where there are . . . difficulties.
And are you going to kill yourself for just that?
It's a poor gait for lovers if they must die for it.
When Aphrodite floods into the heart, she is terrible,
But if you give in, why she gentles you,
Falls as soft as rain . . .
But a body who says no to love,
Who thinks she can forget the laws of Nature,
Aphrodite shakes her, and humbles her soon enough!
[*She speaks with a slow, almost dreamy accent.*]
Aphrodite wanders the air, she is drifted across the sea,
And all things living owe their life to her.
She sows, she breeds and she bestows desire,
All of us who live on earth are born of Love.
And scholars who are very deep in the old books
Will tell you how Zeus himself once longed for Semele
And how Dawn for all her distant, hesitant fragrance
Once caught up Cephalus and took him in her radiant arms to
    Heaven.
But still they live among the Gods, and so I have heard
Feel no strangeness, but go glad that Love took them.
Why not give way yourself? . . .
Your Father should have got you
With other Gods as masters, in some other Heaven and Earth
If you can't take the laws of life as you find them.
Just mind, how many of the most sensible bodies among us
When they see their marriages all here and there,
Shrug, and pretend that nothing has happened.

And how many fathers have mammocked a little for their sons?
No, you can't work out life like the arithmetic.
Take this roof that covers up your house,
Even that doesn't lie quite trimly, but it serves;
You have fallen into a great sea, and how can you hope
To swim ashore? No, child, count your blessings,
And if the good in life comes to more than the bad,
Then, you have done well enough.
Now come, dear child, leave these wrong thoughts, be ruly.
You wouldn't set yourself above the Gods themselves!
Take heart and love! It's what Heaven wills for you.
Yes, yes, I know you're sick. Well, overgo your sickness.
There are old runes, charms and such like:
We shall find some medicine to skin over your troubles.
Men would be hunting long and late, let me tell you,
If our sharp women's wits didn't get there sooner.

PHAEDRA: Now I know what it is that breaks up families,
And whole cities with them—easy, lying words!
You shouldn't tell people just what they want to hear.
We need someone to tell us how to live better.

NURSE: Why be so solemn! It's not fine words that you need.
You need the man. Some one, I say, must be found at once
To tell him the cold fact . . . you need him.
Now don't imagine I should be talking like this
If you simply wanted Hippolytus for your pleasure.
No, it's to save your life. And where's the harm in that?

PHAEDRA: No harm you say! Your very words are filthy.

NURSE: Filthy they may be, but more use to you than your
    fine ones.
Going to it is better, if it saves you,
Than being on the tilt with virtue, and then dying.

PHAEDRA: No more. I won't hear any more, I tell you.
You're too sly and persuasive and I'm so weak with love
I shall drift away with the ebb-tide and be lost.

NURSE: If that's what you think, you shouldn't have sinned
    in the first place.
But sinned you have. So listen, child. Next best is this:
Somewhere in the house, I have just remembered,

I've a love charm, one that will cure this sickness.
There's no disgrace in it, and it'll not harm your mind.

PHAEDRA: This charm, do you drink it, or rub it into the
skin?

NURSE: Whist! Don't ask questions. Think about getting
better.

PHAEDRA: I'm afraid of your tricks. Be careful what you do.

NURSE: Does everything frighten you? Well, what is it now?

PHAEDRA: I'm afraid you will let fall something to . . . him.

NURSE: To Hippolytus? No, no, dear child. Never you fret
now.
Leave all to me.
                [*in a low voice*] Aphrodite, Sea Lady,
Work with me. What else I have in mind
It will be enough to tell . . . you know whom in the palace.

[*Music*]

VOICE 1 [*singing*]: Eros, Eros,
desire,
startling and shadowing the eye
with the dew of longing,
your whispering soldiery
has stormed our hearts
but come now with muted tread . . .

VOICE 2: for neither star-riveted bolt
nor vaulting fire
is as fierce
as that black mane of thunder
hanging in flame
singed from the child fingers of Love,
from Eros,

VOICE 1 [*singing*]: Eros, child of the highest.

VOICE 3: A girl in Oechalia once,
a filly, unbroken, riderless,
who had never hollowed the bed of love

or lain with man in her mind,
Cypris herded in frenzy,
from her home, from her father Eurytus,
like a naiad winding away from Pan,
like a maenad drunk with God
in the coves of the hills,
and flung her to Herakles,
and bridled her
in blood and fire and in hymns of death.

voice 4: Oh sacred wall of Thebes
and Dirce's fountain lips
cry in one bare voice
silence and horror that breeds
in the shadow of Aphrodite.
Yes, Semele she brought to bed
with Bromios the thunder king
by the flame of the two-fanged thunderbolt
welded in marriage to the limbs of death.

voice 1 [*singing*]: For everywhere the dark Goddess broods
and intoning like a bee she looses
a spurt of honey
and a sting.

[*Music ends.*]

phaedra: Quiet, quiet, women. It's all over now.

voice 4: What is happening there in the Palace, madam?

phaedra: Quiet. Let me hear what they are saying.

[*Nurse and Hippolytus are heard within, indistinctly.*]

phaedra: Ah, no, no.

voice 2: What do these cries mean . . .

voice 3: These broken words . . .

voice 4: What can you see?

voice 2: What is it . . . ?

PHAEDRA: The end. Stand near the door and listen for
  yourselves.
The noise shapes itself in the house:
It is him . . . the Amazon's son . . . Hippolytus,
Can't you hear him now brow-beating my nurse?

VOICE 3: I can hear something, but it's all confused.

VOICE 4: He's shouting at her, but what's he saying?

PHAEDRA: Oh, it's all too clear. You must all hear it now.

HIPPOLYTUS [within]: Bawd . . .
treacherous to your master's bed . . .

VOICE 4: You have a treacherous friend.

VOICE 2: Your secret is bared.

VOICE 3: How can we help . . .

VOICE 4: What can we do . . . ?

PHAEDRA: She has told him I am ill . . . everything . . .
She meant kindly, but has left me . . . nothing.

VOICE 4: What now? What will you do?

PHAEDRA: Do? Now? What is left me to do?
Listen, listen . . .

[Fade in]

HIPPOLYTUS: Earth . . . mother of all . . . glaring eye of day
  . . . Sun.
No, I cannot even repeat what I have heard.

NURSE: Softly, Hippolytus, someone will hear.

HIPPOLYTUS: I have heard . . . horror.

NURSE: I beg you.

HIPPOLYTUS: I *will* speak.

NURSE: By this strong, smooth arm of yours.

HIPPOLYTUS: Take your hands away. Don't paw me,
You foul-mouthed creature.

NURSE: By your knees . . .

HIPPOLYTUS: Leave go, will you.

NURSE: To speak would ruin . . .

HIPPOLYTUS: Ruin? Good words ruin?
How can they if what you told me was true.

NURSE: It was only meant for your ears.

HIPPOLYTUS: Shout it aloud if there's nothing to be ashamed
of.
Good words sound better the more people hear them.

NURSE: Oh, wait. Wait. Sweet boy.
You wouldn't hurt your poor friends . . .

HIPPOLYTUS: Friends! I spit at the word.
No one who is filthy like that is my friend.

NURSE: Forgive . . .
Learn to forgive us . . .
It is our human way . . .
We are all flesh . . .

HIPPOLYTUS: Zeus, why did you let her pass into the light,
That glittering false coin, woman?
If you wanted to start the human race
You should never have pitched your stock in women.
No, it would have been better if men had swelled your shrines
With gold or iron or a huddle of bronze
And each man bought himself a brood of children,
Then we might have had value for our money.
Then there would have been no more women,
And our houses would have been clean of the plague.
Women *are* a plague, any way you look at it.
Take the Father who begins it all by begetting them:
He brings the thing up, and when it is full-blown,
To rid his hands of it, must swamp it with a dowry,
A consolation prize for the idiot who takes her,
And plants her like a poisonous flower in his house.
Why, he's even pleased to decorate the vicious doll,
Truss her in silks and bandage her with gold
While his family fortunes wither.

If you must marry, then go and marry a fool,
A nothingness, too stupid to make trouble,
Sitting all day in the house with naked, meaningless eyes.
But most of all I loathe the clever woman,
Knowing too much for her own good. When they're clever
Aphrodite embeds more mischief there
Than in the ninnies' colon—at least you can be sure enough
They won't have the wit to play the fool
The moment your back is turned. I won't have servants
Near them either. No, a wife should be kennelled in the house
With beasts that can bite, but cannot talk
Where there's no one for them to speak to
And no one to answer them back when they open their mouths.
But as it is they shut themselves away
Idling with vice,
And then their servants smear it abroad.
And you, you slut, you crept out, did you,
To drag me to his bed, my father's bed?
I shall flush your words away in the quick
Candour of a stream, hurling the water into my ears.
Did you really think I would come to Phaedra's arms?
Why, when I even heard your scraping voice,
Hiss your suggestion, I felt unclean . . . unclean!
It's only my sense of honour that saves you, woman.
You surprised me to swear an oath to the Gods, otherwise
Nothing could have stopped me telling my father—this!
But now so long as he's abroad I shall keep away
Myself. I shall say nothing till my father returns.
And when he returns, I shall be close behind him,
I shall watch closely how you and your precious mistress
Look him in the face. I've met your shameless impudence
    already.
Oh how I hate the pair of you! How I hate all women!
Though they tell me I am always saying the same thing,
But women are always doing the same thing;
They're rotten to the centre. Animals!
Let someone teach them to smother their hot wishes
Or don't ask me not to despise the lot of them!

[*Fade*]

WOMEN: Haggard life of women.
What art, or argument remains,
What trick of pleading,
when we are caught in passion,
to untie the knot,
to cut the cord of scandal?

[*Fade in*]

PHAEDRA: I have heard the accusing voice.
I have heard sentence . . .
Earth and light.
Is there nowhere now to run from ruin,
nowhere to bury disaster?
Which of the Gods can I cry to?
Would a man stand at my side
and shoulder my evil?
This agony that claws at my life
will whirl me away
in the blind orbit
beyond life itself . . .

VOICE 4: What is done, is done.

VOICE 2: Your servant's shifts have failed you, Phaedra.

VOICE 3: Nothing goes well from now.

NURSE [*approaching*]: Madam, madam—

PHAEDRA: Nurse, you evil woman, do you see what you have
    done?
Oh Zeus . . . Zeus . . . my father . . .
Stab her with dark fire . . . scar her with your voice.
I knew what you meant to do. I told you. I said
"Hold your tongue. Don't say a word to him."
But you . . . you . . . you had to tell him everything.
You had to meddle and now I must smart with scandal.
But now . . . I must find some new way out
Find it quickly . . . for Hippolytus . . . his mind . . .
It will be sharpened to a quick nerve of anger,
He's mad with purity . . . He'll tell his father
What you've blurted out, he'll tell everyone . . .
The whole town will be swollen with low self-satisfied gossip.

Curse you . . . curse you . . . and curse everyone
Whose stupid eagerness
Tries to help those who don't want their help.

NURSE: Madam, like enough you scold and think harsh of
    me.
For you're angry and that blots your mind,
But if you'd listen awhile I've an answer for you.
Weren't you a wisp in my arms? Don't I love you?
All I was wishing was to find some help
For this trouble of yours and I found . . . something else.
Had things gone at a good gait, everyone would have said
How clever I was,
But then we're only clever when our schemes go right.

PHAEDRA: Be quiet. This, after what you have done.
Do you think these sneaking words are going to please me?

NURSE: We've talked too much. Likely I've been foolish.
But it's never too late to mend. Now, madam . . .

PHAEDRA: Don't speak to me. You've said enough. More than
    enough.
Your advice was ugly.
The scheme you tried to force on me was ugly.
Go. I never want to see you again.
Do you hear me. Go. From now on, look to your own affairs.

NURSE: [going, weeping]: Oh, child, child . . .

PHAEDRA: Now there is one sure way to order my life.
You, who are women like myself, my only friends in Trozen,
There is one gift you have for me. Only one.
Be silent. Say nothing of what you have seen and heard.

VOICE 4: We swear . . .

VOICE 3:                    By the name of Artemis . . .

VOICE 2:                              God's daughter

VOICE 4:                                        Never . . .

VOICE 3:              Never to speak

VOICE 2:                        Never to speak.

PHAEDRA: I can only thank you with words. I have been
    looking
Beyond this torment. And I have found it.
A dark and clear way to leave my children their good name.
And to redeem the wreckage of a life. Time,
There is still time.
I must never insult the great house of Crete,
Never meet Theseus again with this between us.
No one shall say that I came to terms with it—my sweet guilt—
Because of one small life.

VOICE 4: The past cannot be undone.

VOICE 2: It is too late.

VOICE 3: What does she mean?

PHAEDRA: What do I mean? Death. Nothing more.
Now I have only to choose—which death.

VOICE 2: No, no, no.

VOICE 3: Don't speak like that.

PHAEDRA: And you, too. Don't give me foolish advice
I shall die today, and Aphrodite at least will sing.
This was what she meant for me.
Oh, I am brimming with an acrid love, torment!
But at least I shall not die without hurting someone else.
I can never forgive him. He despised me
Knowing nothing of the horror of love.
Well, let him take his share.
It may even teach him something of life.

VOICE 2: Would that I might hide in the secret heart of the
    clouds
Under the brows of the hills,
That I might break a bird from the hands of Zeus,
a winged bird among the high plumed flocks;
then might I be upborne
to where the sea waves strain the Adrian shore,
the fair waters of Eridanus,
where those sad daughters of the Sun,
the Heliades,
in pity for Phaethon,

distil into the blue glooms of the sea
the amber glisters of their tears.

  VOICE 3: I would wander to the shore of the singing
Hesperides,
the guardian daughters
of the apple-flushed coasts,
where the ruler of the blind undersea
stems the daring ships,
where God designed the solemn verge of Heaven
that Atlas holds in his arms.
There ambrosia-burdened rivers
lull the bridals of Zeus,
and holy Earth, giver of all good gifts,
gives blessing to the Gods.

  VOICE 4: Oh Cretan boat white-winged
over the droning wave
bringing Phaedra from a house of laughter
to the cold marriage here.
Then from either shore
the Gods spoke by dark signs
when from her Cretan land she came
to brilliant Athens,
the curse crawled from the ship
when they coiled the tangled strands
strict to Munychia's wharf
and first set foot upon the mainland shore.

  VOICE 2: Therefore, her heart is now consumed
by Aphrodite's gift,
by that dry sickness of forbidden love.

  VOICE 3: And at the last dissolved in pain
she is weaving the twists of a noose
to the beams of her bridal roof,
it is groping,
it is winding round the white of her neck,

  VOICE 4: desiring a fair name above her life
she strives to ease her heart
of the bitter weight that is love.

  [*Music ends.*]

NURSE [*within*]: Help . . . help . . . all of you . . . come . . .
   help . . . quickly . . .
She's hanged herself. Phaedra is dead.

VOICE 4: Then it is finished.

VOICE 2: She has gone.

VOICE 3: Caught in the arms of the noose.

NURSE [*within*]: Hurry, hurry, why doesn't someone fetch
   a knife,
Cut the knots that cling to her throat?
No, no, no. Leave it all.
Lay her out quietly. Straighten the poor limbs.
So let the King find her, keeping watch
For him: but when he comes there will be no meeting.

[*Music: Keening Women*]

VOICE 4: And by that cry she is dead already.

[*Superimpose Music: Trumpets*]

VOICE 2: The King . . .

VOICE 3:              The King . . .

VOICE 5: Theseus . . .

VOICE 6:              King Theseus . . .

VOICE 4: The King . . . back already . . .

THESEUS [*approaching*]: You, women, what is this
   commotion in the palace?
What is this look in your eyes . . . what are the servants
Groaning for? And the doors?
Too proud to open and welcome me from Delphi?
Why will no one look at me?
Surely my home-coming deserves more than this.
What has happened? Has someone . . . left us?

VOICE 2: It is a young life you have lost, Theseus.

THESEUS: Ah . . . one of my children . . . torn from me?

VOICE 4: Your children are alive. But you must bear
Their mother's death.

THESEUS: Dead . . . my wife . . . but how?

VOICE 3: By the noose . . . her own hands.

THESEUS: Hanged herself . . . But why? What forced her to
   this?
Come, what was it? Tell me.

VOICE 2: We know nothing more.

THESEUS: Why do I hide my head with these foolish leaves?
Leaves of triumph! Bay leaves from Delphi! You, there,
Loosen the bars on the gates, undo the bolts.

   [*bolts and bars unloosed*]

Let me see her . . . she was my wife . . . let me look at her
   death.

   [*Gates opened*]

   [*Music: Keening Women*]
   WOMEN [*singing*]: Phaedra,
you suffered, you acted,
but what could you do?
And now you have died
for the sin that darkened your eyes
and a God has dimmed your life . . .

   [*Music ends.*]

THESEUS: My tongue hangs heavily like a bell . . .
Through black silence of old blood,
What comes in blood, what crawls,
What stalked the present, what crouched and fell
On the house, on the City . . .

Then sudden water, lost, lost, I am lost,
and ribbed with madness, waves,
coiled hair-like, rise, hiss, clutch,
drop sleek weight and the coast
has wilted under the sea . . .

I warmed a bird in my hand, but it broke away,
lost, cold flare of feathers,
in one tense leap
there among the play of shadows below the world,
there threading through the dream that is not sleep.

Split between sea and Heaven, time stops . . .
a wrong that scars the past, stalks the present.
It is slow, and slowly it shapes,
swells to human form, and desolates at last . . .

> VOICE 4: This agony is shared by many . . .

> VOICE 2: Others before this time lost a loved one . . .

> VOICE 3: A wife,

> VOICE 4: As young, as tender, as Phaedra?

> THESEUS: No, let me run down the darkening spiral,
to the root of the shadows, where
I will house with sorrow,
now, you are not here,
lost, near, remembered, quiet presence . . .
with your last grimace of terrible knowledge
and your secret shrieking in your eyes,
the last pain that clenched your heart . . .
asking without words to be let out
till you found the long kind arms
that crept about your throat!

Will someone tell me how it happened?
Or have you all gone idiot with grief?

No, I can say no more.
Suffer no more . . .
My house is a desert,
My children have no mother;
You have abandoned them: they were born on your body,
You have abandoned me,
Dearest, best of all women,
That ever walked in the day,

or looked
into night's kindling face.

VOICE 4: All that has happened here is darkness and horror.

VOICE 2: But turn away:

VOICE 3: For what comes now
Is darker, more horrible still.

THESEUS: What is this letter crushed in her small cold hand?
It's a message, the last words she ever wrote, and
Her last wishes, too. About her marriage and our children
Perhaps. Poor girl! You have nothing to fear now:
No other woman shall lie in my arms
Or hold the keys of my house. And here, look, yes,
It's the imprint of her ring . . .
It was gold, and it smiles at me . . .
And she's dead. But now let me break the seal
And learn what she has to say to me.

VOICE 3: This is new evil the God blesses.

VOICE 4: I came this way before, and I looked
And I would have died to drown the voice,
To shatter the hanging image,

VOICE 2: But the present is brushing my eyes,
With a shadow, striping the ground
With bird-shadow,
Harsh maze of wings,
An omen . . .

VOICE 3: And evil begins again . . .

THESEUS: Oh, there's more . . .
More than I can speak . . . than I can bear . . .
This tablet does not whisper . . . her dying words
Shriek . . . She shrieked before she died.
I can hear it . . . now . . . it follows me
Over and over again till it slides into music,
Music that is so thin it slices the ear and
Silences everything . . .
Though I can hardly whisper it,
Yet, I will be strong. I shall speak to all the land.

Hear, all the land! Theseus speaks.
Derisive of the rigorous eye of Zeus
Hippolytus, my son, has dared to force my bed,
Dishonouring my wife with his mad hands.
Now, Poseidon, my father, you granted me three prayers.
Here, I shall claim one.
Show me you did not mock me with your promises.
Kill my son . . . Now . . . before the day goes down.

[*Both choruses cry out.*]

VOICE 4: Theseus, in the name of God . . . take your curse
back!

THESEUS: Never! and to make sure I shall force him out of
the land.
So that one way or the other he'll be the loser.
Either Poseidon will keep his word to me,
Will answer my curse and send him down to his death;
Or else he'll wander away his life in strange lands,
And drink the cup of loneliness to its bitter grounds . . .

OLD SERVANT [*approaching*]: King Theseus, look—here *is* your
son, come just in time. You'll find he can explain everything.
Of course you are angry but, sir, you are our King. And as
King you must control yourself and think carefully what is best
for the State.

HIPPOLYTUS [*approaching*]: I heard your voice, Father. It
sounded as though you were angry about something. I left
everything and came at once. [*pause*] But what in God's name
has happened? You look as though you have been crying. Why
does everyone stare at me like this? [*silence*] The Queen—but
what . . . why is she lying there like that? [*sharp intake of breath*]
These marks round her throat . . . She is . . . dead. But I left
her only just now. How did this happen? [*silence*] Why do you
look at me like that, Father, why don't you say something? I
long to help you, but—*why don't you say something?* What
happened—we've got a right to know—your friends, your own
flesh and blood . . .

THESEUS [*abstracted, not answering Hippolytus*]: Friends . . .
The masked faces. The masked voices. How can we know the

real face, the real voice? How can a man tell who his friends are?

HIPPOLYTUS: I'm your friend—you believe that, don't you? [*silence*] Has someone been slandering me, is that it, accusing me of something I never did? I don't know what to make of this.

THESEUS [*carrying on as though Hippolytus had not spoken*]: It's a queer thing, the human heart. To do a thing like this and then . . . Are there no limits to what a man is capable of, is there *no* wickedness we can't expect? [*with a sudden change of tone, turning to the chorus*] Take this man here. Hippolytus, my own son. My own son. He waits till I'm out of the way, then . . . rapes my wife.

[*horrified reaction from both choruses*]

[*cry of "No" from Hippolytus*]

THESEUS: YES, I've got proof—it's here, in the letter she wrote me before she . . . died.

[*confused reaction from both choruses*]

THESEUS: You there, Hippolytus! Take your hands away from your face and look at me. So! *This* is where it has brought you! You weren't like other men, you were so pure. So pure you didn't even know the meaning of the word sex. And religious, too. The Gods' special favourite. Blasphemy, rank blasphemy, that's what it was. Not that it ever took me in. [*Changes tone, back to sarcasm.*] But of course you're an Orphic initiate, too. [*imitating Hippolytus' voice*] "No meat for me, father. Food that has held the breath of life shall never pass these lips." All that ritual hokey pokey, all those big fat books your long-haired boy friends in Athens were always sending you . . . Well, you can drop all that now. It won't wash any longer. You've been shown up for what you are. [*turning violently to the chorus*] Listen, everybody, I warn you. Look out for men like this. They go about preaching at you, telling you to change your lives. It's not your lives they're interested in, it's your wives!

[*reaction from both choruses*]

THESEUS: There she is, dead, dead. Her mouth stopped for ever. But if you think *that'll* save you, you are making the biggest mistake of your career. Nothing you say can outweigh this piece of evidence, the letter she wrote me before she killed herself.

HIPPOLYTUS [*breaking in desperately*]: It's not true, Father, it's not—

THESEUS: She lied, did she? Slandered you, because she hated you, because you were an interloper, a bastard and she was true-born? A bad bargain she made, poor girl, by your account, if she threw away the dearest thing she had—her own life, because she hated you.

[*confused reaction from both choruses*]

[*cries of "Listen to me, Father" from Hippolytus*]

THESEUS: Or will you try and tell me—but why go on? There's no need to prove your guilt. The proof is there—*there,* her dead body proves my case beyond all arguing. Get out, d'you hear me, get out! God help you if you ever show your face here again. And stay out of Athens, too. If I stand for this sort of treatment from you my whole past will rise up against me—every scoundrel I ever brought to book will come to life again and call me fraud.

OLD SERVANT [*sotto voce*]: You must say something, Prince Hippolytus. You're got to defend yourself, now, or you'll be convicted without a hearing.

HIPPOLYTUS: But what can I say?—he makes it all sound so plausible, but it's not true, I swear not a word of it is true.

OLD SERVANT [*soothingly*]: We all believe you, sir. Go over and speak to your father, tell him—

HIPPOLYTUS: But what can I say? I was never any good at explaining myself in public. I can only talk freely when I'm with a few friends.

OLD SERVANT: Perhaps if you swore an oath . . . ?

HIPPOLYTUS: Yes, yes, a solemn oath . . .

OLD SERVANT [*calling out*]: Sir, your son has something to say to you . . .

THESEUS [*violent impatience*]

HIPPOLYTUS [*slowly*]: Father, beneath this Sun that shines above you, upon this earth that you tread, there is no man more innocent than I am. [*change of tone, defiantly*] This is the truth, even if you don't believe it.

THESEUS [*violently*]: Proof, boy, proof.

HIPPOLYTUS: I can prove it, if you'll only listen. Doesn't my whole way of life refute your accusations? I love and honour the Gods—surely, no one would deny that? Then take my friends—they show what kind of man I am. They are people of integrity—people who respect themselves too much to know anyone capable of the thing you accuse me of. For if there's one sin I could never commit, it's this sin you think you have caught me at. My body has never been defiled by the sexual act. I know nothing whatever about it—such things have no meaning for me.

THESEUS [*more impatience*]

HIPPOLYTUS: All right, you're not convinced. But tell me this. Why do you think I did this—where did the temptation lie? Was your wife so beautiful that no one could resist her? Or do you think I seduced her so that I could marry her when you died and become King myself? Do you really believe I'm such a fool? What sane man wants to be King? Everyone wants power, I suppose you'd say. I don't accept that. I covet the honour of being first in the Olympic Games, yes, but as for political power, I'd sooner take second place.

Well, I have argued my case as best I could, but there's one more thing I'd like to say. If I had a witness to my real character and if *she* were still alive to be cross-questioned, then you would see who was guilty. As things stand, I can only give my oath that everything I have said is true. I swear by Zeus, the guardian of all oaths; I swear by the holy earth beneath us, that I never touched your wife, that I never wanted her, that the thought of touching her or wanting her never even passed through my head. If I am guilty, may I die in sorrow: thrown out of my city, an exile begging my bread in foreign lands. It may be she killed herself because . . . she was afraid of something. I can say no more than that. In the eyes of the world she lived virtuously—but if the world could have looked into her mind, could it have said the same? I am virtuous in mind and body: and this is where it has brought me.

OLD SERVANT: King Theseus, your son has proved his innocence. That was a large pledge he gave, swearing an oath by all the gods.

THESEUS: A large pledge, you call it! Does this cool-headed juggler think he can get away with it: first lie with my wife, then tell me he never did me any wrong?

HIPPOLYTUS: If it comes to that, you are keeping pretty cool yourself, for all your ranting. If you were my son and I your father and you did—what you accuse me of, I should kill you, not merely exile you.

THESEUS: Yes, God knows, that's what you deserve. But you are not going to die in any way of your own choosing. A quick death is what we all hope for. I sentence you to the long drawn-out death of exile.

HIPPOLYTUS: If you can prove my guilt I accept your sentence. But give me a little time to collect witnesses and prove my innocence.

THESEUS: Time for nothing. You'll leave Trozen today.

HIPPOLYTUS: Won't you even wait to hear what the Oracle has to say?

THESEUS: My wife's letter is all the oracle I need.

HIPPOLYTUS [half to himself]: You holy Gods! I swore in your name to keep silent—it is this oath that is destroying me. But what's the use? Whatever I said, I should not convince my father. I should be breaking my oath for nothing.

THESEUS: Have the decency to leave the Gods out of it, will you? Oh, this is too much. On your way, boy, on your way.

HIPPOLYTUS: But where can I go? Who will have me with a charge like this hanging over me?

THESEUS: Why, someone who likes entertaining sexual maniacs.

HIPPOLYTUS: If only they could speak, the very walls of the palace would tell you I am innocent.

THESEUS: Very good, that. Walls can't talk, can they? She can't speak either, my poor dead Phaedra. But she witnesses against you all right.

HIPPOLYTUS: If I could stand outside it all for a moment and see myself through someone else's eyes—I think I should break into tears watching what I have to endure.

THESEUS: I'm sure you would. That was always your way—making a cult of yourself instead of showing a proper respect for your parents.

HIPPOLYTUS: My parents, yes . . . My poor mother—you made her suffer as well. Pity the man who comes into the world a bastard.

THESEUS [as the thrust goes home]: All right, that's it. Guards, drag this man away. Do I have to tell you a second time?

HIPPOLYTUS: Keep your hands off me. Drag me away yourself, Father, if you're in such a hurry to get rid of me.

THESEUS: One more word and I will—nothing I'd like better.

[Pause, then Theseus walks away.]

[As he walks away] Captain, I want to hear that Hippolytus has left Trozen within the hour.

[confused noise of voices, stilled as a reprise of music: the Artemis Theme, is heard]

HIPPOLYTUS: No hope now, and my end is certain,
And I must suffer though I know the truth,
I do not know how it should be spoken.
Aloud. Dearest of all Gods, dear child of Leto,
Artemis, we have hunted, we have rested
Under the green eaves of the woods.
Now I must go from brilliant Athens,
Must leave this land, and the city of Erechtheus.

Goodbye, good earth of Trozen. You were a gentle place
For childhood to stray through. Remember me.
I shall never see you again. Come now, you are
My friends. Wish me happiness and go with me
To the border. No man walked nearer to the way
Of God than I. Though my father will not believe it.

[*Music*]

HUNTSMEN [*singing* and VOICES 5 & 6 *speaking*]:
Like the fall of a dry shadow
a doubt darkens my mind:
is there a ruler in Heaven?
For these eyes have saddened at sight
of the star of Athens,
as Athens is the star of Greece,
pursued by his father's rage
to far lost lands.
Oh loud sands that call to the sea,
groves of oaks scarfing our sister hills,
where with his high-tongued hounds
he hunted and killed
with Artemis, terrible, unseen,
by his side.

VOICES 2, 3, & 4 [*speaking*] and VOICE 1 & WOMEN [*singing*]:
You will not ride
tall in your chariot,
taming the quick glitter, the Venetian fillies,
nor the course round Limna resound
to the music of unruly hooves;
never will you rouse again
the tune that lies sleeping
under the slender hair of the lute,
all the garlands will fret away.

BOTH CHORUSES [*speaking*]: where Leto's daughter lies
under the green eaves of the wood,
and young girls who met you in dreams
awake for ever and forget . . .
they forget their dreams
now you have gone away . . .
I could insult the Gods . . .

Sister Graces
    limbs threaded
in the luminous dance
    dancing
in the white blaze of Artemis,
why do you spur innocence
    from his roof-tree,
    his father's house.

[*Music ends.*]

VOICE 2: Look, someone is coming—

VOICE 3: It's Hippolytus' old servant—

VOICE 4: He's hurrying, almost running.

VOICE 2: And his face . . .

VOICE 3: This means bad news.

OLD SERVANT [*approaching*]: Theseus . . . where is Theseus?
Where can I find the King? Tell me,
Is he in the Palace?

VOICE 4:          He's coming out of it now.

OLD SERVANT: Sir, I have sad news for you, sad news too
For all your subjects,
In Athens and in Trozen.

THESEUS:          What is it, man?

OLD SERVANT: It's Hippolytus. He's dead . . . or all but dead.

THESEUS: Dying . . . Who killed him then? Did he meet
    some other husband
Whose wife he had raped, as he raped mine?

OLD SERVANT: His own team of horses . . . They killed him
    . . . and the curse.
The curse you begged from your Father Poseidon.

THESEUS: Thanks to Heaven! Poseidon, you have not played
    false
With your son. You heard my prayer and now he is dead.
Tell me, how did it happen? I want to know everything,
Want to know exactly how the criminal paid for his crime.

OLD SERVANT: We were near the shore, where the sand
     wades into the sea,
Combing our horses' manes, and as we combed them
We were *all* in tears, for the news had broken, sir,
Hippolytus had been banished at your command.
And we were never to see him in this land again.
Then he himself came down to us there on the shore
And told us the same story through his own tears.
And with him there was a crowd, he had so many friends,
Young men of his own age. And after some time
He fought back his tears, and spoke calmly:
"Why am I weeping like this? My father has spoken
And I must obey him. So harness my horses, men . . .
This is no longer my country . . . I have no country,
Now." We lost no time, and quicker than I can tell
We set the mares to harness, all ready for their master.
He snatched the reins from the chariot, then he set his feet
Firmly in the driver's sockets. But first flinging wide his hands
In prayer to God. "Zeus . . . let me die now . . . at this mo-
     ment,
If my heart is evil. Whether I die, or whether I live
Let my father learn he wrongs me . . ." Then he lashed the
     mares,
shouted and they edged to a gallop.
We servants ran hard trying to
follow our master
along the road that leads to Argos and Epidauros,
and soon we struck on desolate land,
a barren finger of land and rock,
where near beyond the borders of Trozen
the narrow sand slides down to the gulf of Sciron.
And then suddenly an empty drumming began
as though some God in his underworld of thunder
were jarring the earth, whose noise troubled us to shudders.
The horses jerked up their heads, pricked their ears to the sky,
while harsh terror took us, all unknowing
from where that sound began. Then, even as we looked
at the sea-loud sands, a steep vaulted wave sprung up
shaped solidly to the sky, till it swamped our eyes
of sight of Sciron's coast,
and masked the Isthmus and the Asclepian rock.

Then it bulged and bristled in a horn of foam,
through a great throat of waters the snorting wave flung on
straight for the shore where the chariot stood . . .
and as that last giddy and horned billow broke,
the wave belched out a bull, a thing of God,
to whose bellows all the land grew resonant
in shivering recognition, and even as we gazed
the sight seemed greater than our eyes could bear.
At once dark panic leapt on the mares.
Our master, like a man much practiced
In all arts of horses, plucked up the reins
And loosely fastening them behind his back
Heaved like a sailor heaving at the oars.
But the horses bore on violently,
Grinding at the fire-born bits between their teeth,
Heedless of helmsman's hand, of traces, of the car.
Whenever like a man taut at the tiller,
He swayed their path towards the gentler ground,
The Bull reared up before them, herding them back;
But if in that crazy course they touched on rocks
In silence it grew near and bounded on beside them.
Till suddenly shouldering the axle on a stone
It fouled the car, and toppled on the flanks,
All lay confused. The naves of the wheels
Burst out, the axle's linchpins groaned apart;
And there he lay, snared in the reins,
Was dragged a prisoner in the obstinate knot,
Slapping that dear head against the rocks,
Stripping his flesh, and his cries grieved at our ears;
"Stop . . . stop . . . you're my own horses . . . I fed you myself.
You are killing me. Oh, Father, this is your curse. Help!
Help! Will no one save an innocent man."
Many would have saved, but were left far behind.
Then loosened somehow from the thongs,
He fell to the ground,
Dying, but with a faint jet of life in his body,
While the horses and the monster were lost to sight
Among that glaring solitude of rocks . . .
Yes, I am only one of your palace servants, sir,
But nothing, nothing will make me believe,
Your son was wicked.

Not if all the women in the world were to hang themselves
And all the timber on Ida
Was scribbled over with lying letters,
He was a good man. I know he was good.

THESEUS: I hated him so much, that as I listened
I felt only pleasure at his end. But now . . .
Suddenly, I remember the Gods . . . he was my son . . .
Now I can feel nothing . . . no joy, no pain.

OLD SERVANT: Sir, what do you wish? Are we to bring him
to you?
Will you take my advice . . . then, be gentle to your son.
He is dying . . . in great pain . . . and there is little time.

THESEUS: Yes. Bring him here. Let me look at him, face
to face.
Once he denied he raped my wife. Now, surely,
He must be persuaded by the violence of Heaven.

[Music]

BOTH CHORUSES [singing]: Oh, Aphrodite,
Cypris,
Who masters the severe mind of the Gods.

VOICE 1 [singing]: The easy hearts of men;
With your helper
Who flits

VOICES 2, 3, 4, 5, 6 [speaking]: In vivid flight
On a shifting rainbow of wings;
Dancing alone above the world,
That turns, and yearns,
And the salt,
Hoarse-throated sea.
Eros, the winged
Goldglaring
Enchanter and death of the heart.
All lures,
All glints and desires
Of the bright quivering air
With a flare
Of wings

He charms the wild young lives
Of the beasts
The mountains bear,
All that moves by field and flood
All the sun's eye warms
And men themselves,
Over all
The Cyprian Goddess broods.
Aphrodite . . .

[*Music: Artemis appears.*]

ARTEMIS: Listen, Theseus, listen. It is Artemis who speaks.
Are you pleased, now you have killed your son?
Lending an easy ear to shadows and uncertainties,
The stories Phaedra laid for your return?
You have wrenched down ruin on your own head.
Why not hide the guilt of your body
                              In Tartarus
Under the dark arches of the world
                              or melt your life
Into the steep life of a bird?
                         No place for you now
In the City of the Just.
                    Listen. The history of your crime.
Your son was innocent.
                    Phaedra loved him,
The prey of Aphrodite
                    my enemy, enemy of all
The pure by nature.
                    Yet Phaedra wrestled with her,
Tried to stifle passion,
                    to stem the dark flood
By her bare will.
                 Twice she was betrayed:
By Aphrodite, then by her nurse.
Who told Hippolytus . . .
                         trapped him into silence . . .
You accused him,
                he kept silent,
                              he remembered the Gods.

And you, you believed it . . .

and your son is dying.

THESEUS: No, Artemis, no . . .

ARTEMIS: Yes. The truth hurts. But there is more to come.
Poseidon promised you three certain prayers.
Whom did you strike down with the last?
Was it some dangerous enemy? No. It was your own son.
Poseidon kept his promise, gave what he had to give,
But how low you appear now in his eyes and in mine.
You would not wait for proof, would not make enquiries,
But launched the curse at your son and killed him.
You are guilty, Theseus,

but there is another,
Aphrodite . . . offended, angry, she began it all.
All that has happened is the shadow of her will.
I watched, and suffered. Why did I let it happen?
There is a law in Heaven: where a God's purpose appears,
We stand aside, we let it take shape as it will.
So I gave way to Aphrodite, yet remember this:
But for that law,
But for my fear of Zeus, the giver of that law,
I would never have abandoned Hippolytus . . .
The man that I loved most . . .
No, I cannot blame you, Theseus, you were deceived,
Three of you have met with sorrow,
Phaedra is dead, he is dying,
And now you stand alone at the heart of the storm . . .

[Fade]

[Music]

[a murmuration of men's voices, approaching]

OLD SERVANT: Look, sir, it's your son—
They are carrying him in now.

VOICE 5: Here is Hippolytus
His young flesh torn, his gold hair
Banded with blood;

VOICE 6: out of clear air,
the hard mane of thunder,

the winged fire of God
falls, and falls again,
convulsing the house . . .

HIPPOLYTUS [*approaching slowly*]: The pain . . . the
pain . . .
my father's unnatural curse
scatters my life . . .
pain . . . puts out its feelers,
a spasm goes blundering through my brain . . .
stop! stop! no further . . . put me down . . .

[*Music ends.*]

Oh that chariot . . . and the horses . . . brutes . . .
they took their food at my hands . . .
and they killed me, yes . . .
they finished what my father began . . .
Oh! for Heaven's sake, men,
lift me gently . . . keep your hands steady . . .
mind my wounds . . . Is there someone there?
There, yes, there, to the right of me . . . who is it? . . . who?
Now keep time as you walk . . . that's it . . . slow . . .
slowly . . .
Do you see me, Zeus, do you see this body of mine?
I gave my heart to the Gods . . . now look at me . . .
Running . . . running along this road of pain . . .
looking for death . . . and none of it had meaning, no,
none of it at all . . . the Gods . . . my father . . .
I was pure and this is what it has come to . . . you can see
my life littered about me . . . nothing is left . . .
only the pain . . . the pain . . . it is coming . . .
let me alone . . . Death . . . only you can heal me . . .
anything . . . a spear . . . one of you . . . a sharp lip like a
kiss . . .
it would let out life, my soul would slip away . . .
Oh Father . . . your curse . . . wickedness . . .
Yet behind all this . . . years, ages, back in family darkness . . .
perhaps an old death . . . blood crawling . . .
the years of it . . . the waiting . . . the impatience . . .
and it falls . . . all of it . . . on me . . . now.
Me . . . only me . . . innocent . . . agony . . .

Oh Death will you come to me . . .
out of the night . . . a mother . . . with your hands my skin
    knows . . .
take me . . . into the night . . .

[*Music: Artemis Theme*]

ARTEMIS [*fading in*]: Only a great heart could pay so
    much . . .
HIPPOLYTUS: Suddenly . . . and I feel it . . . tender
confusion of the air . . . sweet odour of Divinity . . .
Artemis, Artemis . . .
I sense your presence, Lady . . . my pain is lessened . . .
[*in a louder voice*] the Goddess Artemis is in this place . . .

ARTEMIS: I am here and I love you.

[*Music ends.*]

HIPPOLYTUS:                         You see what I have
    come to?

ARTEMIS: Yes, I can see. But I cannot weep for you.
Gods have no tears to give.

HIPPOLYTUS:              I am going . . . away . . .
Your huntsman, your servant . . .

ARTEMIS: You are going away from me. My love goes with
you.

HIPPOLYTUS: I hunted . . . and you were there . . . on foot
    . . . on horseback . . .
And your images . . . dressed them with these hands.

ARTEMIS: Oh, Aphrodite, restlessly wicked, what have you
    done?

HIPPOLYTUS: Aphrodite . . . it was Aphrodite . . . she killed
    me.

ARTEMIS: You gave her no worship. She hated you for that,
Hated your purity . . .

HIPPOLYTUS: Now . . . it is clear. We have had an enemy.
    The three of us.

ARTEMIS: Yes. There was the Queen . . . then you . . . and
  your father
Left alone.

HIPPOLYTUS: Father, you too have suffered.

ARTEMIS: He was blinded too by Aphrodite.

HIPPOLYTUS:                                    Father . . . my
                                          poor father.

THESEUS: Life. I thought I knew it. It has turned on me
  at last.

HIPPOLYTUS: It was all darkness. Even from the beginning.
But worse for you. You must learn it again and again.

THESEUS: My boy, my boy, if I could only die in your place.

HIPPOLYTUS: Poseidon gave you death as a present,
But you gave it to me.

THESEUS: I should have kept it . . . never spoken the word.

HIPPOLYTUS: What, then? You would have killed me. You
  were angry.

THESEUS: It was the Gods! The Gods made me mad . . .
They told me lies . . . all lies . . .

HIPPOLYTUS: We are men . . . weak . . . we cannot curse
  Heaven.
But I will curse . . . I will be strong and curse it . . .
I . . .

ARTEMIS: Peace, now . . . peace.

                    [raised, deliberate tone]

                              My vengeance pursues her
                                    anger
That pursues, Hippolytus, your holiness of mind
Even under the world and as far as the kingdom of shadows.
As you were mortal, and I loved you, there is a mortal
Whom Aphrodite loves more than all other men,
Adonis, his name, and like you a hunter. Be sure,
That I will avenge your death with his death:

I swear it by these hands and I swear it by these arrows
From which none whom I seek out may swerve.

[*softer, more intimate*]

                                                        But, boy,
To ease you a little of your pain, know this;
Dead, you shall have honour in Trozen,
And girls before their wedding day shall clip
The bright tracts of their hair,
And there in the shades you shall reap the shadowy harvest,
The bitter fragrance of tears . . .
                                        as elegy
Always the musical sorrow of young girls
And they will talk together
Of Phaedra's love, and of your death
Remembered always . . .
But, now, Theseus, oh son of Aegeus, take
This son of yours in your arms.
Hold him close . . . for a moment only.
You killed him in the dark. But the race of men
Must act out always the stories the Gods imagine.
And you, Hippolytus, do not hate your father
For what he has done. Now
You have learned the reason why you both must suffer . . .
But now goodbye . . . I must turn away at the end . . .
Must not foul my eyes with sight of your last pain . . .
And it is coming . . . it is here . . . Hippolytus . . .

   [*Fade*]

HIPPOLYTUS: Go, then. Leave me, Lady, invisible sweetness.
Easily you let fall our long companionship,
The times . . . the places . . . we were much together.
But it costs you nothing . . . you go . . . you forget . . .
I am at peace with my father . . . you have wished it.
Now . . . ah . . . darkness creeps across my eyes.
Quickly, hold me, Father.
I am falling into nothing . . .

   THESEUS: Do not die. Tell me, these hands . . .
They killed you.

   HIPPOLYTUS: No, you are free from guilt.

THESEUS: How can you free me?

HIPPOLYTUS:                    I know. I swear it.
And she hears and smiles.
Artemis with her arrows . . .

THESEUS: Dear son, how true to your father.

HIPPOLYTUS: You have other sons whose blood is true.
Pray that they may be, as I am . . . true.

THESEUS: Your heart was too near the Gods to live.

HIPPOLYTUS: It breaks. Now my long goodbye.

THESEUS: Do not leave me alone. Live, live, Hippolytus.
Be strong.

HIPPOLYTUS: I was strong . . . now . . . it is all lost.
There is only death. Quickly, quickly,
Hide my face in this cloak.

### [Dies.]

THESEUS: Oh Athens, and you, Trozen,
You have lost a man indeed and I, my son.
Long and bitterly,
I shall remember you, Aphrodite . . .

[Music: Exodos]

BOTH CHORUSES & VOICE 1 [singing] and VOICES 2, 3, 4, 5, &
6 [speaking] and, if wanted, OLD SERVANT [speaking]:

This sorrow touches all of us,
Like a stealthy cloud darkens all our skies.
And what a storm of tears must follow,
For when the great have died
The noise of mourning wanders far and wide.

### [Their voices die away into silence.]

## 4. The *Phèdre* of Jean Racine (1639–1699)

### Translated by William Packard (1933–   )

[Mr. Packard's translation of *Phèdre* was especially commissioned by The Institute for Advanced Studies in the Theatre Arts, which produced it Off-Broadway in 1966. *Ed.*]

#### CHARACTERS

THESEUS, *son of Aegeus, King of Athens*
PHÈDRE, *wife of Theseus, daughter of Minos and Pasiphaë*
HIPPOLYTE, *son of Theseus and Antiope, Queen of the Amazons*
ARICIE, *Princess of the royal house of Athens*
THÉRAMÈNE, *teacher of Hippolyte*
OENONE, *nurse and confidant of Phèdre*
ISMÈNE, *confidant of Aricie*
PANOPE, *waiting woman of Phèdre*
GUARDS

*The action of the play takes place in Trézène, a city in the Peloponnesus.*

#### ACT ONE

*Scene One:* HIPPOLYTE, THÉRAMÈNE

HIPPOLYTE: I have made up my mind: I go, dear
    Théramène,
and leave the loveliness of staying in Trézène.
Each day I have new doubts, they drive me to distress,
and I must blush with shame to see my idleness.
For more than six long months I've missed my father's face,
I do not know his fate, I do not know the place
that could be capable of keeping such a man.

THÉRAMÈNE: In what new place, my lord, will you try what
    new plan?
So far, to satisfy your great uncertainty,
I've sailed the seas each side of Corinth endlessly;
I've asked about Theseus of those who, it is said,
saw Acheron descend forever to the dead;

78

I've visited Elis, and Tenaros, and I
sailed by where Icarus fell screaming from the sky.
And now with what new hope, in what new place will you
listen for his footsteps or look for what new clue?
Now who knows truly if the king your father be
hidden somewhere that must remain a mystery?
Perhaps we fear for what we both know nothing of,
perhaps this hero has discovered some new love,
some beautiful young girl he's dying to abuse . . .

HIPPOLYTE: Stop now, dear Théramène, you've no right to
    accuse.
He's given up that vice, he's long ago outgrown
such bubblings of the blood, he's happier alone;
for Phèdre has made him shed his old inconstancy,
so she no longer fears an unknown rivalry.
No, no, I only go because I know I must,
and also to escape this place which I distrust.

THÉRAMÈNE: Ah, when did you, my lord, begin to hate and
    fear
this pleasant peaceful place?—for you grew up right here,
and surely you preferred this quiet rest and sport
to all the pomp and noise of Athens and the court.
What danger made you change, what dread drives you away?

HIPPOLYTE: It's not the same, I face a different place today,
since this Phèdre, the daughter of Minos and his wife
Pasiphaë, came here, she has upset my life.

THÉRAMÈNE: I guess at your distress, and I know what is
    true,
For Phèdre weighs on your mind, and she depresses you.
The first time she met you, she hardly let you smile
before she ordered your immediate exile.
And yet her raging hate, which had you in its hold,
has either disappeared, or grown much more controlled.
Besides, what can she do, or bring down on your head,
this dying woman who desires to be dead?
This Phèdre, who wastes away from what she will not say,
grown weary of herself and of the light of day,
can she do anything against you any more?

HIPPOLYTE: I do not fear her hate the way I did before.
No, Hippolyte must flee another enemy:
and that is why I fly from this young Aricie,
last blood of that bad line which worked against us so.

THÉRAMÈNE: What?—even you, my lord, you think she is
    your foe?
She is related to the Pallantides, it's true,
but should she share the blame of that malicious crew?
And should you hate her face, which lights the brightest day?

HIPPOLYTE: If I could hate her face, I would not go away.

THÉRAMÈNE: My lord, let me say this before you go too far—
you are no longer proud of being what you are:
Hippolyte, the sworn foe of love itself and all
the slavish laws of love that made your father fall.
Yet though you may remain cool and aloof in pride,
Venus may still win out, and take your father's side
and, placing you among those men who sigh and pine,
she may force you to kneel before her sacred shrine.
My lord: are you in love?

HIPPOLYTE:                How can you use that word?
You, who have known my heart since first my spirit stirred—
a heart that only knows such distance and disdain,
a heart that hardly can return to earth again.
Son of an Amazon, I drank her milk and drew
that strong and stubborn pride which seems to baffle you;
considering myself, the way a young man does,
I gave myself great praise when I knew who I was.
You who were close to me, who saw to all my needs,
you made me learn by heart my famous father's deeds.
You told me of his life, and once you had begun,
I was on fire to hear whatever he had done:
So you described the way this hero had consoled
mankind for its great loss of Hercules, and told
me how he slew Sinnis, told how he killed Scirron,
and destroyed Procrustes, and slaughtered Cercyon,
took Epidaurus' bones and spilled them in the mud,
then covered over Crete with Minotaur's life blood,
But when you told of deeds that sounded more like crimes,

how Theseus used to break his word a hundred times—
Helen is raped away from Sparta by his lies;
poor Salamis must sit as Periboëa cries—
and there were many more whose names escape me now,
who loved him, and believed that he would keep his vow:
Ariadne, weeping in silence by the sea,
Phèdre, too, whom he seduced, although more happily;
ah, you remember how I begged you to be brief,
such stories made me grave, they stayed and gave me grief;
if it were in my will to wrench them from my brain
so only the brave deeds and glories would remain!
Could I be so enslaved and waste my life away?
Could some god make me cheat, dissemble and betray?
Loose and lascivious, I would have twice the shame
of Theseus—I have none of his great claim to fame:
no name, and no strange beasts defeated, and no right
to fail as he has failed, or fall from his steep height.
And yet suppose my pride should mellow and grow mild,
why should it all be for this Aricie, this child?
Surely I sense, deep in the darkness of my heart,
there is a law that says we two must stay apart?
My father disapproves, and by a stern decree,
forbids that she enlarge her brother's family:
he fears some bright new life from that guilt-ridden line,
therefore each leaf must wilt, and so die on the vine.
This sister must stay chaste forever to the tomb,
and bury their bad name in her own barren womb.
Should I stand by her side against my father's laws?
Show off my arrogance by taking up her cause?
Should I let love set sail the madness of my youth . . .

    THÉRAMÈNE: My lord, once fate takes place and makes men
      face the truth,
not even gods can find what goes on in the mind.
Theseus has made you see, who tried to keep you blind;
his hate has fanned a love, has nurtured a fine fire,
has lent this enemy a grace which you admire.
Why are you so afraid of being so in love?
Perhaps there are strange joys which you know nothing of:
or will cruel scruples rule your conscientious days?

Must you scorn Hercules for his few playful ways?
What brave courageous soul has Venus never won?
And you, where would you be if you were not the son
of Antiope, whose breast encouraged a shy fire
for Theseus your father, the thirst of her desire?
What does it matter now, this high pride when you speak?
Things have already changed, and over this past week
you were not wild, not free, not as you were before,
now racing chariots with loud shouts by the shore,
and now perfecting skills with Neptune as your guide,
taking an untamed horse and breaking it to ride.
The woods do not return the echo of your cries;
weary with some great weight, you die before my eyes.
Now there can be no doubt: you are in love, you burn,
you hide a fatal pain which no man can discern.
Is it this Aricie has made your spirit bow?

HIPPOLYTE: I go, dear Théramène, to find my father now.

THÉRAMÈNE: But will you not tell Phèdre why you refuse to stay,
my lord?

HIPPOLYTE: You can explain, once I have gone away.
I know I should see her; I shall, before I go.
But now, why does Oenone seem to be troubled so?

Scene Two: HIPPOLYTE, OENONE, THÉRAMÈNE

OENONE: Alas my lord alas, whose troubles are like mine?
The Queen almost begins to end her thin life line.
Vainly each night and day I stay close by her side:
she dies of some great pain which she still tries to hide.
Some fatal disarray goes raging through her head,
it keeps her wide awake and takes her from her bed.
This illness makes her long to see the light of day,
yet she insists that I turn everyone away . . .
She comes.

HIPPOLYTE: Enough, I go: I would not want to wait
And let her see a face which she has grown to hate.

## Scene Three: PHÈDRE, OENONE

PHÈDRE: No more, Oenone, no more. Let me stay here and
wait.
My strength is so meager, my weakness is so great.
My eyes are dazzled by the bright light of the day,
my knees are trembling as I feel myself give way.
Alas!

OENONE: See how we weep, O gods, and set us free!

PHÈDRE: All these vain ornaments, these veils weigh down
on me!
What meddling dreadful hands have tried to tie my hair
in such fine tiny knots with such annoying care?
All things on every side conspire to do me harm.

OENONE: The way you say these things, you cause me great
alarm!
When you yourself saw that you were not at your best,
you made me use my hands to get you so well dressed;
and you yourself, because you felt a bit more bright,
wanted to show yourself and feel the full daylight.
So here you are, Madam; yet now you try to hide,
you say you hate the day, so you must go inside.

PHÈDRE: Creator of the day, and of my family,
my mother claimed she came from your fierce clarity;
o now perhaps you burn with shame to see my pain:
Sun, I shall never gaze on your great face again!

OENONE: You choose cruel suicide, is that your last desire?
how often must I hear you curse life's famous fire,
stand here as you rehearse the farewells to be made?

PHÈDRE: Why shouldn't I be there, there in the forest shade?
Why shouldn't I look out and follow with my eye
a cloud of dust, and see a chariot race by?

OENONE: What, Madam?

PHÈDRE: Where am I? and what did I just say?
Have I gone mad, and have my wits begun to stray?
O I have lost my mind, the great gods are to blame.
Oenone, see how my face must blush with such great shame:

I let you see too much, my sorrow was too plain;
my eyes, in spite of me, are filled with tears again.

 OENONE: Alas, if you must cry, then cry for keeping still,
which only aggravates this illness of your will.
So deaf to what we've said, as if you had not heard,
will you be pitiless and die without a word?
What fury must obscure the brilliance of the sun?
What poison has dried up your life before it's done?
The darkness of three nights has crept across the skies
since you have slept, and sleep has rested your sore eyes;
the blazing of three days has chased those nights along
since you took food, and ate to make your body strong.
Have you dreamed up some scheme, some plot to stop your
  breath?
What pride gave you the right to bring about your death?
O you dismay the gods who gave you your own life,
and you betray the man who took you as his wife;
and finally, you cheat your children by this deed,
they will be left to lead a life of endless need.
Suppose on that same day they find their mother dead,
their whole inheritance goes somewhere else instead,
to someone else's son, some enemy of yours,
son of that Amazon from far-off distant shores,
this Hippolyte . . .

 PHÈDRE:  O god!

 OENONE:    That moves you a good deal.

 PHÈDRE: Wretched worthless woman, whose name did you
  reveal?

 OENONE: Now your great hate is not so hard for me to gauge;
it is that fatal name that makes you shake with rage.
Live, Lady, live, let love and duty rule in you.
Live, do not leave it to your children to undo
this Scythian's one son; you must keep his caprice
from bleeding the best blood that can be found in Greece.
Only do not delay, you may die if you wait,
quickly, get back your strength before it is too late,
now, while you still have time, the flame of all your days
may be brought back again to a substantial blaze.

PHÈDRE: This has gone on too long, this guile, this guilty
   heart.

OENONE: What? tell me what remorse is tearing you apart?
What crime obsesses you, that no one understands?
Is there some guilty blood remaining on your hands?

PHÈDRE: Thank god these hands are clean, they've nothing
   to repent.
I only wish my heart were just as innocent.

OENONE: Then what appalling thing is still to happen here
and why does your poor heart still tremble in its fear?

PHÈDRE: No, no, I've told enough. The rest is best unsaid.
I die in silence, so my secret shall be dead.

OENONE: Die then, and try to take your secret to the skies;
just find some other hand to close your sightless eyes.
Because although your life has almost run its course,
my soul shall be the first to seek its holy source.
So many hopeless roads go headlong to the dead,
and my own sorrow now shall choose the best deathbed.
Was I untrue to you about some vow I'd sworn?
Remember that these arms held you when you were born.
I gave up everything, my home, my family—
Is this the way you pay me for my loyalty?

PHÈDRE: What can you hope to gain by using so much
   force?
If I spoke now, you would be frozen with remorse.

OENONE: What evil could exceed what I already see?
—that you should try to die right here in front of me.

PHÈDRE: If you knew my great guilt, what fate makes me
   ashamed,
I would still have to die, but I would die more blamed.

OENONE: Madam, by all these tears I've already shed,
by these knees I embrace, release me from this dread,
tell me what deadly doubts have seized you with such fear—

PHÈDRE: It is your wish. Get up.

OENONE:                              All right. Speak, I can hear.

PHÈDRE: God!—what am I to say, or where can I begin?

OENONE: I do not want to hear your fears that are within.

PHÈDRE: O Venus! Violence! O fatal rage and hate!
My mother's love cast her in a distracted state!

OENONE: Forget such things, Madam, let all such memories
keep in the secret peace of the eternities.

PHÈDRE: Ariadne, sister, O I remember you
were left by those cold stones to die in silence too!

OENONE: Madame, why must you choose such hateful things
    to say
about the blood that moves within your veins today?

PHÈDRE: Since it pleases Venus, this blood which is so base
shall see the last of me and my unhappy race.

OENONE: Are you in love?

PHÈDRE:                      I feel that madness in my heart.

OENONE: Who is it?

PHÈDRE:                Who it is, is the most shocking part.
I love—(his fatal name makes me become undone)
I love . . .

OENONE: Who?

PHÈDRE:          —Do you know the Amazon's one son,
That Prince whom I myself oppressed with hate and shame?

OENONE: Hippolyte? O god, god!

PHÈDRE:                              It's you who said his name.

OENONE: O god, how all my blood runs cold and turns to ice.
O guilt! O great disgrace! O race of hidden vice!
O joyless voyages, through such great storms and wars,
what fortunes made us land on these tormented shores!

PHÈDRE: My illness goes far back. For I had hardly wed
the son of Aegeus, and lain down on his bed,
and tasted the sweet peace of our long reverie
when Athens made me see my matchless enemy.

I saw him, I was lost—I turned red, I turned pale;
disturbances occurred; I felt my feelings fail;
I could no longer see, I could no longer speak;
my body boiled and froze, then everything grew weak.
Great Venus can be seen in these few futile fires
with which she plagues my race with passionate desires.
With reverent strict vows I tried to turn aside:
I built a shrine for her, and tended it with pride;
my knife made sacrifice on beasts of every kind;
I searched through their insides to find my own lost mind.
This was weak treatment for my woeful hopeless love!
In vain I burned incense and watched it curl above:
When I prayed to the god, and said her sacred name,
I still loved Hippolyte; I saw him in the flame,
and at the altar where my prayers rose to the sky,
I worshipped someone I dared not identify.
I fled him everywhere—O sickness of despair;
seeing his father's face, I even found him there!
At last I went to war against this lovely lord;
I persecuted him whom I was so drawn toward.
I banished this bad foe whom I admired so,
pretending some deep grief, insisting he should go,
I pressed for his exile, and my persistent cries
removed him from his home and from his father's eyes.
Then I could breathe, Oenone; once he had gone away
I felt freedom and peace with each new passing day.
Beside my husband now, and hiding my past pain,
I could confine myself to my own home again.
O useless cruel outcome! O destiny of men!
My husband brought me here to settle in Trézène—
once more I face this foe so fatal to my flesh;
my old wound opened wide, and my breast bled afresh.
This is no secret heat concealed within my veins;
this is great Venus now, who plagues me with these pains.
This guilt has made me ill, I loathe my waste of days,
it makes me hate my life and all its idle ways.
In dying now, at least I leave a noble name,
and I do not expose the full scope of my shame.
I could not bear to see your tears or hear your pleas,
so I told everything, with no apologies.
Now leave me to myself, because I choose to die,

and do not lecture me about my reasons why;
now all your foolish pleas to make me live must cease;
let me seek my release, and find my final peace.


### Scene Four: PHÈDRE, OENONE, PANOPE

PANOPE: How I would like to hide the sad news which I
    bring,
Madam, and yet I know I must say everything.
Death has been cruel to you, your husband has been killed;
you are the last to know his greatness has been stilled.

OENONE: Panope, what did you say?

PANOPE:                              That the poor Queen
    must learn
she cannot pray to god for Theseus to return;
because the sailing ships that brought this dreadful word
have just told Hippolyte the news of what occurred.

PHÈDRE: God!

PANOPE:      Athens splits itself, in choosing who shall rule,
Some choose the Prince your son; but others play the fool,
forgetting all the law and what the state has done,
they reach beyond their rights and choose a foreign son.
It's even rumored that a ruthless anarchy
is working to restore the race of Aricie.
This may be dangerous, I thought you ought to know.
Already Hippolyte has made his plans to go;
if he should appear there, there where the storm is loud,
then he may be able to sway that coward crowd.

OENONE: Panope, that's quite enough. The Queen, having
    heard you,
will not neglect this news, and your own point of view.


### Scene Five: PHÈDRE, OENONE

OENONE: Madam, I ceased to plead that you should live
    this through;
I even could agree that I should die with you;

I knew you would ignore all tears or talk of force;
but now this dreadful news dictates a different course.
Your fortune seems to change and wear a strange new face:
the King is dead, Madam, so you must take his place.
His death leaves you one son, you owe him everything—
a slave if you should die; if you should live, a king.
To what discerning friends could he turn with his fears?
His ancestors would hear his innocent outcries,
and they would shake with rage across the distant skies.
O live!—you still possess the honor of your name.
Your sordid flame becomes an ordinary flame.
This passion is no crime, now Theseus has died,
your guilt has gone away, the knots are all untied.
Now Hippolyte is free and you can see him now,
and you can let him come as close as you allow.
Perhaps, because he thinks you are still filled with hate,
he leads a faction now to overthrow the state.
Make him see his mistake, help him to understand.
He thinks he should be King, Trézène is his homeland.
But he knows that the law gives your son all the forts,
all Athens' worldly force, her ramparts and her ports.
Now you both know you have a common enemy,
and so you should unite to fight this Aricie.

PHÈDRE: Your words appeal to me: they please me, I agree.
Yes, I will live: if life will flow back into me,
and if my feelings for my son can lift my soul
and fill me with new hope, I will again be whole.


ACT TWO

Scene One: ARICIE, ISMÈNE

ARICIE: Hippolyte has told you that this is where he'll be?
Hippolyte will come here to say goodbye to me?
Ismène, can this be true?—no one is fooling you?

ISMÈNE: Now that Theseus has died, you will see much
  that's new.
Prepare yourself, Madam, to find on every side
so many friends of yours whom Theseus tried to hide.

Now Aricie is strong, her freedom is complete,
and soon all Greece will be kept captive at her feet.

ARICIE: Ismène, then these are not mere idle fantasies—
I cease to be a slave and have no enemies?

ISMÈNE: From now on, all the fates are tame and will
      behave;
and brave Theseus has joined your brothers in the grave.

ARICIE: Have they said how he died, what led him to the
      dead?

ISMÈNE: Incredible accounts of it are being spread.
Some say that while defiled with infidelity,
this philanderer was swallowed by the sea.
And others also say, and you will hear them tell,
that with Pirithoüs, descending into hell,
he went to see Cocyte, and through that mood of doom,
he showed his own live soul to dead men in the gloom;
but he could not come back from that disgraceful place,
for those were fatal steps which he could not retrace.

ARICIE: Now how could any man, still filled with his life
      breath,
be willing to set forth on the deep sleep of death?
What led him to explore that final finding out?

ISMÈNE: Theseus is dead, Madam, there can be no more
      doubt.
Athens is in a storm, Trézène in an uproar,
and all hail Hippolyte as King from shore to shore.
Phèdre is in this palace, and trembling for her son,
seeks counsel from her friends and pleads with everyone.

ARICIE: Do you think Hippolyte will have more love for me
than his own father had, who gave me slavery?
Will he ease my distress?

ISMÈNE:              Madam, I know he will.

ARICIE: This listless Hippolyte may turn against me still.
How can you dare to say he pities and adores
in me, and me alone, a sex which he ignores?

You know that for some time he has avoided me;
he always finds a place where we will never be.

ISMÈNE: I know the things they say, that Hippolyte is cold—
but coming close to you, he was a bit more bold;
I watched him all the while, I tried to find his pride,
and it occurred to me that everyone had lied.
No, he is not so cold as he has been accused:
when you first looked at him, he seemed to be confused.
He turned his eyes aside to leave your lovely glance,
but they still gazed at you and he was in a trance.
That he should be in love may seem to him absurd;
yet it is in his eyes, if not in his own word.

ARICIE: I listen, dear Ismène, my heart in all its youth
devours what you say, although there's not much truth!
You who are dear to me, you know my great distress:
my heart has only known my own soul's loneliness,
I who have been the toy of accident and chance,
how can I know the joy, the folly of romance?
The daughter of a King from this great ancient shore,
I only have survived the tragedies of war.
I lost six brothers who were strong and brave and free,
the hope and flower of a famous family!
The sword tore all of them, the earth was wet with red,
Erectheus was dead when all these sons had bled.
You know that since their death, there was a stern decree
forbidding any Greek to fall in love with me:
the flame of my desire might kindle in my womb,
and one day light a fire within my brother's tomb.
Besides, you ought to know with what a haughty frown
I viewed this conquerer and what he had set down.
For I had hated love through my disdainful days,
and so I thanked Theseus, and even gave him praise
for making me obey the vows I had begun.
But then I had not seen this fearless hero's son.
Not that my eyes alone were held by his fair face,
and made to dwell upon his celebrated grace—
those gifts which nature gives, which anyone would prize,
he seems to set aside, as something to despise.
I love and value him for what makes him unique:
his father's deeds, and not the ways that he was weak:

I love, and I admire the scope of his high pride,
which never yet was tamed, has never yet been tied.
How Phèdre was taken in by Theseus and his sighs!
I have more self-respect, and my affection flies
from all these easy vows passed out to everyone:
such offers leave me cold, they're something that I shun.
To teach humility to the inflexible,
to speak of suffering to the insensible,
to chain a prisoner with claims that I would make,
which he could strain against, but never really break—
that is what I desire, that will make me complete;
and yet strong Hercules fought less than Hippolyte;
subdued more often, and seduced more easily,
he gave less glory to each lover he would see.
But dear Ismène, alas!—what awful things I dare!
I will come up against more force than I can bear.
Perhaps you may hear me, humble in my despair,
groan under that high pride which now I think so fair.
Hippolyte fall in love?—how could my hope or fear
affect him in the least . . .

ISMÈNE:                Now you yourself shall hear:
for here he comes.


*Scene Two:* HIPPOLYTE, ARICIE, ISMÈNE

HIPPOLYTE:        Madam, before I go away,
I have some things to say about your fate today.
My father has just died. My fears which were so strong
told me the reason why he had been gone so long.
For death, and death alone, could end his splendid deeds
and hide from all the world the life a hero leads.
The Fates in their great greed have taken from our side
this friend of Hercules who shared the same high pride.
I think your hatred may ignore his few defects
and grant his memory these fitting last respects.
One hope has opened up and pleased me in my grief:
I can release your soul and give you some relief.
I can revoke the laws that made you suffer so.
Now you can start to live, your heart is yours to know.

And here in this Trézène, which I come to control
just as old Pittheus, ancestor of my soul,
which calls for a new King, and recognizes me—
I now proclaim you free and give you liberty.

ARICIE: This is immoderate, your Highness is too kind,
such generosity is madness to my mind;
my Lord, it binds me more to all the stern decrees
which you would cast away in an attempt to please.

HIPPOLYTE: In choosing who shall rule, Athens becomes
    undone,
speak first of you, then me, and then the Queen's one son.

ARICIE: Of me, my Lord?

HIPPOLYTE:                I know, no honor to my name,
an ancient famous law seems to reject my claim.
Greece is displeased with me for my strange foreign birth.
But if I could compete against my brother's worth,
Madam, I know so well that my rights would win out,
that I would be made Greek and King without a doubt.
But there are strong restraints which make me rest my case.
I therefore say to you: this is your proper place,
your sceptre is the one your ancestors received
from that first son of earth so secretly conceived.
They say that Aegeus once held it in his hands.
Athens was satisfied in all of its demands
by my own father, who was hailed as its own King,
and your six brothers were deprived of everything.
But Athens calls you now to come within her walls.
There have been groans enough from all these hopeless brawls;
there has been blood enough to soak the open fields
and drown the fertile earth with all the life it yields.
Trézène will obey me. The countryside of Crete
will give the son of Phèdre a sumptuous retreat.
You will take Attica. Now I must go at last
and try to reunite the votes which will be cast.

ARICIE: Astonished and confused by all that I have heard,
I have a secret fear that this is all absurd.
Now am I wide awake, or should I trust this dream?

What gracious god, my Lord, made you adopt this scheme?
How wonderful it is all places know your name!
And how the truth itself exceeds all praise and fame!
Would you betray yourself, like this, all for my sake?
Not hating me may be the greatest gift you make,
and having kept yourself in everything you do
from this hostility . . .

    HIPPOLYTE: Madam, could I hate you?
No matter what they say or how they paint my pride,
do they suppose some beast once carried me inside?
What mind that is unkind, what heart that may be hard,
in viewing you, would not grow soft in its regard?
Could any man resist the charm of what you are?

    ARICIE: What? My Lord.

    HIPPOLYTE:        But I know, now I have gone too
    far.
Reason, I see, gives way to feelings that are real.
I have already said more than I should reveal,
Madam, so I go on: I must inform you of
something which my own heart keeps secret in its love.
You see before you here a wretched restless Prince,
epitome of pride too headstrong to convince.
I who fought love and thought my attitude was right;
who laughed at its captives and ridiculed their plight;
who scorned the worst shipwrecks, the first one to deplore
the storms of mortals which I witnessed from the shore;
now I have been bowed down to know the common lot,
how I have been estranged and changed to what I'm not!
One instant has destroyed my childish arrogance:
this soul which was so bold now yields to circumstance.
For almost six long months, so hopeless and alone,
and bearing everywhere this torture I have known;
divided in desires, I don't know what to do:
with you, I try to fly; alone, I long for you;
far off in the forest, your image follows me;
the brilliance of the day, the night's obscurity,
all show me the sly charm which my high pride ignores;
all render Hippolyte a prisoner of yours.

Now through this mad pursuit, I've lost my self-control,
so I no longer know the scope of my own soul.
I've lost my javelins, my chariot, my bow;
I've lost Neptune's lessons which I learned long ago;
the woods no longer hear loud shouts as I rejoice,
and my horses ignore the sound of my own voice.
Perhaps the telling of a love so wild and free
might make you blush to see what you have done to me.
What foolish things to say from such a captive heart!
And what a sick victim of all your lovely art!
But you should see in me that which is very dear.
Imagine that I speak another language here;
do not reject my love for its vague awkward vow,
for I have never tried to say this until now.


*Scene Three:* HIPPOLYTUS, ARICIE, THÉRAMÈNE, ISMÈNE

THÉRAMÈNE: My Lord, the Queen comes here, and I have
    come before.
She looks for you.

HIPPOLYTE:      For me?

THÉRAMÈNE:            My Lord, I know no more.
But I have just been sent to make sure that you stay.
Phèdre wants to speak to you before you go away.

HIPPOLYTE: Phèdre?—but what can I say?—And what can
    she expect . . .

ARICIE: My Lord, you can't refuse, you owe her this respect.
Although you know too well her old hostility,
her tears require you to show some sympathy.

HIPPOLYTE: And so you go away. And now I do not know
if I've offended you whom I admire so!
I wonder if this heart which I leave in your hands . . .

ARICIE: Go, Prince, and carry out your generous demands.
Arrange that Athens be subject to my decree.
For I accept these things which you bestow on me.
But this impressive state, although it is so great,
is not the gift you give which I praise with most weight.

*Scene Four:* HIPPOLYTE, THÉRAMÈNE

HIPPOLYTE: Are we all ready now?—But see, the Queen
    draws near.
Go now, prepare the way, and gather all our gear.
Set down the plans, the course, the orders, and then come
to free me from this talk which will be tedium.

*Scene Five:* PHÈDRE, HIPPOLYTE, OENONE

PHÈDRE: There he is. My bad blood refuses to obey.
Seeing him, I forget what I have come to say.

OENONE: Remember that your son depends on you today.

PHÈDRE: They say your plans are made, and you are on your
    way.
To all your miseries I offer you my tears.
And I have come to you to speak about my fears.
My son is fatherless; and I can prophesy
that he shall see the day when I myself must die.
A thousand enemies attack this child of mine.
Now you and you alone can keep them all in line.
And yet a new remorse has come before my eyes:
I fear I may have closed your ears against his cries.
I tremble when I think he may receive your hate,
because I am the one you choose to desecrate.

HIPPOLYTE: Madam, I am not base, I could not cause such
    pain.

PHÈDRE: If you detested me, then I would not complain,
my Lord. I know you know I tried to injure you;
but what was in my heart, my Lord, you never knew.
I took enormous care to make your hatred great.
I could not let you live so close to my estate.
Aloud and secretly, I was so proud I swore
that I would have you sent to some far distant shore.
I went on to forbid, by an express decree,
that anyone should speak your name in front of me.
Yet weigh my crime against the pain that is my fate,

and say that my own hate has only caused your hate;
no woman in this world deserves your pity more,
no woman whom you have less reason to abhor.

HIPPOLYTE: A mother's jealousy may make her rarely fair
to some adopted son who comes into her care.
Madam, I know this well. Curses which disparage
are the common outcome of a second marriage.
All mothers would scorn me, and find things to deplore;
perhaps they would have tried to make me suffer more.

PHÈDRE: Ah! My Lord, believe me, that this is not the case!
I do not fit that law which rules the human race!
A very different care consumes me through and through!

HIPPOLYTE: Madam, I see no need for this to trouble you.
Perhaps your husband still bathes in the light of day;
we weep for his return, and heaven may obey.
My father has a god who guards him everywhere;
Neptune will not ignore my father's fervent prayer.

PHÈDRE: One only journeys once to that land of the dead,
my Lord. Since Theseus has been already led
to see those dismal shores, no god restores him now—
no freedom or release will Acheron allow.
But still, he is not dead, because he breathes in you.
Always before my eyes, my husband lives anew.
I see him, speak to him; and my heart . . . O my Lord,
I'm mad, my tortured mind shows its perverse discord.

HIPPOLYTE: I see the power now of love that never dies.
Theseus may be dead, yet he lives in your eyes;
I seem to see his face irradiating you.

PHÈDRE: I long for Theseus, yes, Prince, that much is true.
I love him, not the way the shades of Hades must,
the driven libertine who lives for his own lust,
who may be making love right now in dead men's beds;
but rather faithful, proud, the haughtiest of heads,
so charming and so young, who won all hearts somehow,
a portrait by a god—or as I see you now.
He had your poise, your gaze, your manner and your grace,

a gentle tender smile that lighted his whole face,
when he first sailed the sea, without the least conceit,
receiving the sweet vows of the fair maids of Crete.
What were you doing then? Where were you, Hippolyte?
Why were you not among the famous Greek elite?
Why were you still too young to join these conquerors
who came on their swift ships to land on our far shores?
Seeing the Cretan beast, you could have gained great praise,
by slaying him within his labyrinthine maze.
And so that you would know which way you should be led,
my sister would have come and made you take the thread.
No, wait—I would be there, and well ahead of her,
the love inside of me would be the first to stir.
Prince, I would be the one to help you learn the ways
of staying safe and so escaping from the maze.
I would have taken pains to hasten your return!
A thread is not enough to show you my concern.
I'm sure that it would be a peril I could share,
and I myself could walk ahead of you through there:
so Phèdre would go with you through that great vacant void,
would have emerged with you, or with you been destroyed.

HIPPOLYTE: Gods!—what words have I heard?—Madam,
    recall your vow:
Theseus, my father, is your lord and husband now.

PHÈDRE: My lord, what makes you say I've placed this out of
    mind?
or do I need to have my dignity defined?

HIPPOLYTE: Madam, please forgive me. See how my face
    turns red,
for I misunderstood exactly what you said.
My shame cannot stand here and let you look at me;
I go . . .

PHÈDRE: You understand too well. O cruelty!
I must have said enough to make it all quite clear.
Well then, prepare to see Phèdre in her fury here.
I am in love. And yet, seeing this sentiment,
do not believe I think that I am innocent,
or that the passion which is poisoning my mind

has been encouraged by complacence of some kind.
I am the sick victim of the spite of the skies;
I mightily despise myself in my own eyes.
The gods are my witness, the same great gods who lit
a fire in my blood and then kept fanning it;
these gods who take delight in their deceit and seek
to seduce and undo a woman who is weak.
Now you yourself know well what happened in the past:
I chased you from this place and made you an outcast.
I tried to show myself so odious to you,
by being hateful and inhuman in your view.
What good was this great war I waged without success?
You hated me much more, I did not love you less.
Your sadness gave your face a charm beyond your years.
I languished, I burned up, in fire and in tears.
Your eyes could witness to the truth of what I say,
if you could lift them up and make them look my way.
What am I saying now?—have I become so ill
I could make such a vow, and of my own free will?
I fear for my one son, I must protect this child,
and so I had begun to ask you to be mild.
The feeble weakness of a heart too full to speak!
Alas, for it is you and you alone I seek.
Revenge yourself, my Lord, on my disgraceful shame.
Son of a hero who first gave you your own name,
here is your chance to kill another beast of Crete:
the wife of Theseus dares to love Hippolyte!
This terrible monster should not escape you now.
Here is my heart, right here, it's waiting for your blow.
It is impatient now to pay for its foul lust,
it feels your hand reach out and make the fatal thrust.
So strike. Or if you think your hatred should abstain
from granting me at least this last sweet peaceful pain,
or if you think my blood would soil your hand, my Lord,
then do not make a move, yet let me have your sword.
Now.

OENONE: What is this, Madam? By all gods far and near!
But someone comes. Quickly, you must not be found here;
come, let us leave this place of so much shame and dread.

*Scene Six:* HIPPOLYTE, THÉRAMÈNE

THÉRAMÈNE: Is Phèdre fleeing from us, or is she being led?
And what are all these signs of suffering, my Lord?
Why do you stand here with no color, speech or sword?

HIPPOLYTE: We must fly, Théramène. I feel such wild
    surprise,
I find that I despise myself in my own eyes.
Phèdre . . . No, by all the gods!—Let this deep secret be
kept hidden in the dark through all eternity.

THÉRAMÈNE: If you are going to go, the ship is in the port.
My Lord, before you board, listen to this report:
Athens has made her choice, the voices all avow
your brother is the one. Phédre has full power now.

HIPPOLYTE:    Phèdre?

THÉRAMÈNE:            An Athenian is coming with a scroll
to put into her hands, which gives complete control.
Her son is King, my Lord.

HIPPOLYTE:            You who look down on us,
is she so virtuous that you reward her thus?

THÉRAMÈNE: However, now they say the King is still alive,
that he is in Epire, is well and seems to thrive.
But I have sought him there, my Lord, and I know well . . .

HIPPOLYTE: We must investigate whatever people tell.
Let us look into this, and trace it to its source:
if it should prove untrue, I will pursue my course,
and we will go; and so no matter what it takes,
we'll choose the ruler who is best for all our sakes.


ACT THREE

*Scene One:* PHÈDRE, OENONE

PHÈDRE: I wish that they would take this fame and praise
    away!
Now how can you make me see anyone today?

What have you come to say to comfort my despair?
I spoke my secret mind, and I should hide somewhere.
My passions all broke out more than I meant to show.
I have already said what no one else should know.
God, how he listened so!—and how he seemed to be
distracted and obtuse, misunderstanding me!
And how he tried to find some safe way to escape!
His blushing bothered me and made my shame take shape!
Why did you keep me from my fatal last request?
Alas! when his great sword was resting on my breast,
did he grow pale for me?—or snatch it from my grasp?
No, no, it was enough for my proud hand to clasp
the handle, and I made that instrument abhorred
forever in the eyes of this inhuman Lord.

OENONE: Your misfortunes soar and cause you to complain,
you feed a fire which you must put out again.
Would it not be discreet and wise as Minos was,
to have much nobler cares than your self-pity does?
Instead of mourning for this wretch who flies his fate,
be Queen, and concentrate on the affairs of State.

PHÈDRE: Be Queen!—and make the State come under my
     strong rule,
when I myself stand here, a weak and lawless fool!
When I have lost control of the whole world of sense!
When I can hardly breathe, my shame is so intense!
When I am dying.

OENONE:          Fly.

PHÈDRE:               I cannot turn and run.

OENONE: You dared to banish him, whom now you dare not
   shun.

PHÈDRE: There's no more time for that. He knows my lust
   at last.
All thoughts of modesty and patient tact are past.
I have declared my guilt to this proud hero's eyes;
hope stole into my heart, I could not hold my sighs.
And it was you yourself, ignoring my complaint,
reviving my poor life when I was growing faint,

with flattery and guile, who told me your grand plan:
you made me seem to see that I could love this man.

OENONE: Alas!—these pains are not something I could con-
trive,
and what would I not do to make you stay alive?
If insults have hurt you, and made you try to hide,
could you forget the scorn of such a haughty pride?
With cruel and stubborn eyes, his obstinate conceit
watched as you almost fell and lay there at his feet!
How his great vanity made me hate him again!
If only you had seen, as I could see him then!

PHÈDRE: Oenone, he could subdue this pride that bothers
you.
His ways are just as wild as those woods where he grew.
This Hippolyte is rude and savage in his prime,
and now he heard of love perhaps for the first time.
Perhaps his great surprise gives rise to his silence,
and our complaints perhaps have too much violence.

OENONE: Remember he was formed and born from a strange
womb.

PHÈDRE: That Scythian knew well how true love could
consume.

OENONE: He has a fatal hate which sets our sex apart.

PHÈDRE: Then I shall never see a rival in his heart.
But all of your advice is overdue and blind.
Now serve my love, Oenone, and never mind my mind.
This man opposes love because his heart is hard:
we must find some new way to gain his kind regard.
At least the lure of rule appealed to his high pride;
Athens attracted him, that much he could not hide;
already all his ships are turned towards that great State,
the sails are in the wind, the men can hardly wait.
Find this ambitious youth whose heart is in the skies,
Oenone; and make the crown shine brightly in his eyes.
The sacred diadem is his possession now;
I only ask that I might place it on his brow.
Give him the power now which is not in my hands.

He will instruct my son in how to give commands;
perhaps he may consent to play the father's role.
The mother and the son are placed in his control.
Use every trick you know to move him to my view:
your words will do more good than mine could ever do.
So plead and weep for me; say Phèdre grows weak and dies;
and do not be ashamed of begging with your cries.
You can do anything; I send my hopes with you.
So go: I will wait here to learn what I must do.

### Scene Two: PHÈDRE, *alone*

PHÈDRE: O being who can see the shame of my rebuff,
implacable Venus, am I not low enough?
But you should not prolong this useless cruelty.
My downfall is complete; for you have wounded me.
Now if you truly choose your glory should be known,
attack another heart more stubborn than my own.
This Hippolyte flees you; defying your decrees,
he never sees your shrine nor kneels down on his knees.
He has a pride of mind your name cannot assuage.
Goddess, avenge yourself: we share the same outrage!
Let him love—Here you are, you have come back to me,
Oenone?—Then he hates me; he would not hear your plea.

### Scene Three: PHÈDRE, OENONE

OENONE: Put out of mind this lust, this love that must not
   be,
Madam. Instead, recall your virtue instantly.
The King they said was dead is very much alive;
they know Theseus is here for they saw him arrive.
So now they rush and run to see his famous face.
I searched for Hippolyte in almost every place,
but then a thousand cries went flying to the skies . . .

PHÈDRE: My husband lives, Oenone, give me no more re-
   plies.
I have already sworn a love he must abhor.
He lives: that is enough, now I must know no more.

OENONE: What?

PHÈDRE:                I predicted this; but you preferred to doubt.
My own remorse was weak, and your weeping won out.
If I had only died this morning, all would mourn;
but I took your advice, so I must die forlorn.

OENONE: You are dying?

PHÈDRE:                        My god! What did I do today?
My husband and his son already on their way!
—this witness who has seen all my deceitful charms
will watch my features greet his father to my arms,
my heart still filled with sighs which he would not accept,
my eyes still wet with tears which he could not respect.
To keep the self-respect of Theseus clean and free,
will he now try to hide this love inside of me?
Will he let me betray his father and his King?
Can he contain his rage at this dishonoring?
No, he could not be still. Besides, I know my crime,
Oenone, but I have not grown hard in my lifetime,
like some who even seem to take delight in blame,
who wear a smiling face and never blush with shame.
I know my madness now, I can recall it all.
I feel the ceiling sees, and each great vacant wall
awaits my husband's face, and when Theseus appears,
they will speak my disgrace to his astonished ears.
O let me die, let death deliver me instead.
I wonder can it be so dreadful to be dead?
Death is not terrible to those in misery.
I only fear the name which I leave after me.
My wretched children shall inherit this chagrin!
The blood of Jupiter should help them to begin;
and yet despite their pride in such a great estate,
a mother's wickedness can be a hateful weight.
I fear that they shall hear, alas! the fatal truth,
their mother had such shame when they were in their youth.
I fear in later years, when this guilt multiplies,
that neither one of them will dare to lift his eyes.

OENONE: Believe me, I agree, their future makes me grieve;
I feel you are quite right to fear what you perceive.
But why expose them to such terrible insults?

And why accuse yourself of such grotesque results?
That's that: for they will say that Phèdre, so filled with shame,
is racing to escape her husband's rage and blame.
And Hippolyte is glad to see the end of you,
for by your dying you support his point of view.
Now how could I reply to these things he accused?
Before him I would be too easily confused.
Then I would have to see this Hippolyte rejoice
and tell your tale to all with ears to hear his voice.
I wish I were struck by some fire from the sky!
Now do not lie to me, does he still make you sigh?
How do you see this Prince, so boastful, so upright?

PHÈDRE: I see him as a beast, made frightful to my sight.

OENONE: Then why should he achieve an easy victory?
You fear him. Then strike first, and have the bravery
to say he did this crime which he may lay to you.
For who will disagree, and claim it is not true?
How fortunate his sword is left here in your hands!
All know your present woe, and each man understands
his father heard your words whenever you complained,
and it was due to you his exile was obtained.

PHÈDRE: How can I injure one so innocent of sin?

OENONE: My purpose only needs your silence to begin.
I tremble as you do, and I feel some remorse.
To die a thousand times would be a better course.
But I lose you unless you let me have my way,
and your life is to me worth more than I can say.
I will speak out. Theseus, when my fierce tale is done,
will limit his revenge to banishing his son.
A father, in great rage, still has a father's mind:
and a light punishment is all that he will find.
But if in spite of all some guiltless blood must spill,
why should your honor put such things beyond your will?
For your integrity should not be thrown away,
and it has certain laws you know you must obey,
Madam; and so to save your threatened honor, you
must give up everything, perhaps your virtue too.
Who's there?—I see Theseus.

PHÈDRE:                         Ah!—I see Hippolyte;
in his cruel eyes I see my downfall is complete.
Do what you want with me, my heart is torn and sore.
The way things are right now, I can do nothing more.

### Scene Four: THESEUS, HIPPOLYTE, PHÈDRE, OENONE, THÉRAMÈNE

THESEUS: I am no longer torn by the strong force of fate,
Madam, and to your arms I . . .

PHÈDRE:                         Theseus, you must wait,
do not profane your name by saying anything,
for I do not deserve these greetings that you bring.
You are greatly disgraced. Fate labored to debase
your helpless wife while you were absent from this place.
Unworthy of your words, and of your fine high pride,
from now on I must find the safest way to hide.

### Scene Five: THESEUS, HIPPOLYTE, THÉRAMÈNE

THESEUS: Why this excitement now at the mere sight of me,
my son?

HIPPOLYTE: Phèdre is the one to solve this mystery.
Yet if my earnest wish can move your brave heart, then
let me, my Lord, depart and not see her again.
Your son is so upset that he must disappear
from any place your wife decides she may come near.

THESEUS: My son, you're going to go?

HIPPOLYTE:                         I did not search for
                                        her:
you were the one who made her coming here occur.
When you had left Trézène, my Lord, by your decree,
you also chose to leave the Queen and Aricie.
I took good care of them according to my vow.
But what care makes me stay behind in this place now?
Far in the forests, I have wasted each new day
by chasing frightened game and slaying my small prey.
Why can't I fly from this great laziness I'm in,
and find genuine blood to stain my javelin?

When you were in your youth, and not yet my own age,
strange beasts were beaten down by your enormous rage,
and tyrants felt the crush of your tremendous blow;
the innocent were safe, the insolent brought low;
you made peace on the sea, protecting all our shores.
Travelers did not fear unnecessary wars;
and Hercules, who heard the ordeals you went through,
could lay his labors down and rest because of you.
And I, the unknown son who sees my father's fame,
I even envy now my mother's honored name.
Allow my courage now to be put to good use.
If some beast escaped you and is still on the loose,
then let me try to set its corpse before your feet;
or if I have to die, then let my death be sweet,
so everyone will praise my days so bravely done,
and weigh my famous name, and say I was your son.

    THESEUS: What madness greets my face?—what horror fills
       this place
and makes my family fly off in such disgrace?
If I come back so feared, so little needed here,
gods, why did you help me and make me persevere?
I only had one friend. Desires plagued his life,
he labored in Epire to take the tyrant's wife;
I helped him to attain this passion of his mind;
but an outrageous fate dazed us and made us blind.
The tyrant stepped aside and took me by surprise.
I saw Pirithoüs destroyed before my eyes,
thrown down and torn apart and eaten by strange beasts
who feed on human flesh in their atrocious feasts.
I was shut far away in dark abysmal caves,
a deep and dismal place, and underneath all graves.
Then after six long months the gods came back to me:
and so I could escape by my own subtlety.
The tyrant tried to fight, and when I slaughtered him
his beasts fell on his corpse and tore it limb from limb.
So when with joy I thought at last I could come near
the gift of all the gods that is to me most dear;—
what can I say?—when I myself return all right,
and eagerly expect to satisfy my sight,
my only welcome is a trembling everywhere:

all fly, and all refuse the greetings that I bear.
And I, filled with the fear my coming here has brought,
wish I were still kept in the cave where I was caught.
Speak to me. Phèdre has said that I have been disgraced.
Who betrayed me?—Why has the traitor not been traced?
Would Greece, whom I have saved and served with my brave
      toil,
protect the guilty one on her own sacred soil?
But you do not reply. Then could my own son be
collaborating with his father's enemy?
My mind is overwhelmed with doubt: I must find out
the criminal and what the crime is all about.
So Phèdre will have to say what has been troubling her.


### Scene Six: HIPPOLYTE, THÉRAMÈNE

HIPPOLYTE: Why does my blood run dry and make my
      senses blur?
Is Phèdre now giving in to all her inner strife?
Will she accuse herself and lose her right to life?
Gods!—what will the King say?—What fatal hate has love
spread over all our heads, that we are dying of?
And I, fed by a fire which he cannot allow,—
think how he saw me once, and how he sees me now!
Forebodings fill the air and terrify me here.
But then, the innocent should have no cause to fear.
So let us go, and find some way to state my case
and make my father say that I am in his grace,
because although he may despise this love today,
no power in the world can make it go away.


### ACT FOUR

### Scene One: THESEUS, OENONE

THESEUS: How can I hear these things? What traitor could
      betray
his father's famous name in this disgraceful way?
The pain of my great fate keeps on pursuing me!
I don't know where I am or where I ought to be.

O all my tenderness so callously paid back!
The bald audacity of such a bad attack!
In order to achieve his evil intercourse,
this proud insolent Prince resorted to cruel force.
That was his weapon there, I recognized his sword:
he swore brave deeds the day I gave it to this Lord.
Didn't our common blood give him the least restraint?
And why did Phèdre delay in voicing her complaint?
Or did her silence try to hide the guilty one?

OENONE: Her silence tried to hide that you had been undone.
Ashamed that she should be the cause of all his sighs
and of the lawless fire that kindles in his eyes,
Phèdre would have lied, my Lord, and killed herself outright,
so closing both her eyes, extinguishing the light.
I saw her raise her arm, and I ran to her side;
I made her save her life for love of your high pride.
Now pitying your shock and her disturbing fears,
I have, despite my vows, interpreted her tears.

THESEUS: Dishonesty!—I see why he became so pale,
and when we met again, his feelings had to fail.
I was astonished at his lack of happiness;
his cold embraces stole and froze my tenderness.
But how long has his love so hideously grown?
When he was in Athens was it already known?

OENONE: My Lord, remember how the Queen complained
    to you.
It was this shameful love, which she already knew.

THESEUS: This love began again once back here in Trézène?

OENONE: I've told you everything, my Lord, that happened
    then.
But I have left the Queen alone in her distress;
let me go now and see to her uneasiness.


Scene Two: THESEUS, HIPPOLYTE

THESEUS: Ah, here he is. Good god! Seeing his noble air,
what naive eye would not make the same error there?
Why must the forehead of profane adultery

shine with the sacred grace of virtue's simile?
Are there no secret signs, is there no special art
to know, with no mistake, a false dishonest heart?

HIPPOLYTE: Now let me ask of you what hideous disgrace,
my Lord, is on your mind and showing in your face?
Will you not dare to speak this great shame to my ear?

THESEUS: Traitor and slave!—how dare you stand before me
here?
Sky's brightest lightning bolt should throw you to the void,
almost the last outlaw of those I have destroyed!
After this ugly lust had come into your head
and led you to defame your father's wedding bed,
you still present yourself, and show your hated face,
and so parade your shame throughout this fatal place,
and do not go away, under some foreign sun,
where my own name may be unknown to everyone.
Fly, traitor!—do not try to brave my hatred now,
so go, while my great rage is kept inside somehow.
It is enough for me to bear my own despair
for having brought you forth into the living air,
without your death as well dishonoring my name
and spoiling endlessly the splendor of my fame.
Fly; if you do not wish a swift and fatal blow
to add you to the beasts that I myself brought low,
make sure that that bright sun which shines up in the sky
will never see you breathe beneath its flaming eye.
Fly, I say, forever, now never come back here,
do not let your foul face infect our atmosphere.
And you, Neptune, yes, you: if I was ever brave,
if I have ever raged against the slaves that rave,
remember my reward, your promise to obey
whatever I would ask, whatever I would pray.
In the cruel agonies of a crude prison cell,
I did not cry for help to free me from that hell.
I held myself in check, I waited in my greed,
until some later day saw some much greater need.
But I implore you now. Revenge a father's heart.
I leave this traitor's life for you to tear apart;
stifle his filthy vice in his own blood and lust:
I will worship your worth if you do what you must.

HIPPOLYTE: So Phèdre says Hippolyte is guilty of such
    shame!
Such excellent excess of horror shakes my frame;
so many sudden blows must overthrow me now,
they take away my voice and make me dumb somehow.

THESEUS: Traitor, you may have thought that by your keep-
    ing still
poor Phèdre would try to hide your insults and ill will?
You made one great mistake, just now when you withdrew,
to take away the sword which now accuses you;
or rather, you forgot to make your deed complete,
and take away her life to cover your retreat.

HIPPOLYTE: Now irritated by so foul and black a lie,
I feel I should reveal the truth in my reply,
my Lord, yet I suppress something which touches you.
You should approve my tact, my duty to subdue;
without the slightest wish of stirring up more strife,
remember who I am, and look through my whole life.
Always, some minor sins precede great major crimes.
Whoever breaks the law at first for a few times,
will finally go on to break all sacred rights;
for crime has its degrees, it has its depths and heights;
thus one has never seen timidity grow strong
and leap to the extreme of evil and vile wrong.
More than a single day is needed to create
a monster capable of incest, sin and hate.
Brought up in the chaste gaze of a great heroine,
I never scorned the pride of my own origin.
Old Pittheus, esteemed by all men everywhere,
agreed to teach me when I left my mother's care.
I do not seek to see myself in some great light,
but if I have revealed my worth, however slight,
my Lord, above all things I think I have made clear
my hatred for those crimes I am accused of here.
And Hippolyte is known for this in all of Greece.
My virtue hurts, and yet I work for its increase.
All know I suffer from so strict and harsh an art.
The light of day is not so pure as my own heart.
Yet they say Hippolyte, obsessed with a strange flame . . .

THESEUS: This is the same high pride that damns you to your shame.
I see what evil hides behind your cold disguise:
for only Phèdre alone could charm your brazen eyes;
and for all other loves your sly and lifeless soul
would never once catch fire, but kept its self-control.

HIPPOLYTE: No, my father, this heart—it's too much to conceal—
has not refused a love for someone chaste and real.
Here at your feet I make my great apology:
I love; I love, it's true, what you forbid to me.
For I love Aricie: it is already done;
the daughter of Pallas has overcome your son.
I worship her, and I, defying all your laws,
am lost in my own sighs, of which she is the cause.

THESEUS: You love her? God! But no, this trick is to distract:
act like a criminal to cover up your act.

HIPPOLYTE: My Lord, for six long months, I fought this love for her.
I came here trembling now to tell you this news, sir.
But how? Can anything erase this great mistake?
Could any oath I take persuade you for my sake?
"By this earth, by this sky, by nature all in all . . ."

THESEUS: Always, false hypocrites perjure their own downfall.
No, do not bore me now with more of your fine lies,
if your dishonesty can find no new disguise.

HIPPOLYTE: You think all this is false and full of subtlety.
But Phèdre in her own heart is much more fair to me.

THESEUS: Ah! how your impudence makes me more angry now!

HIPPOLYTE: Where will I be exiled, and how long is your vow?

THESEUS: Far beyond the Pillars of Hercules would be
not far enough, and much too near the heart of me.

HIPPOLYTE: Charged with this awful crime, this foul atrocity,
what friends will pity me, when you abandon me?

THESEUS: Go and invent new friends, whose own dishonesty
congratulates incest, applauds adultery—
outlaws without conscience, traitors who know no law,
able to care for you and share your brazen flaw.

HIPPOLYTE: You keep on speaking of incest, adultery?
I do not speak. But Phèdre comes from her family—
her mother's blood, my Lord, you know it very well,
is worse than mine, and filled with all the filth of hell.

THESEUS: What?—have you lost all sense, that you rage to
    my face?
For the last time, get out, get away from this place:
go, traitor, do not wait for your own father's hand
to drive you forcefully before you leave this land.

### Scene Three: THESEUS, *alone*

THESEUS: Wretched, you are running to your own ruin now.
Neptune, god of that sea which all gods fear somehow,
has given me his word and he will make it good.
You cannot flee a god, let that be understood.
I loved you; and I sense, in spite of your great crime,
the pain you must endure in such a little time.
But you condemned yourself, and now the deed is done.
Has any father been so outraged by a son?
O gods, who see the grief which overwhelms me here,
how could I ever cause this monster to appear?

### Scene Four: PHÈDRE, THESEUS

PHÈDRE: My Lord, I come to you, filled with a ghastly fear.
I heard your strong loud voice as you were speaking here.
I am afraid your threats have ended in something.
If there is still some time, then spare your own offspring;
respect your flesh and blood, I dare to beg of you.
I cannot hear the cries of what you plan to do;
do not condemn me to this future misery,
that your own hand has killed one of your family.

THESEUS: Madam, there is no blood at all on my own hand.
And yet the criminal shall not flee from this land.

For an immortal hand is raised in rage right now.
So you will be revenged, Neptune has made the vow.

PHÈDRE: Neptune has made the vow! What?—just one angry
word . . .

THESEUS: What?—now are you afraid that that will not be
heard?
Instead, join with me now in prayers of righteousness.
Recite his crimes to me in all their foul excess;
arouse my wrath which is too slow and too restrained.
All of his evil deeds have not yet been explained:
your world is furious with insults in his eyes:
your mouth, he says, is full of foul deceits and lies;
he swears that Aricie has all his heart and soul,
that he loves her.

PHÈDRE:            What's that?

THESEUS:                        He spoke with self-control.
But I know how to scorn this artificial trick.
May Neptune's justice come, and be most cruel and quick.
Now I myself will go to worship at his shrine,
and urge him to perform that oath that was divine.


*Scene Five:* PHÈDRE, *alone*

PHÈDRE: He's gone. What news is this which has just struck
my ear?
Now what slow smouldering begins within me here?
O sky, what thunderbolt! what words that shock and stun!
I came here willingly to save his noble son;
breaking away, I left Oenone's own frightened arms,
and gave myself to all these torments and alarms.
What if I were found out, and driven to repent?
I might have just confessed, admitting my intent;
if he had not gone on to interrupt my speech,
I might have let the truth go flying out of reach.
For Hippolyte can feel, and does not feel for me!
His heart to Aricie!—his soul to Aricie!
Ah gods!—to my own love this Lord was so unkind,
with his derisive eye, and his high pride of mind,

that I imagined he, with such a hardened heart,
would have to hate my sex and be set far apart.
But now another has attained this famous place;
in his great scornful gaze another has found grace.
Perhaps he has a heart which some can tempt and lure.
I am the only one that he cannot endure;
so why should I defend what he has been about?


## Scene Six: PHÈDRE, OENONE

PHÈDRE: Dear Oenone, do you know what I have just found out?

OENONE: No, but I tremble now, I must make you believe
I fear for this mad plan which made you try to leave:
for I distrust the path your fatal passions choose.

PHÈDRE: I have a rival now: this is my bitter news.

OENONE: How?

PHÈDRE:              Hippolyte's in love, consumed by a great flame.
That same cold enemy whom no one else could tame,
who praised his own chaste days, and hated others' praise—
this tiger, how I stayed in fear of his wild ways,
and now he has been tamed, he knows a stronger soul,
for Aricie now keeps his heart in her control.

OENONE: Aricie?

PHÈDRE:              Ah, despair which is still unimproved!
Which way is my own heart still waiting to be moved?
All that I have suffered, my passions and my fears,
the fury of my love, the horror of my tears,
and the cruel injury of having been refused,
were all a warning that I would be more abused.
They are in love! but how? right here before my face?
how did they meet? and when? and in what secret place?
You knew of it. But then, why didn't you tell me?
Why didn't you describe this dear conspiracy?
How often have they talked and walked together now?
Far in the forest, did they hope to hide somehow?

Alas! once they met there, they were completely free.
There the wide open sky smiled on their ecstasy;
they did whatever they themselves desired to do;
and each new day was clear and splendid in their view.
While I, the sad outcast of everything in sight,
I tried to hide by day and fly from the bright light:
death is the only god I dared to glorify.
I waited for the day I could lie down and die:
filled with this bitterness, alone in my despair,
still in my illness watched by all eyes everywhere,
I could not find the time to cry as I desired;
that was a fatal joy I privately acquired;
the peaceful features which I wore as my disguise
required that I hide the tears of my own eyes.

OENONE: What true fruit did they taste from their vain en-
deavor?
For they will have to part.

PHÈDRE:              They will love forever.
And right now, as I speak—ah! what a deadly thought!—
they brave the rage of one who raves and is distraught.
Despite the long exile which takes them far apart,
they swear they will remain within each other's heart.
No, no, Oenone, no no, I cannot bear their joy;
take pity on my hate which hastens to destroy.
This Aricie must die. My husband must revive
his wrath against that race he said must not survive.
And he must not lay down a few light penalties:
this sister has surpassed her brother's blasphemies.
My jealousy will speak and seek ways to cajole.
What am I doing now? have I lost all control?
I, jealous! and Theseus becomes the one I seek!
My husband is alive, and love still makes me weak!
For whom? and for whose heart are all my prayers addressed?
Each word I say creates new chaos in my breast.
Now all my hopes fly off beyond all scope of crime.
Incest and fraud exist in me at the same time.
My own cold reckless hands, restless for violence,
are burning to disturb the breath of innocence.
Wretched! and I still live? I am still in the sight
of that great sacred sun which bore me in its light?

My father is the first of all the gods on high;
and my own ancestors still populate the sky.
Where can I hide? far down in the foul dark of hell.
But how? for even there my father casts a spell;
he holds the fatal urn the gods put in his hand:
Minos dooms all who fall to that last ghastly land.
Ah, just imagine how his spirit will despair
when his own daughter comes into his presence there,
confessing all her crimes, with shame in every word,
and sins the underworld perhaps has never heard!
Father, what will you say when I have said it all?
I know, your hand will drop, the fatal urn will fall;
then you shall have to choose what torment you prefer,
so you yourself can be my executioner.
Forgive me: a cruel god has damned this family;
and he still takes revenge in my anxiety.
Alas! and my sad heart has never known the taste
of this forbidden love for which I am disgraced.
Pursued by suffering until my dying breath,
I leave a painful life as I fly towards my death.

OENONE: Ah, Madam, do reject this insubstantial fear.
Do take another look at what has happened here.
You love. And yet we know one cannot conquer fate.
The gods themselves led you into this hateful state.
But then are you so sure your story is unique?
Others, equally strong, have grown equally weak.
For flesh is flesh, and frail—unfortunate, but true.
Since you are human, you must do what humans do.
Your woe is a great weight imposed so long ago.
For the Olympians, the greatest gods we know,
who with a dreadful curse condemn all kinds of crime,
have had their own desires and sinned from time to time.

PHÈDRE: What do I hear? what words of wisdom do you
        give?
You will still poison me for as long as I live,
you wretch! remember that you ruined me this way;
for it was you that made me face the light of day.
Your prayers made me forget the duty that I knew;
I fled from Hippolyte; you forced him in my view.
By what right did your words, which were so full of shame,

accuse his blameless life and darken his good name?
Perhaps he will be killed, perhaps his father's vow
to strike him down is done and he is dead right now.
I will not hear your words. Get out, you worthless beast!
Leave me my last few days and my own fate at least.
Let heaven pay you back for all that you have done!
And may your punishment petrify everyone—
all who, like you, may dare to use deceitful speech,
feeding the weakness of each Prince within their reach,
luring their hearts to go which way they are inclined,
and daring them to do the crimes in their own mind!
O fatal flatterers, the most destructive things
which heaven in its rage inflicts on sinful Kings!

    OENONE [*alone*]: Ah gods look down on me, my faith be-
       gins to fade.
So this is what I get. I have been well repaid.


ACT FIVE

*Scene One:* HIPPOLYTE, ARICIE (ISMÈNE)

    ARICIE: Now you are so unsafe—Speak out, for your own
       sake!
You leave your father here to make the same mistake?
You are too cruel if you turn from my tears of pain
and easily agree not to see me again;
yet if you go away and leave your Aricie,
at least you should assure your own security:
you must defend your name against this shame right now,
and force your father to take back his solemn vow—
for there is still some time. Why, and by what caprice,
does your accuser keep her freedom in such peace?
You should tell Theseus all.

    HIPPOLYTE:          Now what have I not said?
And how could I reveal the shame of his own bed?
Should I describe the truth in all sincerity
and watch my father blush at the indignity?
For you alone have known the worst of what is true.
My heart has only told the gods above and you.
For I loved you that much—from you I could not hide

what I myself despised and tried to keep inside.
But see the secrecy with which my words are sealed:
forget now, if you can, the things I have revealed,
Madam, because I pray your lips which are so fair
may never once repeat this tale of foul despair.
The gods are rational and they deserve our trust;
now for their own sake they shall save me and be just:
unable to escape her punishment in time,
soon Phèdre will pay at last for her most shameful crime.
Your silence is the thing I ask for, at this stage.
And for all else, I give a free rein to my rage:
fly from this hateful state where you have been a slave;
accompany my flight, come with me and be brave;
now tear yourself away and leave this fatal place
where virtue has to breathe the great stench of disgrace;
your hope lies in disguise—to hide your swift retreat,
use the confusion which is caused by my defeat.
I can assure you of the safest means of flight:
the guards here are all mine, the only men in sight;
now we will take our cause to powerful allies—
Argos holds out its arms, Sparta will sympathize:
we can count on these friends to hear our just appeal;
for Phèdre must not succeed, keeping what she can steal,
for she will seize the throne, and once that prize is won,
she will give everything we have to her own son.
This is our perfect chance, and now we must not wait . . .
But what fear holds you back? you seem to hesitate!
It's only your own cause that moves me to be bold:
when I am all on fire, why do you seem so cold?
Does my own banishment fill you so full of fear?

ARICIE: Such a sweet banishment would be to me most dear!
What happiness to be tied to your destiny,
forgotten by the rest of sad humanity!
But not united now by any tie so sweet,
how could I try to leave this place without deceit?
I know that I can go against all stern commands
and free myself right now out of your father's hands:
this place is not the home of my own family;
and flight is right for those who flee from tyranny.
But you love me, my Lord; and there is my good name . . .

HIPPOLYTE: No, you are in my care and you shall know no
    shame.
I have a nobler plan for you and for your life:
fly from your enemies, and join me as my wife.
We shall be free in grief, and under the same sun,
our loving vows shall not depend on anyone.
A marriage does not need bright torchlight and loud sound.
In the ports of Trézène, in the tombs underground,
great ancient sepulchres of Princes of my race,
there is a temple there which is a sacred place.
There men would never dare to make their vows in vain:
for perjurers receive a penalty of pain;
and fearing to find there their own predestined death,
liars will never try to take that fatal breath.
There, if you believe me, we can declare our love
and swear it in the sight of the great gods above;
our witness will be He whom they all worship there;
and our father will be all good gods everywhere.
To the great sacred ones I will address our plea,
to chaste Diana, and to Juno's majesty,
and all the others there, they see my sweet love now,
and they will guarantee the conscience of my vow.

ARICIE: The King comes now: fly, Prince, you must leave
    right away.
No one must know my plans to go, so I shall stay.
But please leave me someone to show me what to do,
to guide my timid steps and lead my love to you.


### Scene Two: THESEUS, ARICIE, ISMÈNE

THESEUS: O gods, enlighten me and give me by your grace
the living sight of truth I search for in this place!

ARICIE: Remember everything, Ismène; prepare our flight.


### Scene Three: THESEUS, ARICIE

THESEUS: You color now, Madam, and you are seized with
    fright;
now why did Hippolyte leave here so secretly?

ARICIE: My Lord, he came to say his last farewells to me.

THESEUS: Your eyes have overcome the high pride of his
    heart;
and his first secret sighs are those you made him start.

ARICIE: My Lord, I cannot lie and hide the truth from you:
nothing could make him take your hateful point of view;
he never treated me like some lost criminal.

THESEUS: I know: he swore his love would be perpetual.
But do not put your trust in his inconstant mind;
for he swore other loves with vows of the same kind.

ARICIE: My Lord?

THESEUS:            You should have trained this Prince to be
    less vain:
how could you bear to share his love without great pain?

ARICIE: How can you bear to say such evil of his ways,
maligning this fair man and darkening his days?
Have you so little wit to understand his heart?
Or can you not keep crime and innocence apart?
Must you see his virtue in some grotesque disguise,
when it so brightly shines before all other eyes?
You damn him to slander and scandal everywhere.
Stop it: you should repent of your relentless prayer;
O you should fear, my Lord, that heaven will fulfill
its own great hate for you and execute your will.
Its fatal rage may take away our prey sometimes.
Sometimes its benefits repay us for our crimes.

THESEUS: No, now you cannot hide how he has been so
    lewd:
your love has made you blind to his ingratitude.
But I have witnesses who testified right here:
and I myself have seen fierce tears which are sincere.

ARICIE: Take care, my Lord, take care: for your heroic hands
have slain the numberless monsters of many lands;
but all are not destroyed, because you did not seek
one . . . But your son, my Lord, forbids me now to speak.
Informed of the respect which he still holds for you,

I would grieve him too much if I said what I knew.
So I shall be discreet, and leave your presence now;
if I stayed I might say more than I should somehow.


### Scene Four: THESEUS, *alone*

THESEUS: What went on in her mind? what did her saying
    hide—
begun, and then cut off, unable to confide?
Were they to baffle me by their hypocrisy?
Or do the two of them resort to torture me?
And meanwhile I myself, despite my self-control,
what is the voice I hear cry out in my own soul?
A secret pity pleads and weeps in my heart's core.
I must seek out Oenone and question her once more:
I must find out the truth, my mind must be made clear.
Now guards, go find Oenone alone, and bring her here.


### Scene Five: THESEUS, PANOPE

PANOPE: My Lord, I do not know what the Queen means
    to do,
but I fear for the state which she now suffers through.
A fatal pale despair is painted on her face,
already, the great dread of death has left its trace.
Already, leaving her and flying shamefully,
Oenone has thrown herself into the raging sea.
Now no one knows what cruel madness made her obey;
we only know the waves have taken her away.

THESEUS: What do I hear?

PANOPE:                           Her death has not disturbed the
    Queen;
the anguish of her soul is so grotesquely seen.
Sometimes, as if to ease the torment of her fears,
she holds her children close and bathes them with her tears;
and then, rejecting them, renouncing tenderness,
she pushes them away, far from her best caress;
she walks as if she lived in some oblivion;
and her distracted gaze does not know anyone;

three times she tried to write; and then, changing her mind,
three times she rose and tore the letter up unsigned.
See her, my Lord, see her, and listen to her cry.

THESEUS: O gods! Oenone is dead, and Phèdre desires to die!
Recall my son, he must defend himself somehow;
now let him speak to me, I want to hear him now.
The fatal vow must wait, it cannot be begun,
Neptune; I almost wish my prayer could be undone.
Perhaps I have believed people I should not trust,
I may have raged too soon and asked you to be just.
Now into what despair am I led by my vow?

### Scene Six: THESEUS, THÉRAMÈNE

THESEUS: Théramène, is it you? And where is my son now?
I trusted him to you in his most tender years.
But now I see you weep: what is behind these tears?
Where is my son?

THÉRAMÈNE:     Too late, this should have come before!
Your suit is useless now: Hippolyte is no more.

THESEUS: O gods!

THÉRAMÈNE:     I saw him die, this loveliest of men,
and this man had no guilt, my Lord, I say again.

THESEUS: My son is no more now! I would have been his
     friend,
but the impatient gods have rushed him to his end!
What blow has taken him? What great stroke of the fates?

THÉRAMÈNE: When he had left Trézène and gone beyond
     the gates,
he drove his chariot; and with a solemn air,
his silent grieving guards were all around him there;
sadly he chose the road to Mycenae, and he
relaxed the reins so that his horses all ran free;
these handsome animals, which once were his own choice,
and eager to obey the loud sound of his voice,
now galloped with sad eye and raced with heavy head,
as if responding to his own keen sense of dread.
A frightful cry, which came from far along the shore,

cut through the quiet sky with an ungodly roar;
and from the earth itself there came a great loud shout
which terrorized the air and echoed all about.
Afraid in our stark hearts, our own life blood froze cold;
the horses heard and reared and could not be controlled.
Just then, erupting from the surface of the sea,
there rose a mound of foam which burst ferociously;
the wave approached, and broke, and vomited to sight,
amidst the waves of foam, a monster of great height.
Its large forehead was armed with long and pointed horns;
covered with yellow scales, the beast could be sea-born,
a fiery dragon, a wild and raging bull;
the hair along its back was twisted, thick and full;
its shrieking shook the shore and cut across the air.
The sky with horror saw the savage monster there;
the earth quaked, and the sight poisoned the atmosphere;
the same great wave of foam it came on, fled with fear.
Everyone flew, we knew that now no one was brave;
we sought the safety that a nearby temple gave.
But Hippolyte remained true to his origin,
halted his horses there, took up his javelin,
threw at the monster's side, and with a perfect aim,
he tore a ghastly wound in its enormous frame.
The great beast leaped ahead and shrieked with rage and pain,
came where the horses were, fell to the earth again,
rolled over, roared, and showed its throat, began to choke,
and bathed the horses there with fire, blood and smoke.
Fear overwhelmed them then, none of the horses heard
their master shouting out his stern commanding words;
he pulled back on the reins, his strength was infinite,
but their mouths overflowed with blood around the bit.
Through all this violence they say that one could see
a god with a great whip beating them ruthlessly.
Spurred on by their own fear, they raced across the rocks;
the axle screeched and broke from such outrageous shocks:
the chariot flew off its few shattered remains;
but Hippolyte was caught all snarled up in the reins.
Forgive my sorrow now: for knowing what I know,
the sight of this will be a constant source of woe.
For I saw your own son, my Lord, I saw your son
dragged by his horses there wherever they would run.

He tried to call a halt, they bolted at the sound,
they ran until he was torn open on the ground.
The field could feel the pain, and our hearts were downcast,
and then the mad horse race began to slow at last:
and finally they stopped near the great ancient tomb
where all his ancestors are kept in the cool gloom.
I ran there breathlessly, and his guards followed me:
his blood had formed a trail which everyone could see;
the rocks were wet with it; there was red everywhere,
even the rough thorns bore his bloody shocks of hair.
I reached him. I cried out: and then, trying to rise,
the dying Hippolyte opened and closed his eyes:
"The sky," he said, "has seized a sinless life from me.
When I have died, dear friend, take care of Aricie.
If my own father should someday be told the truth,
and pities the sad fate of an insulted youth,
tell him, to please my blood and give my spirit peace,
that all these injuries to Aricie must cease;
let him give her . . ." And then, at last, the hero died,
leaving his poor torn form to lie there by my side:
a figure which the gods decided to despise,
which his own father now would never recognize.

THESEUS: My son! My only hope now taken far away!
O gods! In your high pride you served me well today!
I know grief is the fate I must forever face!

THÉRAMÈNE: Then timid Aricie came up to that sad place:
she came, my Lord, because you made her try to fly;
she swore to be his wife by all the gods on high.
She came up close; she saw the grass was wet and bright;
she saw (and what a thing for a sweet lover's sight!)
without color or form, how Hippolyte stretched out.
For a long time she stood, and she had a strong doubt;
not knowing her own love who lay there at her feet,
she looked around awhile and called for Hippolyte.
But satisfied at last this had to be her love,
she gazed up to the sky and blamed the gods above;
then cold and so alone, and losing all restraint,
she fell there at his feet, insensible and faint.
Ismène was close to her; and lost in tears, Ismène
made her come back to life, or back to grief again.

And I myself came here, hating the light of day,
to tell you everything he wanted me to say,
and finishing, my Lord, this last unpleasant task
which his fine dying heart had strength enough to ask.
But now I seem to see his deadly enemy.


### Scene Seven: THESEUS, PHÈDRE, THÉRAMÈNE, PANOPE (GUARDS)

THESEUS: My son has lost his life: this is your victory!
It is no wonder now I tried to see his side,
deep in my heart I sensed a doubt I could not hide!
But Madam, he is dead, so you should claim your prey;
enjoy his having died, guilty or not, today:
for I agree my eyes must be forever blind.
He was a criminal, you proved it to my mind.
His death gives me enough to occupy my grief,
without more questions now, to test my disbelief,
since it would do no good nor cause my son to live—
a greater source of pain is all that it would give.
Let me go far from here, and far away from you,
perhaps the sight of death will vanish from my view.
I choke with memory, and to escape this curse,
I would exile myself from the whole universe.
Everything rises up against me to complain;
the fame of my own name increases my great pain:
if I were less well known, I might hide easily.
I hate all gifts the gods have ever given me;
I shall regret their great murderous favors now,
and never weary them with any further vow.
What they have given me, cannot at all repay
for that which they have now chosen to take away.

PHÈDRE: No, Theseus, let me speak, for I cannot keep still;
I must show you your son in his own guiltless will:
for he was innocent.

THESEUS:                Ah! unfortunate son!
And it was on your word that this damned thing was done!
O cruel! and do you think that I could now forgive . . .

PHÈDRE: Moments are dear to me, so hear me while I live:
I am the one in whom this passion had begun,
by casting a foul eye on your respectful son.
The gods lodged him in me until I was obsessed:
detestable Oenone accomplished all the rest.
She feared that Hippolyte, informed of my mad lust,
would tell you of this love which gave him such disgust:
and so this meddling wretch, seeing that I was weak,
hurried to greet you here, and she began to speak.
Escaping from my rage, she then began to flee
and sought her judgment in the silence of the sea.
The sword would have served me, and made me face my fate,
but I felt the command of virtue was too great:
I wanted to come here, to say what I have said,
so then I could descend more slowly to the dead.
Medea's poison now runs all along my veins,
and I can feel it work, I understand these pains.
Already, its cruel death is coming on my heart,
I feel an unknown cold in every body part;
already my dim eye no longer comprehends
my noble husband whom my being here offends;
and death, which takes away this great disgrace in me,
gives back the light of day in all its purity.

PANOPE: She has just died, my Lord.

THESEUS:                              If this catastrophe
could only wipe away the fatal memory!
I know my error now, and since it has been done,
I must mingle my tears in the blood of my son!
And I must go embrace his mangled body now,
to expiate the shame of that great hateful vow.
He has deserved his name, his honors will increase;
and so that we are sure his soul will rest in peace,
I shall, despite the guilt of her whole family,
proclaim to all the world my daughter Aricie!

# 5. The *Phaedra* of Kenneth Rexroth (1905—    )

CHARACTERS

FIRST CHORUS, *two people*
SECOND CHORUS, *four people*
HIPPOLYTUS
PHAEDRA
THESEUS

*The Greek Heroic Age.*
*Before the palace at Athens.*

*At the back of the stage, a screen, seven feet high and ten feet wide with a rough black and white sketch of a small, primitive, columned building, of the wooden Doric type postulated in histories of architecture. Along the bottom of this screen is a step about one foot high. At right and left are screens, seven feet high and four feet wide, hinged to the wall or wings, which can be pulled back, on a cord, towards the audience, by members of the Second Chorus.*

*On the step, at right and left, sit the First Chorus. At right is a young girl, barefoot, dressed only in a single black cloth, tightly wrapped like a sarong—a street prostitute. At left is a fat old man, with shaved head, wrapped in a white cloth, a small brass bowl beside him—a beggar. The First Chorus speak with great dignity and treat the principals with a certain condescension. All business with the principals is done by them, except Hippolytus' last entrance.*

*The Second Chorus sit, two and two, along the walls on either side, in front of the screens. They are inconspicuously dressed, possibly in long dull blue gowns. They are the musicians, mob, commentators, prop men, and sound effects.*

*On her entrance Phaedra may be dressed in gauze trousers, jeweled brassiere, heavy jewelled girdle, extremely high-heeled slippers, a headdress like a Chinese bride's, a great deal of jewelry, bracelets and anklets—a newsboy's idea of a harem queen. These are all removed for her first dance. Afterwards, she wears the same costume as the prostitute, but without jewels.*

*Hippolytus wears a white cloth, with his arm and chest bare.*

*The cloth is tied with a cord around his waist, draped over his shoulders, the way Indians are supposed to wear blankets, but somewhat shorter. He is barefoot. This is the same costume as the beggar's.*

*Theseus is dressed in a simplfied version of a light-armed Greek soldier's costume, carries a short sword and a fiddle-shaped shield.*

*The couch is a stout folding camp bed, covered with a white blanket. The cup is a plain white hemispherical bowl about eight inches in diameter. There should be a set of fragments of a similar cup. The sword is in a plain scabbard, has a cruci-form hilt, and looks rather like a child's wooden sword.*

*There is no curtain. At the beginning the Choruses walk on, take their places, tune their instruments and begin. At the end, players and Choruses rise and file out, in "reverse precedence," as at Mass.*

*The dances in all these plays should be restrained and formal and very slow. They should under no circumstances resemble the expressionist dance fashionable in America in the Thirties.*

*The make-up should be as formal as possible, or, much bet-ter, the three principals and the First Chorus should wear masks. If masks are used, the corpses should be dummies.*

*Except for the jewelry, the colors should be exclusively black and white.*

*The instruments for the music for these plays should in-clude viola, flute, percussion—wood and drums—very little or no metal, and plucked strings—either an Irish harp, a zither, dulcimer or guitar.*

1 CHORUS: What hour is this, what day?

We have seen the eclipsed sun
Cut by the sea horizon,
The light rush from the gray sand,
The still sea turn black, the sky
Turn black, and the stars come out,
And the wind rise with the dark
With an uncanny rustling
Noise like stiff pleated tissues
Moving with the shadow's edge.

The owls called in the shadow.

We watched from the dark seashore
And the secret icy hair
Of the sun sprang on the sky,
And the ring of the sun's blood.

Behind us all the cocks crowed
In every blackened farmstead,
And every dog cried with fright.

They rose from the sea and sprang
Apart, and all day the sun
Looked as though it had been bled,
All day the black moon followed,
Hidden across the bright sky.
Soon in the red evening
It will hang in the sunset,
Thin as imagination.

    II CHORUS: Our country is very sick.
Crops wither and men quarrel.
Something is wrong with our queen.

A city is like a hive—
Evils possess its rulers
And its life becomes deranged.
The life of the people hangs
On the womb they crown with gold.
Men and beasts become sterile
When it sickens and withers.

Nightmares escape from her dreams
And tramp the seeded furrow.

If she does not heal or die
Soon, we will all have perished.

Theseus wanders in Hell
On a fool's errand; his heir
Plays hermit in the forest,
Forsakes a king's duties for
A saint's gelded wantonry.

Life should flow from our rulers—
They rape the queen of the dead,

Couple with ghosts, lie between
The freezing limbs of the moon.

Hippolytus is the worst.

There was no better prince once.

It was a pleasure to see
Him staggering hot with wine,
Under each arm a young girl,
Squirming in her red drawers.

He certainly liked young girls.

Yes, the younger the better.
Every year he deflowered
Half the town's crop of virgins.

That's the duty of a prince,
To open bellies for new
Infant armies to march out.
He's a lucky man who gets
A girl unsealed by a prince,
Their daughters make the best wives,
Their sons the bravest soldiers.

He's changed.

Seeing that leper
Turned his royalty sour.

Was it a leper? I heard
He stepped on a corpse one night
When he was drunk and roaring.

I heard he saw a crazy
Blind, bald, toothless, old woman;
And they told him she was once
Herakles' sweetheart and taught
Him to love in his young days.

Do you see that beggar there,
Sitting on the palace steps?
I think he really scared him.
They say he was a king once.
Theseus took his city,

Killed his children, raped his wife,
And hamstrung all his horses.
Now he idles in the woods,
And lives on nuts and berries,
Sleeps with the moon in summer,
And nests in a temple porch
In the wintertime. They say
Those cropped ears can hear
The foolish words of the dead,
The wise words of the undying.

They are hitching up the chariot.
I guess he is leaving soon.

He didn't stay long this time.

[*Hippolytus enters.*]

HIPPOLYTUS: Are the horses ready? Hurry.
I can't get away quick enough.
I feel as though I'm chained with gold
Inside a jewelled prison cell
That gets smaller every hour,
A harem full of manacled
Skeletons and behind the stone
Eyes in the dry skulls of the king's
Councillors—spiders and sowbugs.

1 CHORUS: You leave a lot undone.

HIPPOLYTUS: Leave it
To the sick queen and her vapors.
Let my father's politicians
See to the quarrying of stone.
Let them build banks, tombs, whorehouses.
Tell them to convert the palace
Into a pyramid. I'll sleep
In it when I have turned mummy.

1 CHORUS: In the mountains the wind rustles
The leaves. Deep in the night the deer
Cry out beyond the edge of dreams.

The black queen has married the sun.
All the next fortnight she will grow
Big with the sun's blood inside her.

HIPPOLYTUS: Deep in the forested mountains
There is a meadow where a wild
Apple tree grows. For fourteen days
The buds will open one by one
As the moonlight grows in the tree.
The sun's blood will stream from the moon's
Veins into the veins of the tree,
And the mist of vision descend
In perfume and light around me.

I CHORUS: They say there was a city there,
Greater than Knossos or Athens.
Ten thousand years ago its walls
Were smashed down, its temples looted,
Its girls' gauze bottoms and spiced breasts
Left splattered on the smoking stone.

Now that tree changes all the dust
Of riot and debauchery
To pride and chastity and peace.

HIPPOLYTUS: Vein and artery are braided
Into the branches of that tree.
It is the cord that feeds my heart
From her pure compassionate heart—
Artemis, who hears the world's cry.

I CHORUS: Your chariot is ready now.

HIPPOLYTUS: Good-by, pesthouse. I only hope
I never have to smell your stink
Of lust and murder anymore.

[*He goes out.*]

II CHORUS: They say she is worse, the last
Three days she has refused food.

She is weak now and can scarce
Walk.

Before, she paced her room
Continuously, or called
For her chariot, only
To send it away unused;
Or she rode out aimlessly,
And then returned suddenly,
Forgot what she had gone for;
Or she took the reins herself,
And drove like mad, hair flying,
Lashing the horses, headlong
Nowhere, and then she'd stop short
And stare and fall in a muse.

Sometimes she would spend the day
And night sleeping like a corpse.
Another time her lamp
Would burn all night and we
Would hear her moving around.

She is certainly beautiful.

It is terrible to see
Such beauty destroy itself.

They say it takes two thousand
Years to make beauty like that.

She sat at the loom doing
Nothing. The shuttle fell from
Her hands, or else she flung it
Back and forth between the threads,
Empty.

She called for music,
And then said the sound was like
Hot nails driven in her ears.

For a week she drank thick wine
Day and night. It didn't seem
To affect her, now she won't
Even taste wine; and at last
She has refused to touch food.

They are bringing her outdoors.

She wants to lie in the sun.

Maybe it will do her good.

[*Phaedra is carried in on a couch.*]

PHAEDRA: Take me back. You shouldn't have moved me.

1 CHORUS: You said you wanted the sunlight.

PHAEDRA: I know. But I don't want it now—
Not that violent animal,
Tearing at my eyelids and bowels.

1 CHORUS: Phaedra. The sun will give you strength.

PHAEDRA: I don't want his strength. I've my own.
It is strength that makes these white thighs
Too weak to walk. I have ample
Strength at my spine's black root—
I don't need all his cheap blonde noise.

1 CHORUS: Please sit up. Please. Please try to eat.

PHAEDRA: Damn you to Hell. Let me alone.
I have more than enough to eat.

1 CHORUS: This beautiful, beautiful flesh—
Why do you try to destroy it?

PHAEDRA: Don't worry. It won't be injured.
This stuff is immortal, passing
From dying spirit to spirit.
Wisdom, lust, chastity and war—
All the gods try to destroy it —
But they never will. They themselves
Live on human flesh. You know that.
Or have you everything backwards,
Like all the other buffleheads?
Give me your hand.
Touch my belly.
This is the phoenix' nest. Someday
I shall burn myself up in it,
And walk from the smoke a virgin.
Come back.

Are you afraid of me?
Give me some wine.
It is pretty,
Isn't it? You know my sister
Bathes in it with her black lover.
People that see them go crazy.
"The gold lion watches himself
In the unruffled forest pool.
He is immortal. His image
Is immortal." That is my flesh.
It will never, never, never,
Die.

    1 CHORUS: Lean back. Let me comb your hair.

    PHAEDRA: Give me the mirror.
It drinks me.
It has drunk up the smiles of girls
Ever since Daedalus made it—
Before I was born, in Crete.
That octopus carved on its back
Is fat with all those painted lips
Sucked under in its polished lie,
Drowned with the fleeting, pouting smiles
Of expected kisses frozen
Upon them.
Women made these holes
In space, into the other world.
The inhabitants of that world
Peer and mock at us, grimacing
In the elastic masks of our
Identities.
And memory—
This is memory. All the world,
Everything, falls in here. This thing
Sends its radiant loneliness
Out like a cloud, and draws it back,
And everything with it. It is
The way the thing breathes. Take it
Away.
Apathy. Do you know
What real apathy really is?

Mountains are apathetic, too.
I see the sun on the mountains
Of ice that I have never seen.
Against their apathy I have
Only pain trickling from their cold
Like a waterfall. That water
Flows through endless, immense forests,
Sinuous and sweet, between the pines
Of two thousand years. The rabbit
Drinks, and the weasel, in the night
Of eyes. Young men go naked there.
What did I say?
You know, at night
The air is full of flying knives—
Daylight my brain is the center
Of a mirror without limit.

    I CHORUS: What is it haunts you? Into what
Cobweb of fire have you fallen?

    PHAEDRA: I didn't ask to be involved.
I never wanted to be here.
O God how I wish I were home—
Back home in the ruined city—
My father killed at the altar
In the heart of the labyrinth—
Nothing left but the broken walls—
The crumbling frescos scrawled with smoke
And the obscenities of Greek
Infantrymen.
I don't want this.
There will never be anything
Like it again. These savages
Will perfect a new savagery.
Once more the art will be refined
Of fanning every appetite
And stifling every desire.
But there will be a difference—
And I shan't be royal priestess.
Do you know that these arms that I
Can hardly lift have held the coiled
Adders of double death like flowers?

This will-less hand has struck the dark
With the double axe of lightning?
And here I am, a pirate's whore.
It's not the change that you might think.
A princess is a kind of whore,
The peasant's gorgeous imagined
Bedfellow. We serve to provide
Insatiable appetites
That keep men busy. If it weren't
For us there'd be no history.
Our emperors find us frigid.
When our empires fall, and we pass,
Raped, to barbarian chieftains,
I suppose they wonder, lying
Against our chilly backs, what all
That getting and spending was for.
Still, we teach them to read and bathe.
Enslaved by blood and freed by lust,
The court ladies of dead Knossos
Become prostitutes in Athens.
But not me. I'll never be freed.
I am the proof of the pudding—
What it was all for—my sister
And I, all that blood, nastiness
And ruin. She was abandoned
To a drunken Indian, and I
Am being smothered to death.
I'm hot.
Take these clothes from my body.
This barbarian frippery
Dries up my womb like acid hate.
I wish I were naked in cold
Water. I want to be taken,
Plunged in a freezing cataract,
My flesh burst with monstrous male flesh.
My mother's demoralized womb
Bore me, that first had borne the bull.
Saluting soldiers, and shivering
Peasants and prostrate worshippers—
Their appetites sent them to Hell,
Chasing each other like lewd dogs.

Let them howl. I am escaped clean.
Only love's absolute will fill
The desire they have left with me.
The best do *not* rot away, I
Am where I do not want to be,
Trapped in a net of illusion,
A stranger amongst savages,
But I am not terrified. Do
You hear me? I cannot be touched.
Help me up.
I want to stand up.
Hold me.
Stop that fumbling.
I am
Going to dance.

I CHORUS: Phaedra.

PHAEDRA: Shut your
Mouths and hold me.
I will be all right.
And take off my clothes.
All of them.

[*They support her as she begins her dance. When she breaks
away she staggers, but gains strength rapidly.*]

I CHORUS: It is the Minotaur dance,
That she danced with her brother,
In the dark on the bloody floor.
The dance of the fire tangle
That rules the knotted bowels,
The dance of the netted sun,
The black sun in the red earth.

II CHORUS: It is a terrible dance
To watch; ordinary folks
Should not look at things like this.

I CHORUS: She taught the king the heron dance—
The rigid erotic hover
Of the male and female virgins—
The labyrinthine procession;
But Theseus will never see her

Dance like this. It is what his dance
Is for; but he will never know.
For ages the Athenians
Will tread those steps that she taught him;
But they will be pointless, headless.
There will be no one at the heart
Of the labyrinth—no one there
To do what she is doing now.

[*At the end of the dance she sits down abruptly, woodenly,
and stares straight ahead. The right screen reveals Hippolytus.
He does not speak or move. She turns her head stiffly and sees
him.*]

PHAEDRA: The heart steals the lizard's instant.
I am nailed to the wall.

HIPPOLYTUS: I came back. I have lost my sword.

PHAEDRA: I found it. I have it here.

II CHORUS: His sword was hidden in her
Bed, in cloth that smells of her.
His face blenches, but he comes
Forward to take it from her.

PHAEDRA: Why are the hilt and scabbard
Sealed together, the seal stamped
With a five rayed star? I tried
To draw the blade and could not.

HIPPOLYTUS: It is my father's sword, which he
Left with me, and I have taken
An oath that it shall not be drawn.
The witch Medea forged it.
It is an heirloom in Athens.
It has been drawn enough. Too much.
He gave a symbol of power;
But I took from him a symbol
Of my responsibility.
I have sworn never to draw it,
And never to be without it.

PHAEDRA: You spend all your time hunting;
Don't you ever need your sword?

HIPPOLYTUS: Do you want to know my secret?
I will tell you. I do not hunt.
That is just a tale to mislead
My father. Have you ever seen
Me bring home game? Have you ever
Seen blood on my spear or arrows?
He thinks I give the venison
Away to beggars and peasants.
Have you ever seen me eat meat?
I tell him I have a surfeit
At the campfire and need a change.
I have vowed never to take life.
I have taken on the penance
For a career of lust and blood.

PHAEDRA: I thought you were devoted
To Artemis the huntress.

HIPPOLYTUS: Artemis the huntress of souls,
The healer and the avenger,
The lady of the moon filled lake.
She is living retribution,
The peace that unties illusion,
Renunciation that gains all,
The myriad breasted virgin,
The mirror that reflects the sun—
Pure in the dark night of the soul.

PHAEDRA: I am amazed. I cannot
Believe it is you speaking.
I have loved and hated you,
And for all the wrong reasons.
I saw and loved your pride, but
I have hated you, thought you
One of these Hellenes, sensate
Till they are insensible.
They're so sure, and plot the moon's
Course with their machinery.
Someday they may discover
It's held in its orbit by
The menstruation of women.
Come here.
Come and take your sword.

II CHORUS: The sword lies in her soft lap.
As he takes it by the hilt,
Her hands cling to the scabbard.

PHAEDRA: Someday you will draw this sword
That Artemis seals shut now.
When you do, you will kill me.

II CHORUS: Hippolytus is afraid
Of her. He takes the sword, but
His whole body is trembling.

PHAEDRA: Je fonds comme la neige
Sur les montagnes d'été.

II CHORUS: She spoke in her own language.
Hippolytus has not moved.

Now she weeps violently.

HIPPOLYTUS: What did you say? Why do you cry?
I never hated you. Always
I have pitied you. Certainly
I do not hate you now. Tell me.
What is the matter? I know now
I have not been alone. I can
Tell you now how much I love you.

PHAEDRA: You do not know, as I know,
You can never understand
As I can—I do not weep
For our private misery,
But for the chaos of the world.

HIPPOLYTUS: I do not know what to say. I
Do not think I understand you.
You have a riddle for a heart,
And I am only a young man.
I have been tortured by conflict.
I have tried to find my duty.
I do not know if I have failed.

PHAEDRA: Realization is hard
To recognize. It's like pain
In a nerve you've never used—
Like the pains of childbearing.

HIPPOLYTUS: I'm not sure. I believe I'd know.

PHAEDRA: If you saw her, are you sure
You'd recognize Artemis?

II CHORUS: Hippolytus is dead white.
He can hardly move at all.

HIPPOLYTUS: I think I would. I think I have.
I want . . .

PHAEDRA: Do you want me?

HIPPOLYTUS: I want
What you want.

PHAEDRA: No you don't. But I
Will take you. Maybe it is what
I want.

HIPPOLYTUS: I want you to take me.

I CHORUS: They are dancing together.
The prince and the young queen dance.
They dance the dance of the world
That they alone rule over.

It is hard for him to dance.
He must follow her swift steps
As she dances on bright air.

On the rock in the sea's waste
The sea eagle lives alone.
She nourishes her children
On the poisonous sea snakes.
She flies in front of the sun,
Two snakes twisting in her claws.
Once a year her husband flies
To her from the land over
The sea. They mate in mid-air.
The sun is at the zenith,
The full moon at the nadir.
The heart hangs in a gold web.
Moonlight streams up through the earth.
The birds have vanished in fire.

[*The stage is darkened gradually to black out at the climax
of their dance—after a brief interval the lights come up to
moderate dimness—Hippolytus and Phaedra are gone. The
girl sings.*]

I CHORUS: Lie still. Let your mirror lie.
Lover, look not on the rose
Love has shattered in your hair.
Kiss me. Turn and go to sleep.
Lie still. Our youth goes by us
Like dreamless sleep, soft footed
As our heartbeats and as quick.

[*Phaedra and Hippolytus enter.*]

II CHORUS: They are coming out.

They look
Like dead people.

The queen moves
As though she had lost her skin.

You think so? I think the prince
Looks as if there was nothing
Inside his skin.

I suppose
Love like that is wonderful.
But I could do without it.

PHAEDRA: Stop. Look at the million stars.
Do you suppose that someday
They will put us in the stars?
And when you rise they will yoke
Bullocks to the sharpened plow,
And when I set, call the ships
From wandering in the islands.
Stop. No more.
Don't kiss me now.
Maybe they'll separate us
With the river of heaven,
And allow us only once
A year, when we lie against
The sun, to come together.

It's likely to be like that.
We will have to pay for this.
Life, like any property,
Is acquired by theft.
My love.

HIPPOLYTUS: I have never known anyone
Like you. I did not know there was
Anything in the world like this.
I can never love you enough.

PHAEDRA: O lover, lover, lover—
I can't call you that enough.
I knew, but I have never
Found it before. I have been—
For all my lust—a king's wife.
That Aphrodite who turns
Men's hearts inside out never
Haunted the bedside during
My scrimmages with Theseus.

HIPPOLYTUS: Hush. Let me forget my father.
Tonight we are going to start
To make ourselves new memories.

PHAEDRA: People have tried that before.
Memory, unhappily,
Is not some wandering ghost
That the mind can dispossess,
But living bone that our acts
Made powerful over us.
I'd like to forget so much—
But I can never forget.
He may return at any time.

HIPPOLYTUS: Impossible. Come back from Hell?
He has broken in his last gate.
This one will stay shut behind him.
He's there to stay. No lovesick girl
Will give him a clue to that maze.

PHAEDRA: I am afraid you do not
Know the vast frivolity
Of the economy of Hell.

Orpheus overturned it
With a song; and Theseus
Never lacks for stratagems.

HIPPOLYTUS: I don't want to hear it. Kiss me.

PHAEDRA: Besides. If we really have
Found the bliss we think we have,
The glamor of it will shine
Even in that cloudy place,
And he will sense its meaning;
Or else our lust will call him home.
One or the other, someday
He will turn up, the kidnapped
Persephone tagging him
Like a frolicking kitten.
The world's destructive children
Dictate their own terms to fate.
It's people like you and me
Fate traps and the Furies haunt.

HIPPOLYTUS: I'm sorry. I can't be worried.
You lie here philosophizing,
And all I can think of is this curve
Of this smooth belly—these dimples
Where this proud back and buttocks join.

PHAEDRA: O my love—
Is that what you are?
I call you that.
I hope you are.
I can't believe it.

HIPPOLYTUS: How can you say that? For ten years—
Since he brought you back from Crete—
I hardly dared to look at you
For fear I would reveal myself.
You have stood by me in his court,
And your perfume swept over me,
And I have been struck blind with it,
And not known what I was doing.
Or the thought of you has stopped me
In some drunken brawl, and my brain
Has been stripped and sprayed with pepper.

Do you think a live man will take
A goddess as love's surrogate,
If he can have mortal female
Flesh in which to clothe his worship?
While her immortality poured
Into me I could forget you.
The rest of the time I could force
Myself to think of you as his
Embodied lust and disaster.
If I'd not forgotten my sword,
I'd be in the mountains tonight,
Drunk with her immortality.
Maybe I'd never have come back.
I think she might have opened to me
Fully, taken me into her,
Merged my will with her turning disc.
It is too late now, and I feel
This has not been an act of will.
It should have been made to happen—
Not just have happened anyhow.

PHAEDRA: Lover.
Do you know what you're
Saying?
Have you found vision
In a trance under a tree?
Or have you found it elsewhere?
I lay completely open
To you. Did you find it then?

HIPPOLYTUS: I think I did. I know I did.

PHAEDRA: You know indeed.
Do you know
I am a monster's sister?
Do you know what vision costs?
We are each of us tied up
In the inside of a glove.
A great pride or a great lust
Can cut the knot and reverse
The glove. There's no other way—
Vision—evisceration.

The pride must be forged so pure
It fits the lust as a sword
Fits the wound as it cuts it.
That sword with the blade sealed shut
Is the sword of perfect pride.
Have you the right to a sealed
Scabbard?

HIPPOLYTUS: Once more I do not know
If I understand you at all.
But I wonder. Are you so sure
You have the power to be the wound
Only an undrawn sword can cut?
I would rather lie under your
Dragging hair and drink your kisses
Than bandy mysteries with you.
I know that I have wanted you
For years, and at last I have you,
And I am going to keep you.
It's my love against your wisdom.

PHAEDRA: My wisdom is not so deep
That you can't understand it.
It is just the end product
Of a hundred sailors' queens
That slept as deep in the bride
Beds of Knossos as they sleep
On the floors of looted tombs.

HIPPOLYTUS: Kiss me. I'll pay you in full.
What do you want? There is nothing
I have that I haven't given.

PHAEDRA: That will you took ten years to
Sharpen, what should you have done
With it once it was perfect?

HIPPOLYTUS: Would I have given it to you?
Is that what you mean? I don't know.
I doubt if you want submission.

PHAEDRA: Want it? Dear child. I can get
Submission from Theseus
Or any blue-eyed sailor.

Those boys you sent to Knossos,
The lovers of the serpent
Priestess who coupled with her
In the room that my brother
Kept drenched with the blood of girls—
Why do you think they were killed
Before they saw the daylight?
I can only be possessed
By an act that is its own
Memory.
You have it wrong—
Your wisdom against my love.
Only the wise can be proud.
Only the imbecile love.

HIPPOLYTUS: There's been a labyrinth too long
Under your feet, and now you have
An inhuman, labyrinthine heart.
I want the ordinary bliss
Of a human woman's body,
Not a wedding with black nothing.

PHAEDRA: You forgot your Artemis.
You would have been her husband,
Dark moon or full.

HIPPOLYTUS: I can choose.
I choose the bright hair on your womb.
I reject these strands of blackness
You are trying to spin around me
Like a hungry female spider.

PHAEDRA: All right. I make the same choice.
I can take you to a place
Beyond memory, beyond
The sound of talkative Greeks.
There is a place, a crossroads
In the Italian jungles,
Where fugitives from burned out
Troy and Knossos have settled.
It is a country of wolves,
A city with a single

Mud street and cabins of mud
And sticks; but men of our race,
My people and your mother's,
Struggle with oblivion there.
Thin-lipped men with narrow waists,
And long narrow faces,
The wisest men left alive,
Wiser than Egypt's mummies,
Drain the marshes and teach the
Foolish aborigines.
They'll die out. They're not enough.
The wilderness is too big.
A thousand years of rural
Idiocy may go by.
But their building and teaching
Will last in those savage brains.
And someday they will pay the heirs
Of Theseus in his own coin.
I could make you a king there.
My royalty is holy
There; I am the only one
Left who can perform those rites.
And I could be your wife there,
Not a Greek's elegant whore,
But the sacred wife who lights
The hearth fires of a new race.
And you could draw that sword there
And bathe me for my marriage
In the immortal blood of bulls.

   HIPPOLYTUS: I will let my father found states.
I don't even want to head one.
I have no desire to butcher
Bulls just to make men immortal.
I would prefer that history's
Senseless wheel ran down and the wheel
Of man's appetite that wants to
Go on spinning forever, stop.
They are firewheels made by torches
Whirled in the dark.

PHAEDRA: What do you want?

HIPPOLYTUS: You. For the rest, I'll wait and see.
Time is a coiled snake, and deadly
If trod upon.

PHAEDRA: That sounds wise.
It's just procrastination.
I can take what I can get?
All right. I take everything.
It's now or never? This now
Is never. Kiss me. Take me.
You can have the power now
To take me beyond return.
But what returns if you do,
Is your responsibility.
Now do you know what I mean?

HIPPOLYTUS: I understand you. I can see
Fire spray from our union and burn
Down the world, and burn us with it.
Let it burn. We are all burning.
This hand burns. Look at the others
That fall like burning leaves, senseless
Through Hell's cold circles forever.
Your eyes are burning, and the stars
They watch burn, and the reflection
Of the stars in your eyes burns too.
Let this fire fall away in fire,
Like water poured into water.

[She stands.]

PHAEDRA: Stand up.
Give me back your sword.
Drink before you burn. This cup
Is the brain pan of Minos.
In the starlight, the red wine
Is black as blood in a ditch.

[As Hippolytus drinks from the cup which she holds up to
him, he drops her dress and she draws the sword.]

II CHORUS: Look. They are dancing again.

Again? How can they stand it?
Twice in a day would kill me,
And they haven't eaten yet.

If I was Hippolytus,
I would be afraid of her,
Waving that sword and drinking
She might cut someone with it.

They look like crazy people.

Like people that died crazy.

I CHORUS: Surefooted as sleepwalkers,
They dance on the shifting beams
Of doom's unmeasured levers.

The snake stirs in the earth's core.

The sun hangs in the Bull's horns,
Caught in the Hyades' net.
The moon moves from the Bull's loins.

The snake climbs the last mountain.

The double-headed eagle,
The firebird, flies from the fire.

The five planets crown the snake.

Act and power are mirrored
Pictures in each other's eyes.

The snake crawls into the sun.

The torch goes out, the firewheel
Vanishes in the orb of fire.

The sun's seed is drenched wth blood.

Worlds bloom in their flaming hair.

An invisible crystal
Hangs where the sun has gone out.

[When the climax of the dance is reached they sustain it,
perfectly still, for several seconds, and then spring apart, each

*with one mechanical leap, downstage. Phaedra right, Hippolytus left.*]

II CHORUS: What is the matter with them?

I CHORUS: They came together like snow
Whirled in a coiling blizzard.
They mingled like falling rain.
They broke like a falling stone.

[*Neither move. The left screen reveals Theseus. Phaedra
runs across the stage with small, swift dance steps, the cup and
sword still in her hand, presses against his body and looks into
his face.*]

PHAEDRA: The lictors of Hell, are they
Sentient beings, or merely
Automata created
Especially for the purpose?

[*She runs out, left.*]

THESEUS: What's the matter with her? Is she drunk?

II CHORUS: He circles away from him,
His eyes are like a wolf's eyes.

His father is astonished.
His feelings are very hurt.

THESEUS: What's the matter with you? Aren't you
Glad too see me? Stop staring at me.
You can be sure that I'm still alive.
I've had a hard trip and I need rest.
They locked me in the bottom dungeons
Of Hell, but their walls are as flimsy
As smoke, and I walked right straight through them.
Persephone wouldn't come with me.
Although she is a living woman,
She is at the mercy of the dead,
And wanders in the devil's prayers.
However, I had a night with her
Before they caught me. She liked it, too.
I was her first real man in six months.

We were the only live things in Hell
Except for a bull that got lost there
Years ago. They were afraid of it.
When they found out they could not hurt me,
They tried to get the bull to kill me.
I just got on the poor thing's back, rode
Him out through the closed gates, and came home.
I put him in the stable with your
Horses, you want to watch out for him.
I'm the only one he'll let touch him.
He's a sort of relative, in fact
The bull that the queen's mother once loved.

HIPPOLYTUS: The queen has been violated.

THESEUS: What? What did you say? Speak distinctly.

HIPPOLYTUS: I have violated your queen.
I have raped your wife. What are you
Going to do about it?

THESEUS: Nonsense.
What are you talking about? You mean
You gave her comfort in my absence?
Look, my boy, I am a man of the world.
What do you think I thought would happen?
Do you think that I thought that I could leave
A passionate woman to the care
Of a hot-blooded young sport like you,
And nothing happen? You are my son.
I'd be ashamed if nothing happened.
We were never happy. I never pleased her.
She wanted something I haven't got.
I planned it this way. If I hadn't—
I'd have sent you to the provinces,
And left her in the care of eunuchs,
I'm glad it turned out well. I hope
You give her pleasure and me grandchildren.
If you'd both like, you can have Crete
For your province. Restore the country.
Well? Speak up. Stop that foolish staring.

HIPPOLYTUS: You infamous, infamous man.
I don't wonder Hell spewed you out.
You're a walking Hell of your own.
You have destroyed a dozen wives,
And all your children, and cities
Full of other men, and their wives
And children, the poems of poets,
The visions of artists, the dreams
Of the wise, you destroy them all.
You think there's nothing you can't smash.
You can't smash me. I defy you.
I am where your power ends. Here.
Me. Do you hear me? I smash you.
Let me go. Let me out of here.

[*He goes out, right.*]

THESEUS: Fiddlesticks. He will get over that.
He won't be able to keep away
From her if she gets him that excited.
She never had that effect on me.
If I had been better educated,
And had better manners, and a stock
Of high-flown talk . . . I've had a hard life.
I'm not young. His mother was my type.
They'll make a fine pair—like his mother
And I did once, but not so brawny.
Where is the queen? Go and bring her back.

[*The girl goes out, left. The beggar points as she pushes
out the screen and reveals Phaedra, standing against the wall,
dead, covered with blood from the waist down.*]

I CHORUS: She is dead.

A few moments
Ago she was still living.
I could see her standing there
Listening to you and your son.

The sword is drawn at last. She
Has impaled herself on it.

[*Theseus crosses the stage. He lifts her face, brushes the
hair from her forehead, looks silently into her dead eyes, finally
lets her head fall with a sigh.*]

THESEUS: She dropped the cup, but there's no wine spilled.
She must have drunk it all. That's a lot
Of wine for a young woman to drink,
Her father was a big-headed man.
She must have been drunk. I guess she was
Out of her senses when she did it.

[*The Second Chorus bring in Hippolytus, dead, his arms
and legs obviously broken, smeared with dirt and blood.*]

THESEUS: What has happened? Is he badly hurt?

II CHORUS: When he went to get his horse
The bull trampled him to death.
We were too late to save him.
One of the grooms was killed, too.
The bull broke down the barn doors,
And escaped in the darkness.

THESEUS: Let them lie together on this couch.
Just a little while ago, I guess
They must have been happy lying here.
What a terrible thing to happen.
And so suddenly. I should have stayed
Away. I am a good-natured man.
But everywhere I bring disaster.
I am just Theseus, a bawdy
Old campaigner, why should things like this
Have to happen to me all the time?

I CHORUS: The sword of a Russian witch,
Proud past belief, the evil
Memory of a bestial
Queen long dead.

They could not win.
Her love was not strong enough,
And her vanity took flesh.

His frail pride could not withstand
That lewd hungry animal.
It walked forth alive from him.

Out of vision generate
The perfected grace of bliss,
The terrible things that wait
Behind substance, seeking form.

Impure intention is damned
By the act it embodies.

Each sinned with the other's virtue.

They go out of the darkness,
Onto a road of darkness.

The wind turns to the north, and
The leaves rattle. An unknown
Bird cries out. And the insects
Of a day die in the starlight.

# ✠ Chapter IV ✠
## Moslem Parable

In some ways the Moslem versions of the story of the Chaste Youth and the Lustful Stepmother are the most complex, because they combine features of several of the other variants. The earliest of them is the "Yusuf" chapter of the *Koran,* perhaps the only complete and coherent narrative in that inspired but often disjointed scripture. The Koran's very disjointedness may be evidence that the Prophet—or rather Allah through the Prophet— was alluding in it to already familiar lore that did not need to be given either in full detail or in continuous order. The story of Yusuf is remarkable in how little it shares in this literary defect of the *Koran.* Like so much else in that book, it trickled down to the Arabs of the desert as part of an oral literature deriving from "The People of the Book," as both Jews and Christians were denoted by Mohammed. This heritage, it must be assumed, included not merely the Biblical texts, but also Apocryphal and Pseudepigraphal matter, and possibly also much Talmudic, Midrashic, and early Christian commentary.

It should be noted here, perhaps, that much of what has since come to be regarded as Jewish tradition in this story was lore borrowed by the Jews from the Moslems in the post-Islamic period. This is apparent in Louis Ginzberg's interesting collection of *The Legends of the Jews,* which correctly assigns a Moslem origin to various elements of the present story, including the name given to the heroine—"Zuleika," as Ginzberg transliterates it.

In addition to the Hebrew-Christian sources of the story of Yusuf and Zulaikha must be mentioned the classical legend of Hippolytus and Phaedra. If the latter cannot be proved to have borne directly upon the *Koran* chapter of Yusuf, there is at least no doubt of its having influenced later versions of the Moslem story as told by Persian, Turkish, and Indian poets. For it must be remembered that where Islam went, this favorite story of the most faithful of The Faithful also went. Yusuf became the very symbol of the great monotheistic idea of Abraham, who is, of course, the fountainhead of Islam as of

Judaism and Christianity. Yusuf was, besides, a type of ideal beauty, the Adonis of his world, as the Moslem poets never tire of reiterating. Although his character remains fundamentally as it is given in the book of Genesis, his personality takes on the colors of the Moslem world view.

The *Koran* account, although it does not yet name the wife of Potiphar, clearly takes fuller notice of her than did Genesis and shows a softening attitude toward her. On her husband's part there is, to be sure, a bit of harem cynicism regarding women, but she is nevertheless given an opportunity to repent and to make a public confession of her evil plotting against the innocent Yusuf. One may see in this, if one wishes, the moderating effect of the Phaedra legend as sieved through Hellenistic romances, or, simply, Mohammed's larger tolerance for the female in Arab society. In any case, the Koranic account assigns to Potiphar's wife one of the major scenes of the narrative: the one in which her envious women friends are invited to a gathering where the handsome object of the mistress' much discussed passion is displayed to them. In their distraction at the beauty of Yusuf, they all cut their hands with the sharp knives provided them for peeling fruit. It is a rare set piece in the Moslem story, made much of by later narrators, and heartily accepted by Thomas Mann as an authentic part of the Joseph legend. Besides the women friends of Zulaikha, the *Koran* also introduces as minor characters the household witnesses to Yusuf's innocence. (These are changed in Jami's later version to a precocious infant in the cradle.) Potiphar's wife does not yet have, however, the female attendant later assigned to her after the manner of the Greek legend.

Since the entire chapter is a revelation from Allah, it is frequently punctuated by reminders that the Deity, through the Archangel Gabriel, is the narrator. Hence the august impersonal "We." The didactic tone of a revelation is never lost, despite the fascinating involutions of the narrative. The account is thus dominantly Hebraistic (again in Arnold's sense), being a preachment from which the pious hearer may learn the path of righteousness, truth, and obedience. The Hellenization was to occur later and largely at the hands of the Persian poets, who were inheritors not only of the Prophet's message, but also of Iranian, Greek, and Byzantine humanism.

✠

Hermann Ethe, a German orientalist of the nineteenth century, counted some eighteen poetical versions of the Yusuf and
Zulaikha story in Persian. One of these is generally attributed
to Firdausi, the epic poet, whose other analogue, "Siyawush
and Sudaba," is included in this book. There has been some
doubt raised about his authorship of the Yusuf and Zulaikha,
but in any case the poem in question is an early work of
Persian literature. E. J. W. Gibb observes that it is still the
story of Yusuf alone. The later tendency was for the narrative
to center on the two leading characters, to become in fact a
romance, one of the great love stories of Moslem literature.
Perhaps the best—certainly the best-known—of the later accounts is the verse-novel by the fifteenth-century Persian poet
Jami, who was a Moslem mystic, a member of the Sufi order.
In his hands, the tale became not just a preachment in behalf
of the True Faith, not even just a romantic idyll, but also a
parable of the Sufi's pantheistic striving after the divine nature.

Jami's long poem begins with an invocation of the Prophet,
continues with a eulogy to Beauty and Love, and only then
takes up the narrative of Yusuf. Working as on a large mural,
Jami sets the action of the story in three places: in the Holy
Land, in the North African kingdom of Mauretania, and in
Egypt. We are introduced to the family of Jacob and to his
problematically gifted son, who early shows powers of divina-
tion with dreams. Next, with a scene shift, we are shown the
young child Zulaikha, daughter of the king of Mauretania,
whose subsequent fateful life is early projected in three visions
she has of the handsome Yusuf, with whom she falls hopelessly
and forever in love. Since the person in her vision identifies
himself as a future vizir of Egypt, she prevails upon her father
to send her on a mission of betrothal to that kingdom. She is
married sight unseen to the Grand Vizir of Egypt, only to
discover too late that he does not correspond to the figure in
her dreams.

Her agony begins here, for we learn that the Vizir is a
eunuch of the temple. Thus, when she later sees Yusuf as a
foreign slave in the Egyptian mart and prevails upon her husband to buy him for her household, we are back in the familiar

Biblical situation, but with an entirely different attitude toward the heroine, who may now at last be said to deserve that designation.

The course of Zulaikha's incontinent passion for the youth is told in full detail and with profound psychological acumen. This is an affair of the heart and not merely the lust of a wanton stepmother. She at first tries to sublimate her feelings by treating Yusuf as an adopted son, and like Anpu's wife offers to make fine clothes for him to wear. She later finds herself longing for him, sends her nurse to woo him (after the manner of Phaedra), receives the inevitable refusal and then begins experiencing the protracted and frightful anguish of unrequited love.

In frantic desperation—but with time obviously not a factor —she has a palace built and decorated with murals suggestively depicting herself and her slave in the act of love. Yusuf, responding now in the fashion described by the Midrashic commentators, is on the verge of yielding, especially as he is terrified by his mistress' threat of suicide (borrowed, as in *The Testament of Joseph,* from the Greek romances). He is saved only by what the *Koran* had described darkly as "the demonstration of his Lord," which Jami interprets as Yusuf's realization that Zulaikha is a worshipper of pagan idols. In a fierce Hebraistic recollection of his pious mission, he breaks away, leaving behind his telltale robe.

Between the investigation by the puzzled Vizir and Yusuf's imprisonment, the author introduces the scene of the women of Memphis and their bleeding hands. But more significant is the change that begins to occur in the character of Zulaikha. During Yusuf's imprisonment, she finds herself not so much desiring him as being concerned about his welfare. Thus the stage is set for her repentance and for the confession, by her and her women friends, of their previous malicious designs on the innocent youth. Yusuf's release from prison is effected, as in the Biblical account, by his interpreting of Pharaoh's dreams; and his elevation to high office follows in the manner prescribed by the universal story of the Fortunate Youth.

This is where the poem might have ended, but the poet carries the repentance of Zulaikha one step further to bring about her regeneration. Purified in the fire of her consuming passion, she at last wins her way to a true love of Yusuf. The external sign of this is her destruction of the pagan idol she has worshipped, which takes care of the orthodox moral of the tale. But beyond that, she has become a prototype of the Sufi mystic enthusiast whose worship of beauty and love must pass from the realm of the senses to a sort of Platonic realm of essences. A final ironic twist is given the story when the united lovers, who have been betrothed at the command of the Archangel Gabriel, find themselves in reversed roles: Yusuf chasing Zulaikha in a moment of backsliding, and she reminding him that, in the matter of robe-snatching, the score between them is now even.

The Sufistic or allegorical character of the story has made it palatable to saints and sybarites alike in the Moslem world. A Turkish version by the poet Hamdi, begun under the influence of Firdausi's eleventh-century poem and completed after a reading of Jami's in the fifteenth century, adds an amusing embellishment. Zulaikha places one hundred beautiful damsels at Yusuf's disposal, with instructions that the one favored by him is to inform the mistress, so that she may take the place of the handmaid on the following night. Yusuf destroys her plan by forthwith converting all hundred of the beauties to the Sufistic belief in the Unity!

✠

Apart from its strictly Moslem career, the story of Yusuf and Zulaikha has had considerable circulation in Western and Christian countries. With the growth of Near Eastern studies in the late eighteenth century, especially in Germany, the Moslem form of the story began to insinuate itself into European accounts of the Biblical hero. Grimmelshausen's *Yusuf und Zulaikha* (1753) is only the first of a number of treatments by German authors including Bodmer, Hofmannsthal, and Mann. Both Goethe and Byron were fascinated enough by the name of Zulaikha to use it in their own verses.

The poem by Sir Edwin Arnold, below, is derived entirely from the *Koran* and from Jami's verse-novel. Its bias, however, is distinctly Christian-British-Victorian. The late nineteenth-century English reader might enjoy the Arabian Nights sensual-

ity of the attempted seduction without yielding the moral
satisfaction of seeing evil resisted by a pious hero. Concentrat-
ing on the climactic scene, Arnold draws upon Jami's description
of the palace of pleasure, although giving more than a hint,
in his slow-moving verse form, of Tennyson's "Palace of Art."
The purely sensuous delights of the latter are here grossly
sensual, to be sure, but the hero's plight has similar overtones
of an ethical struggle. Arnold calls Potiphar Lord Itfir; he alters
the name of Zulaikha to Asenath—an inexcusable confusion,
since the Bible story has made Asenath known to us as the
later true wife of Joseph. (A commoner confusion, as in
Josephus' *History of the Jews,* has been to take Joseph's wife
Asenath as the daughter of Potiphar because her father was
called Potiphera of On.) Arnold's poem is perhaps most
interesting as a document in the growing cultural interchange
between the colonizing and the colonized portions of the world
during a century that saw the first real penetration of Asian
spiritual ideas into Europe. It illustrates, too, what that other
Arnold called the excessive Hebraizing tendency of the British
people.

Similar use of the Moslem legend is found in Louis
Parker's *Joseph and His Brethren,* a Biblical pageant play,
which in the early twentieth century provided the aging actor
father of Eugene O'Neill with the dual roles of Pharaoh and
Jacob. In this play, Potiphar's wife, called Zulaikha, is not
simply the wanton of Genesis 39; if anything, she is worse,
playing a "heavy" or "siren" role as in motion-picture treatments
of the theme. Parker introduces the girl Asenath as the true
love of Joseph and creates a triangle similar to Racine's. Unlike
the Moslem story, however, Parker's play centers on the twelve
brothers. The envious Simeon is allowed to become involved
in a plot with Zulaikha against Joseph, after the discovery of
which she deservedly has her eyes put out by Potiphar in a
manner already prepared for by the Buddhist and the medieval
analogues of the tale. The hybridization of the story, with a
purely melodramatic intent, is well illustrated by this pageant
play.

# 6. "Yusuf", Chapter XII, Verses 21–35, 50–54, *Koran*

Translated by E. H. Palmer (1840–1882)

[I have provided a paraphrase of the omitted verses, 36–49. *Ed.*]

And the man from Egypt who had bought him said to his wife, "Honor his abiding here; it may be he will be of use to us, or we may adopt him as a son."

Thus did We establish Joseph in the land; and We did surely teach him the interpretation of sayings; for God can overcome His affairs, though most men do not know.

And when he had reached his strength We brought him judgment and knowledge, for thus do We reward those who do good.

And she in whose house he was desired him for his person; and she locked the doors and said, "Come along with thee!" Said he, "Refuge in God! Verily, my Lord has made good my abiding here; verily, the wrong doers shall not prosper."

And she was anxious for him, and he would have been anxious for her, had it not been that he saw the demonstration of his Lord; thus did We turn evil and fornication away from him; verily, he was of Our sincere servants.

And they raced to the door and she rent his shirt from behind; and they met her master at the door. Said she, "What is the recompense of him who wishes evil for thy family, but imprisonment or a grievous torment?"

Said he, "She desired me for my person." And a witness from among her family bore witness: "If his shirt be rent from in front, then she speaks the truth and he is of the liars; but if his shirt be rent from behind, then she lies and he is of the truth tellers."

And when he saw his shirt rent from behind he said, "This is one of your tricks; verily, your tricks are mighty! Joseph! turn aside from this. And do thou, woman, ask pardon for thy fault; verily, thou wert of the sinners."

And women in the city said, "The wife of the prince desires her young man for his person; he has infatuated her with

love: verily, we see her in obvious error." And when she heard
of their craftiness, she sent to them and prepared for them a
banquet, and gave each of them a knife; and she said, "Come
forth" to them. And when they saw him they said, "Great
God!" and cut their hands and said, "God forbid! This is no
mortal, this is nothing but an honorable angel." Said she, "This
is he concerning whom ye blamed me. I did desire him for his
person, but he was too continent. But if he do not what I bid
him he shall surely be imprisoned and shall surely be among
the small!" Said he, "My Lord! Prison is dearer to me than
what they call on me to do; and unless Thou turn from me
their craftiness I shall feel a passion for them and shall be
among the ignorant!" And his Lord answered him and turned
from him their craftiness; verily, He both hears and knows!

Then it appeared good to them, even after they had seen
the signs, to imprison him until a time.

[Joseph expounds the dreams of his two fellow prisoners.
One of them, when released, at length remembers his
promise to mention Joseph's name before the king, which
he does when the king has had his famous dream of the
seven fat kine and the seven lean, and of the seven green
ears of corn and the seven dry. *Ed.*]

Then said the king, "Bring him to me."

And when the messenger came to him, he said, "Go back
to thy lord and ask him, 'What meant the women who cut
their hands? Verily, my Lord knows their craftiness!' "

He said, "What was your design when ye desired Joseph
for his person?" They said, "God forbid! We know no bad of
him." Said the wife of the prince, "Now does the truth appear!
I desired him for his person and, verily, he is of those who tell
the truth."

"That" (said Joseph) "was that he might know that I did
not betray him in his absence, and that God guides not the
craft of those who betray! Yet I do not clear myself, for the
soul is very urgent to evil, save what my Lord has had mercy
on; verily, my Lord is forgiving and merciful!"

And the king said, "Bring him to me. I will take him
specially for myself." And when he had spoken with him he
said, "Verily, today thou art with us in a permanent place of
trust."

# 7. *Yusuf and Zulaikha* by Jami (1414–1492)

Translated by Ralph T. G. Griffith (1826–1906)
and by Alexander Rogers (1826?–1911)

[What follows is in the main an abridgement, to about one fourth of its size, of Griffith's translation, which was itself a slight abridgment of Jami's poem of some seven thousand couplets. Besides the subtitles (see below), I have supplied elliptical periods for omissions. The last scene of the story is given in Alexander Rogers' translation since Griffith did not see fit to retain it in his English version. Jami's story tells of a "king in the West" who had a fair daughter named Zulaikha. When there appeared in several of her dreams the figure of a handsome young man, she "was forever undone." In the last of these visions, he tells her that he is Grand Vizir in Egypt. She therefore prevails upon her father to send a marriage embassy to the Vizir. The offer is accepted and she sets out for Memphis to meet her betrothed, whose entourage is on its way to receive her. While they are camped side by side, she cannot restrain the desire to have a look at him. But when she peeks through a tear in his tent, she is horrified to discover that he is not the man of her visions. The Archangel Gabriel, messenger of Allah, appears to inform her that:

> The Vizir is not he whom thou longest to gain,
> But without him thy wish thou canst never attain.

There is a switch of the scene to Judea and to an account of Yusuf's birth to Jacob and Rachel, his boyhood among his envious brothers, his remarkable powers of dream interpretation, the offense given to his brothers, and their sale of him to the nomadic Ishmaelites. Brought to Egypt, he is offered for sale at the slave-market just as Zulaikha is sadly returning with her Vizir husband to his home. On an impulse she looks out of her litter:

> She raised the curtain, her glances fell
> On the form and features she knew so well.

She persuades her husband to purchase the youth, offering her own casket of jewels to meet the high price placed on the handsome slave. When an agent of the king is about to win the bidding, she persuades her husband to plead with Pharaoh to give him up to her as a son, for we learn that her husband is an emasculated priest of the Egyptian temple. Having obtained him, she now indulges Yusuf as an adopted son, bedecking him with fine

clothes and maternal affection until a new passion begins to arise
within her. *Ed.*]

1. THE WOOING OF YUSUF

When on Yusuf, seen in her vision, as yet
No waking eye had Zulaikha set,
One wish alone in her heart might dwell,—
To look on the form which she loved so well.
When the sight of her darling had blessed her eyes,
Her bosom yearned for a sweeter prize,
And her loving arms round that form to wind
Was the longing thought of her heart and mind,
With a kiss on his ruby-red lips impressed,
By his arm encircled, to take her rest.
When a youth in the spring through a garden goes,
His heart marked like a tulip, for love of the rose,
First on its petals he looks with delight,
And then plucks the fair flower that has charmed his sight.
With winning art would Zulaikha woo;
But Yusuf far from her gaze withdrew.
Tears of hot blood would Zulaikha shed;
But her tears were idle, for Yusuf fled.
Zulaikha's soul with deep wounds was scarred:
But the heart of Yusuf was cold and hard.
Still on his cheek would Zulaikha gaze;
But Yusuf never his eye would raise.
For a glance from her darling Zulaikha burned;
But Yusuf's look from her look was turned.
His eye he kept lest his heart might err,
And no fond glance would he bend on her.

What rest has the lover who pines alone,
If his darling's eye may not meet his own?
He sheds his tears, and he heaves his sighs,
Hoping to gaze on his loved one's eyes.
If still those eyes to his love she close,
With the blood of his heart he must weep his woes.
     When this heavy load on her bosom lay
Zulaikha wasted from day to day.
In the chilling autumn of pain and grief
The tulip banished the pink rose-leaf.
Under the weight of her sorrow she sank,
And the stately young cypress tree withered and shrank.
Gone was the splendor her lips had shed,
And the light that had shone from her cheek was dead.
Faint and weary she hardly through
Her long sweet tresses her fingers drew.
Scarce would she look at her mirror; she
Kept her eyes bent down with her head on her knee.
No borrowed bloom on her cheek was spread,
For the blood that she wept from her heart was red.
The world about her was black, and why
Should she darken her orbs with the jetty dye?
If under those lids the dark tint had lain,
The tears that she shed would have washed them again.
When Zulaikha's heart with her wound was torn
She rebuked her spirit with queenly scorn:
"Shame on thee! Disgrace on thy name thou hast brought
By love of the slave whom thy gold has bought.
A lady thou on a princely throne,
Wilt thou stoop to make love to a slave of thine own?
The chains of thy love on a monarch fling:
A prince's daughter should love a king.
But of all that is strange 'tis most strange that he
Should shrink from love offered by one like thee.
If the dames of Memphis but knew thy shame,
Where were the end of their scorn and blame?"
     Thus spoke Zulaikha; but still she felt
That he alone in her fond heart dwelt.
Him she could not banish, but strove awhile
To charm her pain with this simple guile. . . .

In course of long sorrow Zulaikha knew
That her nurse was faithful and helpful and true.
"Thou hast served me often," 'twas thus she prayed;
"Help me again, for I need thine aid.
To him as my messenger take thy way,
Be thou mine eloquent tongue, and say:
'Delicate plant, ever tended with care,
Lovely with blossom but wayward as fair;
In the garden of beauty no cypress tree
Lifts up its head to compare with thee. . . .
Angels enthroned in the heavenly height
Bend their heads to the ground when thy face is in sight.
If, by favor of Heaven, so high is thy place,
Have mercy and show thy poor captive grace.
They say that Zulaikha is witchingly fair,
But ah, she has fallen a prey to thy snare.
She has carried from childhood the wound in her breast
Which for many long days has deprived her of rest.
In three nightly visions thy face was shown,
And no peace in her heart from that time has she known.
Now chained like the waves of the wind-rippled sea,
Now roaming ere morn like the zephyr is she.
She is worn by her sorrow as thin as a hair,
And her longing for thee is her only care.
All the gold of her life for thy sake has she spent;
Have pity at last: it is sweet to relent.
Pure and fresh is the Water of Life on thy lip:
What harm if a drop from the fountain she sip?
With full clusters laden, what harm to allow
One taste of the fruit that hangs ripe on the bough?
On thy ruby lip let her feed her fill,
And perhaps the wild storm of her breast will be still.
Let her pluck the dates from that palm-tree's height,
Or lay down her head where thy foot may light.
What wilt thou lose of thy rank, my king,
If thine eye one glance on thy servant fling?
In all the pride of her station, she
The least of thy handmaids would gladly be.'"
    He heard the speech. In reply to the dame
From his ruby lips opened this answer came:
"Skilled in the secrets thou knowest so well,

Cheat not my soul with thy ravishing spell.
The slave of Zulaikha and bought with her gold,
My debt for her kindness can never be told.
To this stately mansion she raised my clay,
And nurtured my soul and my life each day.
If I counted her favors my whole life through,
I never could pay her the thanks that are due.
On the line of her pleasure my head I lay,
And I wait ever ready to serve and obey.
But warn her never to hope that I
My God's commandment will break and defy.
Ne'er let her tempt me in hope to win
The soul which I strive to keep pure from sin.
I am called his son by the Grand Vizir;
He counts me true and my love sincere.
Shall I, the young bird whom his care has bred,
Bring shame on the house where I long have fed?
God in various natures has sown the seeds
Of divers wishes and thoughts and deeds.
The pure in nature will fear disgrace;
But base are his actions whose birth is base.
Can a dog be born of a woman? Where
Does barley wheat or wheat barley bear?
In my bosom the secrets of Jacob dwell,
And my heart keeps the wisdom of Gabriel.
Am I worthy of prophethood? Well I know
To holy Isaac that hope I owe.
A rose am I and a secret I hold;
In Abraham's garden my petals unfold.
May sin never drive me—forbid it, God!—
Aside from the path which my fathers trod.
Bid Zulaikha spurn the wild thought, and free
Her own kind heart from the sin, and me.
My trust in the God whom I serve is sure
To keep my life undefiled and pure."

The answer was brought to Zulaikha; despair
Made her senses as wild as her own wild hair.
From her eye's black almond there came a flood
Of thick tears mixed with her own heart's blood.
She reared up her stately cypress, and flew

Till its shade o'er the head of her darling she threw.
"My head," she cried, "at thy feet shall be,
But ne'er shall my breast from thy love be free.
My love of thee throbs in each hair of my head:
Self-thought and self-feeling are vanished and dead.
That vision of thee is my soul, and the snare
Of thy love is the collar which slave-like I wear.
Have I a soul? 'Tis but longing for thee;
A body? Its spirit is hasting to flee.
But how of the state of my heart shall I speak?
'Tis one drop of the torrent that pours down my cheek.
In the whelming sea of thy love I drown:
Its waters rush o'er me and weigh me down.
When the leech with his lancet would ease my pain,
Love of thee, and not blood, gushes forth from the vein."
      Then Yusuf wept at her words. "Ah, why
Those tears?" said Zulaikha, and heaved a sigh.
"Thou art mine own very eye, and while
Tears of sorrow are dewing it how can I smile?
For each big drop from thine eye that flows,
A flame of fire in my bosom glows.
A miracle this of thy beauty, that turns
Water itself into flame that burns."
      He saw her anguish, he heard her sighs,
And the tears flowed down from his lips and eyes:
"My heart is broken," he said, "when I see
How woe ever waits upon love of me. . . ."

      Zulaikha answered: "My lamp and eye,
I need no moonlight when thou art nigh.
If I may not be dear in thy sight, to be
The least of thy slaves were enough for me.
But canst thou not treat her in gentler mood,
And free her from sorrows of servitude?
No outward sign will thy handmaid show,
But her heart will long and her bosom glow.
Why dost thou deem me a foe? Thou art
Dearer to me than mine own dear heart.
And where is the fool who would add a care
To double the load which his heart must bear?
What dost thou fear from my hate? My heart

By the sword of thy love has been cleft apart.
Ah, kiss me; the touch of thy lips will restore
The rest of my soul that I sorrow no more."
"Nay, my sweet mistress," thus Yusuf replied:
"In duty's bonds I am.chained and tied.
From the path of service I may not stray:
There thou commandest and I obey.
More than such duty forbear to claim;
Make not thy love my dishonor and shame.
Assign me some labor that far from thy side
My days still for thee may be occupied.
Against thy light orders I will not rebel,
But remember thy bounties and serve thee well.
By faithful service a slave like me
Made glad by kindness at length is free.
True service rejoices a master; but still
A slave he continues who serves him ill."
"Rare jewel," she answered, "compared with thee
The meanest slave's rank were too high for me.
For each slight task, when my voice is heard,
A hundred servants obey my word.
Their ready service can I refuse,
And thee for the task or the message choose?
The eye is counted of higher worth
Than the foot which is fashioned to tread the earth.
Thorns in the path of thy foot may lie,
But lay not upon them thy precious eye."
      Again said Yusuf: "Dear lady, round
Whose heart the bands of my love are bound,
If thy love like the light of the morn be true,
Only my will must thou seek to do.
My wish is only to serve thee; thou—
Or thou art no friend—must the wish allow.
To please the heart that he loves, a friend
Regards as his being's true aim and end.
'Neath the foot of friendship his will he sets,
And self in the love of his friend forgets."
      He spake in the hope that a task might bar
All converse with her and keep him afar.
He knew that her presence was trouble and fear:

In distance was safety, and woe to be near.
In fire and tempest the wool that flies
When it may not contend with the flame is wise.


## 2. THE PALACE OF LOVE

Deep in despair was Zulaikha, slain
With the love of the boy whom she wooed in vain.
One night she summoned her nurse to her side,
Where gently she bade her be seated, and cried:
"Strength of this frame when my limbs are weak,
Lamp of my soul when thy light I seek,
Thy nursling owes thee each breath that she draws;
If she lives, the sweet milk of thy love is the cause.
Love more than a mother's, too deep to be told,
Has raised me up to the rank I hold.
How long must I pine with my fond bosom scarred,
How long from that soul of the world be debarred?
Wilt thou not aid me, and tenderly guide
My feet to the harbor that still is denied?
What profits it me that my palace walls hold
My friend and myself, if that friend is so cold?
The lover, whose darling refuses to hear,
Is far from his love, though he seems to be near.
If spirit from spirit be still far away,
What fruit has the meeting of water and clay?"
"Sweet child of the Peris," the nurse replied,
"Though what were a Peri if set by thy side?
God gave thee thy beauty to steal from the wise
Their heart and their face with thy ravishing eyes.
If a painter of China thy form portrayed,
And hung in a temple the picture he made,
The very idols to life would spring,
And their souls be the slaves of so fair a thing.
On the mountain height if thy cheek were shown,
Love would throb and thrill in the hard flint stone. . . ."

"How can I tell the cruel scorn,"
Zulaikha said, "that I long have borne?
Can I show my beauty to one whose eye

Is bent on the ground when my step is nigh?
Were I the moon, he would turn away:
The sun, he would shrink from his golden ray.
If, his own eye's apple, I lent him light,
Scarce would he welcome the boon of sight.
Ah! if a glance on mine eye he would throw,
The pangs that I suffer perchance he might know.
Those griefs would find place in his heart; but he
Would never languish for love like me.
'Tis not only his beauty that kills me; no,
'Tis the cold, cold heart, where no spark will glow.
Ah! if but a pang for my sake he had felt,
Thus with my lover I never had dealt."
"Thou whose beauty casts on the sun a shade"—
The nurse to her lady this answer made—
"I have wrought a plan, and I trust that rest
Will at length be thine from the thought in my breast.
Bring forth thy treasure stored up of old,
Lade a camel with silver, a mule with gold.
I will build a palace like Iram fair,
And a skilful painter shall labor there
To paint on the walls with seductive charms,
Zulaikha folded in Yusuf's arms.
If, for a moment, he visit the place,
He will see thee locked in his own embrace.
Then will he yearn for thy touch, and at length
The love of thy beauty will grow to its strength.
Soon will he yield with his senses on fire,
And naught will be left for thy heart to desire."
    She heard the counsel: her heart was bold:
She brought forth the stores of her silver and gold;
And her wealth, fond fancies therewith to build,
She gave to the nurse to be spent as she willed.

They who raised the dome of this story say
That the nurse, whom the plan of her brain made gay,
Called in a wise master, his aid to lend,
With a hundred arts at each finger's end;
A skilled geometer, trained and tried,
Through the maze of the stars a most trusty guide. . . .

There was life and soul in the drawing when
The lines were sketched by his artist pen.
If his fingers had graven a bird of stone,
It had risen up in the air and flown.
By the nurse's order his hand of gold
Began the work on the plan she told.
There was hope in the sheen of the polished walls,
And the dawn of bliss gleamed through the stately halls. . . .

The painter there, to his orders true,
The forms of Zulaikha and Yusuf drew,
Like lovers both of one heart and mind,
With the arm of each round the other twined.
Like heaven was the ceiling, for wrought thereon
The sun and the moon in their glory shone.
In the prime of Spring on the walls outspread
To the wondering view was a bright rose-bed,
And the eye might mark in each narrow space
The rose-sprays twined in a close embrace.
Wherever the foot on the carpet stepped
Two lovely roses together slept.
Search through the palace, no spot was there
But showed a type of that beauteous pair.
Under the foot, overhead, and around,
An emblem of two happy lovers was found.
The love of Zulaikha still grew meanwhile,
And rose each day with the rising pile.
As the idol-house met her eager gaze,
With fiercer fire was her heart ablaze.
There thrills a new pang through the lover's breast
When he looks on the picture of her he loves best,
The fair lines of her features his woes recall,
And he sinks in his sorrow love's helpless thrall.

Zulaikha opened her hand and decked
The finished work of the Architect.
Tissue of gold on the floor was strown,
And its beauty enhanced with a golden throne.
Jewelled lamps on the walls were hung,
And odorous herbs were beneath them flung.
She gathered together all things most fair,

And unrolled the carpet of pleasure there.
But amid the charms of the sumptuous hall
She longed only for Yusuf, far dearer than all.
A heavenly palace is dark and dim
To a lover whose darling is far from him.
   She would summon Yusuf, once more they would meet:
She would set him high on a princely seat,
She would woo his beauty and win success
With her tender guile and her soft caress,
Or feed on his lips and beguile her care
With the tangled locks of the rebel's hair.
But to conquer his heart she would add a grace
To her peerless form and her perfect face.
Her beauty needed no art, and yet
A current stamp by its aid was set.
The rose of the garden is fair to vew,
But lovelier still with her pearls of dew. . . .

Across her bosom, like sweet flowers grown
To perfect beauty, a scarf was thrown.
Then she drew on a delicate smock and her skin
Filled with roses the folds of the jessamine,
Which looked to the eye like a stream that flows
Over a garden of tulip and rose,
A wondrous stream, of fine silver made,
Where two fishes* at rest on two arms were laid.
On each wrist a fair bracelet shone to enfold
Each glittering fish with a collar of gold.
So by her cheek and her hand was it shown
That her charms from the moon to the Fish† were known.
Next the lady her form arrayed
In precious tissue of China brocade.
She shone so bright in that robe, Chinese
To her as an idol had bent their knees.
On her jet-black garner of hair was set,
Of pearl and gold mingled, a coronet.

  * Her long shapely hands.
  † Her cheek is the moon above the earth, and her hand the Fish on
which the earth rests. [*Mah* (moon) and *mahi* (fish) in Persian thus
permit a pun while denoting something like "from alpha to omega."
*Ed.*]

No peacock, proud of his jewelled plumes,
Could move more bright through the splendid rooms.
She reckoned on conquest, for who could withstand
The charms seen in the mirror she held in her hand?
Those charms she assayed, and the mirror told
That the beauty she trusted was current gold.
As she thought of her treasures her joy rose high,
And nothing was wanting save one to buy.
    She sent her maidens and bade them call
Yusuf to visit her new-built hall.
He came, bright, noble, and mild, like the sun
And the moon and Mercury joined in one.
No mixture of clay made his nature base,
And light, all light, were his brow and face.
One glance from that eye, and the world is aglow:
He speaks, and all nations his utterance know.
    Zulaikha saw, and the flames rose high,
Like the spark that falls where the reeds are dry.
"Purest of creatures, thou lamp to guide
The eyes of those who see best," she cried.
"O servant faithful and prompt to obey,
High favor and grace should thy care repay.
Thy dutiful love I can never forget,
And my glory and pride is my collar of debt,
Come, and to-day will I labor to show
Some slight return for the debt I owe:
Nay, long in the record of time shall live
The meed I bestow and the thanks I give."
    With gentle charm and resistless sway
To the first of the chambers she led the way.
    Soon as the door of pure gold he passed,
With the lock of iron she closed it fast.
The door she closed, but the secret nursed
Deep in her heart from her lips outburst.
Thus she addressed him: "O thou, the whole
Wish and desire of my hungry soul,
Thy vision appeared in my dreams and beguiled
The sleep from mine eyes when I yet was a child.
That vision brought frenzy and anguish to dwell
Forever with me: I loved thee so well.
Ere yet I had seen thee, to find thee here

I came from my country and all that was dear.
A helpless exile I sat and grieved,
And no sweet comfort my woes relieved.
After long pain I was blest to behold
Thy face; but hope fled, for thine eye was cold.
Look on me no longer with eyes so stern:
Oh, one word of love, one word, in return!"
    He bent his head as he answered: "Thou
To whose bidding a hundred high princes bow,
Release me from this sore burden of woe,
And freedom of heart on thy slave bestow.
Dear lady, longer I would not be
In this curtained chamber alone with thee,
For thou art a flame, and the wool is dry:
The wind art thou and the musk am I.
Is the wool secure when the flame burns fast?
Should the musk be left to the boisterous blast?"
His eager words to the winds she threw:
To the second chamber the boy she drew.
Again she fastened the door: again
The heart of Yusuf was rent with pain.
She lifted the veil of the days gone by
And poured out her grief with a bitter cry:
"How long wilt thou scorn me, Oh! thou more sweet
Than my soul, and rebel when I fall at thy feet?
I lavished my treasure to buy thee, I gave
My faith and my prudence to make thee my slave.
For I hoped in my heart that, pledged to obey,
Thou wouldst be my comfort and joy and stay.
But no order I give thee wilt thou fulfil,
And thou seekest each path save the path of my will."
"Sin is not obedience," he answered; "shame
Ne'er may be linked with true duty's name.
Each act defying the Master's law
Is in true service a breach and flaw:
And never mine be the power or will
To break His law by a deed so ill."
Onward from chamber to chamber they strayed,
And in each for a little their steps delayed.
New arts of temptation in each she plied,
In each new magic and charms were tried.

Through six of the rooms she had led him, still
She won not the game though she played with skill.
Only the seventh was left: therein
Lay her strongest hope that at last she might win.
In this way was nothing of dark despair,
For black to her eyes seemed white and fair.
If no hope from a hundred doors appears,
Eat not thy heart nor give way to tears.
For yet one door thou mayst open and see
A way to the place where thou fain wouldst be.


### 3. THE TEMPTATION

These are the words of the bard who sings
This ancient story of mystic things.
To the seventh chamber their steps they bent,
And Zulaikha cried in her discontent:
"Pass not this chamber unnoticed by,
And lay thy foot on this loving eye."
    He entered and sat where she bade him: again
She fastened the door with a golden chain.
No spy, no stranger might there intrude
To break the charm of the solitude.
'Twas made for the loved and the lover alone,
And the dread of the censor was there unknown.
The loved one's beauty was there more bright,
And the lover's heart sang a song of delight.
No more was the bosom's soft flame concealed,
And the spirit of love had a limitless field.
    Full, eyes and heart, of the flame she fanned,
She seized in wild passion her darling's hand,
And with gentle magic of words most sweet,
Half led and half drew his slow steps to a seat.
She threw herself there by his side. Then broke
A flood of hot tears from her eyes, and she spoke:
"Look on me, look on me once, my sweet:
One tender glance from those eyes, I entreat.
Then if the sun saw my glad face, he
Moon-like might borrow new light from me.
How long wilt thou see my poor heart's distress?

How long will thy heart be so pitiless?"
　　She told her love, and her sorrow woke
With a pang renewed at each word she spoke.
But Yusuf looked not upon her: in dread
He lowered his eyes and bent his head.
As he looked on the ground in a whirl of thought
He saw his own form on the carpet wrought,
Where a bed was figured of silk and brocade,
And himself by the side of Zulaikha laid.
From the pictured carpet he looked in quest
Of a spot where his eye might, untroubled, rest.
He looked on the wall, on the door; the pair
Of rose-lipped lovers was painted there.
He lifted his glance to the Lord of the skies:
That pair from the ceiling still met his eyes.
Then the heart of Yusuf would fain relent,
And a tender look on Zulaikha he bent,
While a thrill of hope through her bosom passed
That the blessed sun would shine forth at last.
The hot tears welled from her heart to her eyes,
And she poured out her voice in a storm of sighs:
"List to my prayer, thou sweet rebel, and calm
The pangs of my heart with thy healing balm.
Thou art Life's Water: these lips are dry;
Thou art life forever: I faint and die.
As thirsty eyes when no water they see,
As the dead without hope, so am I without thee.
For many years has my heart in its love for thee bled.
And, fasting, outworn, I have tossed on my bed.
Oh, let me no longer in misery weep:
Give my body its food, give mine eyelids their sleep,
Oh, hear my entreaties: on thee I call
In the name of God who is Lord over all;
By the excellent bloom of that cheek which He gave,
By that beauty which makes the whole world thy slave;
By the splendor that beams from thy beautiful brow
That bids the full moon to thy majesty bow;
By the graceful gait of that cypress, by
The delicate bow that is bent o'er thine eye;
By that arch of the temple devoted to prayer,
By each fine-woven mesh of the toils of thy hair;

By that charming narcissus, that form arrayed
In the sheen and glory of silk brocade;
By that secret thou callest a mouth, by the hair
Thou callest the waist of that body most fair;
By the musky spots on thy cheek's pure rose,
By the smile of thy lips when those buds unclose;
By my longing tears, by the sigh and groan
That rend my heart as I pine alone;
By thine absence, a mountain too heavy to bear,
By my thousand fetters of grief and care;
By the sovereign sway of my passion, by
My carelessness whether I live or die;
Pity me, pity my love-lorn grief:
Loosen my fetters and grant relief:
An age has scorched me since over my soul
The soft sweet air of thy garden stole.
Be the balms of my wounds for a little; shed
Sweet scent on the heart where the flowers are dead.
I hunger for thee till my whole frame is weak:
Oh, give me the food for my soul which I seek."
"Fair daughter," said he, "of the Peri race—
But no Peri can match thee in form or face—
Tempt me no more to a deed of shame,
Nor break the fair glass of a stainless name.
Drag not my skirts through the dust and mire.
Nor fill my veins with unholy fire.
By the Living God, the great Soul of all,
Inner and outward and great and small,
From whose ocean this world like a bubble rose,
And the sun by the flash of His splendor glows;
By the holy line of my fathers, whence
I have learned the fair beauty of innocence;
From whom I inherit my spirit's light,
And through them is the star of my fortune bright;
If thou wilt but leave me this day in peace,
And my troubled soul from this snare release,
Thou shalt see thy servant each wish obey,
And with faith unshaken thy grace repay.
The lips of thy darling to thine shall be pressed,
And the arms that thou lovest shall lull thee to rest.
Haste not too fast to the goal: delay

Is often more blessed than speed on the way,
And the first paltry capture is ever surpassed
By the nobler game that is netted at last."
    Zulaikha answered: "Ah, never think
That the thirsty will wait for the morrow to drink.
My spirit has rushed to my lips, and how
Can I wait for the joy that I long for now?
My heart has no power to watch and wait
For the tender bliss that will come so late.
Thy pleading is weak, and no cause I see
Why thou shouldst not this moment be happy with me."
    Then Yusuf answered: "Two things I fear—
The judgment of God, and the Grand Vizir.
If the master knew of the shameful deed,
With a hundred sorrows my heart would bleed.
Full well thou knowest my furious lord
Would strike me dead with his lifted sword.
And think of the shame that the sin would lay
On my guilty soul at the Judgment Day,
When the awful book is unclosed wherein
Recording angels have scored my sin."
    "Fear not thy master," Zulaikha cried;
"At some high feast when I sit by his side,
A poisoned cup from this hand shall he take,
And sleep till Doomsday shall bid him wake.
And the God thou servest, I hear thee say,
Pardons His creatures who err and stray.
Still, their sole mistress, the keys I hold
Of a hundred vaults full of gems and gold.
All this will I give to atone for thy sin,
And thy God's forgiveness will surely win."
    "Ne'er can my heart," he made answer, "incline
To injure another by deed of mine;
Least of all my lord, who with tender thought
Bade thee cherish and honor the slave he bought.
And will my God, whom no thanks can pay,
Take a bribe to pardon my sin to-day?
Shall the grace which a life cannot buy be sold
By the Living God for thy gems and gold?"
    "O King," she said, "to high fortune born,
May throne and crown be thine to adorn!

My soul is the mark of the arrows of pain,
And excuse on excuse thou hast marshalled in vain.
Crooked, contemptible, all unmeet
For a noble heart is the way of deceit.
God grant that my heart from deceit may be free,
And let me not hear these pretences from thee.
I am sorely troubled: oh, give me rest;
Grant, willing, unwilling, this one request.
In words, idle words, have my days passed by,
And ne'er with my wishes wouldst thou comply.
A truce to pretences, or thou wilt repent
That thine eye would not glow nor thy heart relent.
A fierce flame has lighted the reeds of my heart;
Thou canst look on the flame and stand heedless apart.
What boots it to burn in this flame of desire,
If thine eyes be undimmed by the smoke of the fire?
Come, pour a cool stream on the hot flame, if I
Fail to melt thy cold heart with the heat of a sigh."
For new excuses his lips unclosed,
But with swift impatience she interposed:
"My time thou hast stolen while fondly I hung
On the guiling words of thy Hebrew tongue.
No more evasion: my wish deny,
And by mine own hand will I surely die.
Unless thy warm arm round my neck I feel,
I will sever that neck with the biting steel.
If fondly around me thou wilt not cling,
A streak of my blood shall thy neck enring.
A lily-like dagger shall rend my side,
And my smock in blood like a rose shall be dyed.
Then shall my soul and my body part,
And thy guile no longer distress my heart.
My lifeless corpse the Vizir will see,
And the crime of the murder will rest on thee.
Then under the earth, when the doom is passed,
Near this loving heart thou wilt lie at last."
She drew from the pillow, distraught with grief,
A dagger gray as a willow leaf.
And, fierce with the fire of fever, laid
To her thirsty throat the bright cold blade.
Up sprang Yusuf; his fingers' hold

Circled her wrist like a bracelet of gold.
"Master this passion, Zulaikha," he cried;
"Turn from thy folly, oh, turn aside.
Wilt thou not strive for the wished-for goal?
Wilt thou abandon the aim of my soul?"
She fancied his heart was relenting; she thought
His love would give her the bliss she sought.
The gleaming steel on the ground she threw,
And hope sprang up in her breast anew.
She sugared his lip with a touch of her own:
One arm was his collar and one his zone.

    With a long sweet kiss on his lips she hung,
And an eager arm round his neck was flung.

    One nook of the chamber was dark with the shade
Of a curtain that glittered with gold brocade.
And Yusuf questioned her: "What or who
Is behind the curtain concealed from view?"
"It is he," she answered, "to whom, while I live,
My faithful service I still must give:
A golden idol with jewelled eyes—
A salver of musk in his bosom lies.
I bend before him each hour of the day,
And my head at his feet in due worship lay.
Before his presence this screen I drew
To be out of the reach of his darkened view.
If I swerve from religion I would not be
Where the angry eyes of my god may see."
And Yusuf cried with a bitter cry:
"Not a mite of the gold of thy faith have I.
Thine eye is abashed before those that are dead,
And shrinks from the sight of the lifeless in dread.
And God almighty shall I not fear,
Who liveth and seeth and ever is near?"

    He ceased: from the fond dream of rapture he woke;
From the arms of Zulaikha he struggled and broke.
With hasty feet from her side he sped,
And burst open each door on his way as he fled.
Bolt and bar from the stanchions he drew—
All open before him as onward he flew.
Of his lifted finger a key was made,
Which every lock at a sign obeyed.

But Zulaikha caught him, with steps more fast,
Or ever the farthest chamber he passed.
She clutched his skirt as he fled amain,
And the coat from his shoulder was rent in twain.
Reft of his garment he slipped from her hand
Like a bud from its sheath when the leaves expand.
She rent her robe in her anguish; low
On the earth, like a shadow, she lay in her woe. . . .


4. THE ACCUSATION

The pen that has written this tale relates,
That when Yusuf fled through the palace gates,
Soon as his foot in the court was set,
The Grand Vizir and his lords he met.
The master looked on his troubled face
And questioned him wherefore he fled apace.
Yusuf was ready with apt reply,
And with courteous words put the question by.
The Grand Vizir took his hand in his own,
And they came where Zulaikha sat brooding alone,
She saw them together, and cried, dismayed,
To her own sad spirit, "Betrayed! betrayed!"
Moved by the fancy, in loud lament,
The veil of the secret she raised and rent:
"O Balance of Justice, what sentence is due
To him who to folly thy wife would woo?
And, false to his duty, has plotted within
The folds of his treason a deed of sin?"
"Speak, fairest one, speak: let thy tale be clear.
Who has thus dared?" said the Grand Vizir.
"The Hebrew servant," she cried, "has done
This thing, whom thy favor hast made a son.
Freed from the trouble and toil of the day,
Here in my chamber asleep I lay,
He came to the bed where alone I repose,
And would pluck the flower of the spotless rose;
But the hand of the robber my slumber broke,
With a start and a cry from my rest I woke.
He started in fear when I raised my head,

And swift to the door of the chamber fled.
He fled amain, but I followed fast
And caught him ere yet from the palace he passed.
I caught his garment, my strength outspent,
And it split as the leaf of a rose is rent.
The garment he wears on his shoulders view,
And see that the words which I speak are true.
Now were it best for a little time
To send him to prison to mourn his crime;
Or let the sharp lash on his tender skin
Cure the wild boy of his wish to sin.
Let the scourge be heavy, the pain severe,
That others in time may be warned and fear."
The Grand Vizir in amazement heard:
His visage changed and his heart was stirred,
From the path of justice he turned aside,
And his tongue was a sword of rebuke as he cried:
"Treasures of pearl and of gold I gave,
When I weighed out my jewels to purchase my slave.
I made thee my son of mine own free grace,
And gave thee beside me an honored place.
I gave thee Zulaikha for guardian to tend
Thy youth with her maidens and be thy friend.
The slaves of my household obeyed thy will;
They were gentle in speech and ne'er wished thee ill.
I made thee lord over all that I had,
And never would suffer thy heart to be sad.
A folly and sin was this thought of thine:
May God forgive thee the base design.
In this evil world, full of grief and woe,
Kindness responsive to kindness we owe.
But thou, all my love and my trust betrayed,
My tender affection with ill hast repaid.
Thou has broken the bond which the meal had tied,
And the pledge which the salt had sanctified."
    At the wrathful words of the Grand Vizir
He shrank like a hair when the flame is near.
He cried to his master: "How long, how long
Wilt thou burden the guiltless with cruel wrong?
False is the tale that Zulaikha has told:
Her lie is a lamp when the flame is cold.

From the man's left side came the woman. Who
Will hope that the left will be right and true?
From the day Zulaikha beheld me first,
A frantic passion her heart has nursed.
About me ever she comes and goes,
And with soft allurement her fancy shows.
But ne'er I lifted mine eye to her face,
Ne'er have I looked for a kiss or embrace.
Who am I, thy servant, that I should be
The tempter of her who is sacred to thee?
From earthly wealth I had turned away,
To the pangs of exile my heart was a prey.
A word from Zulaikha bade doors unclose,
And opened a way to a hundred woes.
She called me hither—her spells were sweet—
And drew me aside to this lone retreat.
With passionate pleading her love she pressed,
And made my bosom a stranger to rest.
By many a bar for a while detained,
The gate of the palace at length I gained.
She followed fast as I fled, and tore
Behind from the shoulder the coat I wore.
This is the story I have to tell:
This, only this and no more, befell.
If thou wilt not believe I am free from guilt,
In the name of Allah do what thou wilt."

　　Zulaikha heard, and in self-defence
Called Heaven to witness her innocence.
She swore an oath on each sacred thing,
By the throne, and the crown, and the head of the king,
By the rank and state of the Grand Vizir
Whom the monarch honored and held so dear.

　　When trouble and doubt in a suit arise,
An oath the place of a witness supplies.
But ah, how oft, when the truth is known,
Has the shameless lie of that oath been shown!
Then she cried, as her tears in a torrent ran:
"From Yusuf only the folly began."
Tears, ever ready to flow, supply
Oil for the lamp of a woman's lie.

Fed with this oil the flame waxes in power
And destroys a whole world in one little hour.
  The oath of Zulaikha, the sob, the tear,
Shut the blinded eye of the Grand Vizir.
He gave a sergeant his order, like
The strings of a lute the boy's heart to strike,
That the vein of his soul might be racked with pain,
And no trace of compassion or mercy remain;
That the boy should be lodged in the prison till
They had thoroughly fathomed the secret ill.
His hand on Yusuf the sergeant laid,
And straight to the prison his way he made.
The heart of the captive with woe was rent,
And the eye of complaint on the sky he bent:
"Thou who knowest all hearts," he cried,
"And every secret which men would hide;
Who discernest the true from the false, whose might
Save Thine only can bring this secret to light?
Since the lamp of truth in thy heart Thou hast placed,
Let me not with the charge of a lie be disgraced.
Bear witness against mine accuser, I pray,
That my truth may be clear as the light of day."
  He spoke in his sorrow; and straight to its aim
The shaft of his prayer from his spirit came.
In the court was a dame, to Zulaikha allied,
Who was night and day by Zulaikha's side.
With her babe on her bosom but three months old
She seemed her own soul in her arms to hold.
No line in the volume of life had it read,
And its tongue like a lily's no word had said.
But it cried: "Vizir, be thy judgment more slow,
And beware of the haste that will end in woe.
No stain of sin upon Yusuf lies,
But he merits the grace of thy favoring eyes."
  In courteous words spake the Grand Vizir
In reply to the speech which he marvelled to hear:
"O thou whom God teaches to speak while yet
With the milk of thy mother thy lips are wet,
Speak clearly and say who lighted the flame
That has threatened the screen of my honor and fame."
"No informer am I," said the babe, "to reveal

The secret another would fain conceal.
The tell-tale musk is so black in its hue,
For no folds will imprison the scent that steals through;
And the screen of the petals that round her cling,
Gives a charm to the smile of the rose in Spring.
No secret I utter, no tale I tell,
But I give thee a hint which will serve thee well.
Go hence to Yusuf; examine and note,
As he lies in the prison, the rent in his coat.
If the rent in the front of the garment appear,
The skirt of Zulaikha from soil is clear.
There is then no light in the charge he brings,
And the stain of a lie to his story clings.
But if rent be the back of the garment, he
From charge of falsehood and slander is free.
Then faithless Zulaikha has turned aside
From the path of truth and has basely lied."
       The Grand Vizir to the prison went,
And summoned Yusuf, to view the rent.
He saw that the garment was torn behind;
And he cried to that woman of evil mind:
"Thou hast forged a lie, and thine art has sent
The innocent boy to imprisonment.
What hast thou gained by thy crafty toils
Since the shame of thy deed on thyself recoils?
Thou hast left the straight path and hast sullied thy name,
By wooing thy slave to a deed of shame,
From the path of honor thy feet have strayed,
And on him the guilt of thy sin thou hast laid.
The arts and wiles of a woman rend
The heart of a man, and they never will end.
Those who are noble they bring to naught,
And the wisest hearts in their toils are caught.
O that men from the plague of their arts were free!
O that treacherous woman might cease to be!
Begone: on thy knees in repentance fall,
And pray for forgiveness, thy face to the wall.
Let the tears of contrition thy penitence grace,
And the blot from thy volume of life efface.
And, Yusuf, set on thy lips a seal:
This tale of dishonor to none reveal.

Enough that thy speech—for thy words were wise—
Has shown thee guiltless and opened mine eyes."
    He spoke; then he turned from the prison: and food
For tale and jest was his clement mood.
Ah yes; it is good to forgive and forget;
But bounds e'en to mercy itself should be set.
If the man be too mild when the woman sins,
There ends good-nature, and folly begins.
Too patient a part, should thy wife offend,
Makes a rift in thine honor which naught can mend. . . .


### 5. THE WOMEN OF MEMPHIS

The women of Memphis, who heard the tale first,
The whispered slander received and nursed.
Then, attacking Zulaikha for right and wrong,
Their uttered reproaches were loud and long:
"Heedless of honor and name she gave
The love of her heart to the Hebrew slave,
Who lies so deep in her soul enshrined
That to sense and religion her eyes are blind.
She loves her servant. 'Tis strange to think
That erring folly so low can sink;
But stranger still that the slave she wooes
Should scorn her suit and her love refuse. . . .
There is many a woman, fair, good, and kind,
To whom never the heart of a man inclined;
And many a Laili* with soft black eye,
The tears of whose heart-blood are never dry."
    Zulaikha heard, and resentment woke
To punish the dames for the words they spoke.
She summoned them all from the city to share
A sumptuous feast which she bade prepare.
A delicate banquet meet for kings
Was spread with the choicest of dainty things. . . .
Bands of boys and young maidens, fine
As mincing peacocks, were ranged in line;

* [Laili was the legendary beauty with whom Majnun (the crazed one)
was in love. Ed.]

And the fair dames of Memphis, like Peris eyed,
In a ring on their couches sat side by side.
They tasted of all that they fancied, and each
Was courteous in manner and gentle in speech.
    The feast was ended; the cloth was raised,
And Zulaikha sweetly each lady praised.
Then she set, as she planned in her wily breast,
A knife and an orange beside each guest:
An orange, to purge the dark thoughts within
Each jaundiced heart with its golden skin.
One hand, as she bade them, the orange clasped,
The knife in the other was firmly grasped.
Thus she addressed them: "Dames fair and sweet,
Most lovely of all when the fairest meet,
Why should my pleasure your hearts annoy?
Why blame me for loving my Hebrew boy?
If your eyes with the light of his eyes were filled,
Each tongue that blames me were hushed and stilled.
I will bid him forth, if you all agree,
And bring him near for your eyes to see."
"This, even this," cried each eager dame,
"Is the dearest wish our hearts can frame.
Bid him come; let us look on the lovely face
That shall stir our hearts with its youthful grace.
Already charmed, though our eyes never fell
On the youth we long for, we love him well.
These oranges still in our hands we hold,
To sweeten the spleen with their skins of gold.
But they please us not, for he is not here:
Let not one be cut till the boy appear."
    She sent the nurse to address him thus:
"Come, free-waving cypress, come forth to us.
Let us worship the ground which thy dear feet press,
And bow down at the sight of thy loveliness.
Let our love-stricken hearts be thy chosen retreat,
And our eyes a soft carpet beneath thy feet."
    But he came not forth, like a lingering rose
Which the spell of the charmer has failed to unclose.
Then Zulaikha flew to the house where he dwelt,
And in fond entreaty before him knelt:
"My darling, the light of these longing eyes,

Hope of my heart," thus she spoke with sighs,
"I fed on the hope which thy words had given:
But that hope from my breast by despair is driven.
For thee have I forfeited all: my name
Through thee has been made a reproach and shame.
I have found no favor: thou wouldst not fling
One pitying look on so mean a thing.
Yet let not the women of Memphis see
That I am so hated and scorned by thee.
Come, sprinkle the salt of thy lip to cure
The wounds of my heart and the pain I endure.
Let the salt be sacred: repay the debt
Of the faithful love thou shouldst never forget."
    The heart of Yusuf grew soft at the spell
Of her gentle words, for she charmed so well.
Swift as the wind from her knees she rose,
And decked him gay with the garb she chose. . . .

    Like a bed of roses in perfect bloom
That secret treasure appeared in the room.
The women of Memphis beheld him, and took
From that garden of glory the rose of a look.
One glance at his beauty o'erpowered each soul
And drew from their fingers the reins of control.
Each lady would cut through the orange she held,
As she gazed on that beauty unparalleled.
But she wounded her finger, so moved in her heart,
That she knew not her hand and the orange apart.
One made a pen of her finger, to write
On her soul his name who had ravished her sight—
A reed which, struck with the point of the knife,
Poured out a red flood from each joint in the strife.
One scored a calendar's lines in red
On the silver sheet of her palm outspread,
And each column, marked with the blood drops, showed
Like a brook when the stream o'er the bank has flowed.
    When they saw that youth in his beauty's pride:
"No mortal is he," in amaze they cried.
"No clay and water composed his frame,
But, a holy angel, from heaven he came."
" 'Tis my peerless boy," cried Zulaikha, "long

For him have I suffered reproach and wrong.
I told him my love for him, called him the whole
Aim and desire of my heart and soul.
He looked on me coldly; I bent not his will
To give me his love and my hope fulfil.
He still rebelled: I was forced to send
To prison the boy whom I could not bend.
In trouble and toil, under lock and chain,
He passed long days in affliction and pain.
But his spirit was tamed by the woe he felt,
And the heart that was hardened began to melt.
Keep your wild bird in a cage and see
How soon he forgets that he once was free."
    Of those who wounded their hands a part
Lost reason and patience, and mind and heart.
Too weak the sharp sword of his love to stay,
They gave up their souls ere they moved away.
The reason of others grew dark and dim,
And madness possessed them for love of him.
Bareheaded, barefooted, they fled amain,
And the light that had vanished never kindled again.
To some their senses at length returned,
But their hearts were wounded, their bosoms burned.
They were drunk with the cup which was full to the brim,
And the birds of their hearts were ensnared by him.
Nay, Yusuf's love was a mighty bowl
With varied power to move the soul.
One drank the wine till her senses reeled;
To another, life had no joy to yield;
One offered her soul his least wish to fulfill;
One dreamed of him ever, but mute and still.
But only the woman to whom no share
Of the wine was vouchsafed could be pitied there.

When many rivals compete, the prize
Waxes more dear in the winner's eyes,
When another loves the fair maid you seek,
The love grows strong that before was weak,
And the flame that languished bursts forth anew
When eager rivals come near to sue.
The flame fed afresh on Zulaikha's mind,

And her heart more strongly to Yusuf inclined.
Again she spoke to that lovely band,
Whom love had wounded in heart and hand:
"If ye think I had reason, forbear to chide
And blame me for love which I could not hide.
The door of friendship is open; be
Friends in my trouble and prosper me."
       They swept the chords of love's lute and raised
Their voices in tune and excused and praised.
"Yes, he is lord of the realm of the soul;
There his is the right and the sway and control.
What creature that looks—nay, even what stone—
On that lovely face, calls its heart its own?
If thy love for him be thy sum of distress,
Thine excuse is sufficient, his loveliness.
Breathes there a mortal beneath the sky,
Who can look unmoved on that witching eye?
The heaven has oft compassed the earth, but where
Has it seen a darling so bright and fair?
Thou hast loved the sweet youth, but thou art not to blame,
Thy soul is afire, but thy love is no shame.
May his strong heart touched by thy passion relent,
And shame make thy darling his coldness repent."
They ceased. On Yusuf their eyes they bent,
And addressed him thus in admonishment:
"Joy of the age, from the east to the west,
The fame of thy virtue by all is confessed.
This garden, where roses with thorns we see,
Has ne'er grown a rose without thorns like thee.
Stoop down for a little, and add a grace
To that height by descent from thy lofty place.
Zulaikha is dust for thy feet to tread,
Trail thy skirt for a while where that dust is spread.
How, O pure one! wilt thou be hurt
By touching the dust for a time with thy skirt?
One wish has Zulaikha: no longer refuse
To grant the sole favor for which she sues. . . .
Or if thy fancy perchance prefer
More winning beauty and turn from her,
To us in secret thy heart incline,
And be ours forever as we are thine.

See, in our charms we are matchless; see,
Moons lighting the heaven of beauty are we.
Shame makes Zulaikha her own mouth close
When we open our lips whence the honey flows.
How can Zulaikha with us compare?
So sweet are we and so bright and fair."
    He heard the voice of the charmers, and knew
That their zeal for Zulaikha was all untrue.
They would lead him to swerve from his faith and err,
But more for the sake of themselves than of her.
His heart was troubled, he turned aside,
And no tender look to their looks replied.
He lifted to heaven his hands and prayed:
"O Thou who givest the needy aid,
Friend of the humble recluse, the sure
Help and refuge of all who are pure;
Against the oppressor a strong defence,
The lamp and beacon of innocence;
Their wiles torment me. The bolt, the bar,
The chains of the prison were better far.
Years in a dungeon were lighter pain
Than to look on the face of these women again.
Thus our hearts grow blind that we cannot see,
And we wander farther and farther from Thee.
If Thou wilt not turn their devices aside
Who had strayed from the path and their faith denied,
Who will not permit me to rest and be free—
If Thou wilt not aid me, ah, woe is me."
    For prison he prayed. Nor would God deny
The boon he sought with his eager cry.
But had Yusuf asked at His hands release,
The boy unimprisoned had gone in peace;
From the snares of the women the bird had flown,
And the pains of the dungeon he ne'er had known. . . .


## 6. ZULAIKHA'S AGONY

    But they left not Zulaikha a moment's rest,
On her sorrowing soul their advice they pressed.
"Poor suffering creature," 'twas thus they cried,

"Unworthiest thou to be thus denied;
No Houri's child is like Yusuf fair,
But he will not listen to grant thy prayer.
We gave him rebuke and advice enough,
And the file of our tongue we made sharp and rough.
But his heart is hard, and he will not feel;
The file, though rough, would not bite the steel.
Let the forge—his prison—be heated, so
The stubborn iron will melt and glow.
When the metal grows soft in the flame, the skill
Of the smith can fashion its form at will.
If the softened iron thou canst not mould,
Why hammer in vain when the steel is cold?"
        She trusted the words that the charmers spoke,
And hope in her bosom again awoke.
She would prison the treasure her heart loved best,
And make him suffer that she might rest.
When love is not perfect, with one sole thought—
Himself—is the heart of the lover fraught.
He looks on his love as a charming toy,
The spring and source of his selfish joy.
One rose will he pluck from his love and leave
A hundred thorns her lone heart to grieve.
        As Zulaikha sat by her husband's side,
She poured out the rage of her soul and cried:
"This boy has brought me to grief and shame;
The high and the humble reproach my name.
Men and women the story tell,
How I pine for the youth whom I love too well;
That I am the game he has struck with his dart,
And laid on the ground with a bleeding heart.
Barb upon barb in my breast, they say,
Has drained the blood from the stricken prey;
No hair on my head from that love is free,
And my very self is a stranger to me.
To send him to prison and thus repel
The growing slander, methinks, were well,
And in every street of the town to proclaim
By the voice of the crier the traitor's shame;
Thus shall be punished the slave who allows
His eye to look on his master's spouse,

And with lawless feet, on the carpet spread
For the lord who owns him, presumes to tread.
The tongue of reproach will be silent when
My avenging wrath is made known to men."
    The plan she spoke to his willing ear,
Delighted the heart of the Grand Vizir.
"I have pondered it long," was the answer he made;
"Long on my soul has the trouble weighed;
But I never have pierced a pearl so fine,
Or devised a plan to compare with thine.
The boy is thine own, as thou wilt, to treat;
Sweep thou the dust from the path of thy feet."
    She heard his speech with a joyful smile,
And she turned to Yusuf the rein of her guile:
"O wish of my heart and desire of mine eyes,
The only treasure on earth I prize,
My lord's permission has left me free
To deal as my will may incline with thee.
Thy head, if I will, in a prison must lie,
Thy foot, if I order, will tread the sky.
Why still rebellious? why still so blind?
Bend thy proud spirit at last and be kind.
Oh, come, tread the path of agreement and peace;
Me from torment, thyself from affliction, release.
Come, grant me my wish; I with thine will comply;
In the zenith of glory thy name shall be high.
Beware, beware, or the door will unclose
Of a prison fraught with a hundred woes;
And to lie there in sorrow and chains will be
Less sweet than to sit and smile softly on me."
He opened his lips in reply: but well
You know the answer I need not tell.
In Zulaikha's bosom resentment woke,
And thus to the chief of the guard she spoke:
"Off with his robe and his cap of gold;
In coarsest woollen his limbs enfold.
His silver with fetters of iron deck,
And bind the slave's collar about his neck.
Guilty of crime, make him sit on an ass
And through every street of the city pass;
And let a crier's loud voice proclaim

That the treacherous servant, lost to shame,
Who dares on his master's carpet to tread,
Shall thus with scorn to his prison be led."
  The multitude gathered on every side,
And "God forbid," in amaze they cried,
"That from one so fair should come evil deed—
The robber of hearts cause a heart to bleed.
Of the race of the angels he surely is one,
And no deeds of Satan by them are done.
No evil act will the lovely do,
For the sage has said, and his words are true:
'The fair in face are not soiled with sin;
Less fair are their looks than their souls within.
But he who is hideous in form and face,
Has a heart in his breast that is yet more base.'
And we see the truth of the maxim still,
Ne'er the hideous do good nor the lovely ill."
Thus to the dungeon the boy was driven,
And there to the charge of the jailer given.
Within the prison the saint was led,
And life seemed to return to the corpse of the dead.
A cry of joy from the captives rose,
And happiness came to that house of woes; . . .
When the glad commotion was hushed and still,
To the jailer Zulaikha declared her will:
"Spare him: with kindness the captive treat;
Strike the ring from his neck and the chain from his feet.
Strip off the rough gown from his silver skin;
Bring silken raiment to robe him in,
Wash the dust of toil from his head, and set
On his brows the bright round of a coronet.
A separate house for his rest prepare,
And lodge him apart from the others there.
The door and the walls with sweet scent perfume;
Brighten each window and arch of his room;
And over the floor be a carpet laid
Of silver tissue and gold brocade."
  Within the chamber the captive passed:
The carpet of prayer on the ground he cast,
And raised—for such was his wont each day—
His tranquil face to the arch to pray.

He joyed to have fled from the women's snare,
And his burden was light for his heart to bear.
Woe never visits the world but it brings
Sweet scent of the coming of happier things;
And the weary captive who lies in chains
Feels the breath of a blessing to lighten his pains. . . .
The light that the rose-cheek of Yusuf shed
Made the house of bondage a bright rose-bed;
But Zulaikha, whose palace had been more fair
Than a garden of roses when he was there,
Felt a deep gloom on her spirit press,
When she saw not the light of his loveliness.
Sad was her heart in that dungeon's hold,
And one sorrow by parting became twofold. . . .

Each thing he had touched, as it met her eye,
Drew from her bosom a long deep sigh.
Sad was her soul, and her eyes were dim,
As she caught up the raiment once worn by him.
But the touch was to her as the breath of the rose,
And soothed the fierce pain of her burning woes.
About her own neck his collar she tied,
With a hundred kisses of love applied:
"This is my collar of glory, nay,
The band of my heart," she would cry, "and its stay."
To place her arm in his mantle's sleeve
Would for a moment her pain relieve;
As she thought of her love it was touched and kissed,
And with silver filled of her dainty wrist.
She pressed to her eyes—and the touch was sweet—
The skirt that had lain on her darling's feet,
And, hopeless to fasten her lips on them,
Deluded her soul with a kiss of the hem.
Pearl and ruby in showers she spread
Over the cap that had decked his head.
For once it had shaded the beautiful brow
To which the whole world loved in worship to bow.
To the zone that had girded his waist she gave
The honor due from a faithful slave;
As a token most dear of her vanished fawn
Round her neck for a snare was the girdle drawn.

With dim eyes weeping, her hands displayed
The glittering folds of his robe of brocade.
She bathed its skirts with her tears, and the gleam
Of the rubies she dropped was on band and seam.
    Thus was the grief of Zulaikha renewed
Through the dreary day by each thing she viewed.
As she knew not the value of present joy
The fierce flame of absence must bliss destroy.
Zulaikha sorrowed, but sorrowed in vain;
Only patience was left her to heal her pain.
Yes, patience would bring her the balm of rest,
But how could she banish her love from her breast? . . .

    Zulaikha fain from herself would fly,
And, of good despairing, would gladly die.
The wall and the floor with her head she smote,
The bloodthirsty dagger was raised to her throat.
She sought, like a watchman, the roof at night
To cast herself down from the giddy height.
She twisted a cord of her hair, and strove
To stifle her breath with the noose she wove.
She sought release for her weary soul—
A poisonous draught from life's pleasant bowl.
She sickened of all, and would fain destroy
Her life with each thing that was once her joy.
    The pitying nurse sought her lady's side,
Kissed her hands and feet and blessed her and cried:
"May thy darling return to dispel thy woe;
May thy cup with the wine of his love o'erflow!
May a happy meeting thy bliss restore,
With no fear of parting for evermore!
How long shall this folly subdue thee? Arise,
Throw off thy madness, again be wise.
This sad heart bleeds when thy grief I see:
What woman ever has acted like thee?
Patience—list to the voice of age—
Patience alone will thy grief assuage.
Impatience has brought thee this fever of pain:
Let patience allay it with soothing rain.
When o'er thee the whirlwinds of sorrow pass,

Flee not before them like scattered grass.
Keep thy foot in thy skirt with undaunted will,
And stand firm in thy place like a rooted hill.
Patience will lead thee to lasting bliss,
And the fruit of thy longing thou shalt not miss.
Every triumph from patience springs,
The happy herald of better things.
Through patience the pearl from the raindrop grows,
And the diamond shines and the ruby glows;
The full ear springs from the scattered seed,
And food from the ear for the traveller's need.
So moons come and vanish till babes are born,
And with moonlight beauty the world adorn." . . .

When the day of a lover is merged in night
Again wakes his pain with redoubled might. . . .
In the wild impatience that drove her mad,
The night to Zulaikha was gloomy and sad;
The darling who ravished her heart was away,
And her night was moonless and sunless her day.
There was splendor of torches, yet dark was each place
Where shone not the light of her loved one's face. . . .

Thus till a watch of the night was spent
She poured out her anguish in wail and lament.
Then strength departed, endurance died;
The brook of her patience was empty and dried.
Then the flame of her longinging flashed forth: with eyes
Streaming she called to her nurse: "Arise,
I can wait no longer: arise, let us go
Unseen of all to the house of woe.
There we will hide in some corner; thus
The Moon of our prison will shine for us.
With the rosy cheek of one's darling, there
No prison may be, but the spring is fair.
Let others be glad when gay gardens they see:
This bud of the prison is all to me."
In graceful motion away she sped,
And the nurse followed close where the lady led.
She came like a moon to the prison wall,

And the warder rose at her secret call.
He opened the gate as he moved the bar
And showed her the moon of her love afar. . . .
     Silent and hidden she moved no limb,
Far from herself but so near to him.
But she wept in her heart, and the tears she shed
Turned the jasmine hue of her cheek to red.
With pearl she mangled the ruby, and tore
The rich ripe dates that the palm tree bore.
Then her grief burst forth, and while hot tears ran
From their fountain in torrents, she thus began:
"Eye and lamp of the lovely ones, thou
Whom the fairest would follow with prayer and vow,
In my breast thou hast kindled a flame of fire;
From my head to my foot I am all desire.
But no drop of pity hast thou bestowed
To quench the flame when its fury glowed.
Thou hast gored my breast and no pity felt
For the cruel wound which thy hand has dealt.
Hast thou no ruth, O most heartless, none
For me rejected, oppressed, undone?
I bear from thee daily fresh grief and scorn:
Ah, woe is me that I ever was born!
Or if she had borne me, a babe unblest,
Would I ne'er had lain on my mother's breast,
Ne'er on kindly milk from her bosom fed,
But deadly poison had sucked instead."
     Thus sad Zulaikha wept and complained;
But cold and unyielding his heart remained.
Unmoved was his soul, or no sigh betrayed
That his ruth was stirred as she wept and prayed.
     The night passed away: the pure skies o'erhead
Wept tears like those which the holy shed.
Loud sounded the drum from the palace, high
Rose through the air the Muezzin's cry.
The watch-dog's baying was hushed, and round
His throat for a collar his tail was wound.
Up started the cock from his sleep; his throat
Sent forth to the morning its clarion note.
Then Zulaikha rose; from the jail she withdrew,
But its threshold she kissed ere she bade it adieu. . . .

Through the weary day till the night brought ease
Such was her bondage, her words were like these.
While the light of her heart in that prison lay,
This is the story of night and day.
Still to the prison at night she went,
And by day her eyes on its roof were bent.
Day after day, week after week,
She looked on that wall and she gazed on his cheek.
She had made him a home in her heart: no care
For her life, for the world, could find entrance there.
Lost to herself she thought of him still,
From her heart's tablet washing all good and ill.
When the call of her maidens rang loud and clear
She scarce came to herself, though she seemed to hear.
Then to those maidens she oft would say:
"My senses are gone, ah, forever, astray.
Attention from me it is hopeless to seek;
Touch me and shake me before you speak.
I may come to myself, by your touches stirred;
Mine ear may be opened, your message heard.
My heart is with him in the prison: hence
Springs all the trouble that steals my sense.
She in whose bosom that fair moon lives,
No care and no thought to another gives."

   Fierce fever followed her heart's wild pain,
And the point of the lancet must open a vein.
They who stood round saw each blood-drop spell
A letter of Yusuf's name as it fell.
This word on the ground, so that all might note,
The lancet-reed of the surgeon wrote.
So full of her love were the vein and the skin
That nothing save Yusuf might dwell therein. . . .


   Rise, Jami, thou! A new life begin;
Seek the mansion eternal and enter in.
Thou knowest the way which thy feet should tread:
Ne'er the path of the sluggard to bliss hath led.
Quit self and this being forever: set
Thy feet no more in the worldling's net.
Once thou wast not, and no loss was thine:

Now be rich forever, this life resign.
Seek not thy bliss in thyself; refrain
From the fruitless hope that will bring no gain. . . .


## 7. YUSUF'S RELEASE

So while the prison where Yusuf lay
Smiled with his presence and all was gay,
Each prisoner, happy in heart, forgot
The bond and the chain and his dreary lot.
But if ever a captive sickened there,
The weary victim of toil and care,
Yusuf watched tenderly o'er him till he
Was made whole from the pain of his malady.
Was the soul of any oppressed with grief
Yusuf was ready to lend relief,
With a smile so sweet and a voice so kind
That the mourner was cheered and his heart resigned.
If a penniless wretch of his lot complained,
As the new moon filled or the full moon waned,*
Yusuf took from the wealthy a golden key,
Relieved the debtor and made him free.
If a rich man dreamed a sad dream and was caught
In the threatening whirlpool of wildered thought,
The dream was explained by those lips, and he
Was saved from the depth of the surging sea.

Two lords, once high in the ruler's grace,
Had fallen low from their lofty place,
And, doomed in that prison long days to spend,
Had won the love of that faithful friend.
Each dreamed a dream one night, and the breast
Of each was moved with a wild unrest;
For one had the promise of freedom, one
Was warned that the days of his life were done.
So weighed those dreams, both of hope and dread,
On the heart of each, uninterpreted.
They came to Yusuf and prayed him unfold
The secret drift of the dreams they told.

* As the days came near on which he was bound to pay debts.

"Thou on the gallows," he said, "must swing;
And thou wilt return to the court of the king."
    True were his words. To the youth restored
To his place of honor beside his lord,
Ere he turned to the court from his bonds set free,
Thus spoke Yusuf: "Remember me.
If fortune favor thee, time may bring
A happy hour to address the king.
Thou wilt gain thy reward if thou speak to him then
As he sits in the hall with his noblemen.
'A stranger,' say, 'in the prison lies
Barred from the sight of thy pitying eyes.
It beseems not a heart that is righteous like thine
To suffer the guiltless in bonds to pine.'"
    But when that servant his rank regained,
And the cup of the grace of his master drained,
For many a year his glad heart forgot
The prayer of Yusuf or heeded not.
The tree of his promise brought forth despair,
And Yusuf yet lingered a captive there. . . .

    The heart of Yusuf all hope resigned
That his own device would his bonds unbind.
His hope was only in Him from whom
Comes help to us all in the days of gloom,
And, free from self thought in his low estate,
He was guided by God the Compassionate.
    Clear to the ruler of Egypt's sight
Appeared seven kine, as he dreamed one night;
Each more fair than the other, all
Were healthy and handsome and fat from the stall.
After them others advancing were seen,
Equal in number, but weak and lean.
By these the former were overpowered
And, like the grass of the field, devoured.
Seven ears of corn then were seen to rise,
That might gladden the heart and delight the eyes.
Then seven thin ears, grown each from a stem,
Followed and withered and ruined them.
    In the early morn when the king awoke,
To each wakeful heart of his dream he spoke.

"We cannot interpret it," all replied;
"Thought and conjecture are here defied.
The dream is a riddle no wit may explain,
And wisest are they who from guess refrain."
Then he who had knowledge of Yusuf flung
Aside the veil that before him hung,
And said:—"A youth in the prison lies,
In solving riddles supremely wise.
His wit can interpret each dream, and he
Will bring up the pearl when he dives in the sea.
Permit me to tell him this secret thing,
And the drift of thy dream from his lips will I bring."
"What need," said the king, "of permission to speak?
What better than sight may the blind man seek?
And from this moment the eye of my mind,
Till I master this secret, is dark and blind."
He ran to the prison with utmost speed,
And gave to Yusuf the dream to read.
"Years," he explained, "are those ears and kine,
Whose looks of those years are the mark and sign.
The fair fat kine and the full ears well
The nature and hope of those years may tell.
The meagre ears, the kine thin and weak,
Of years of dearth and misfortune speak.
In the former seven the kindly rain
Will fill the fields full with rich grass and grain,
And all the land will be glad and gay.
But seven will come, when those pass away,
To ruin the gifts of the years before;
And the hearts of men will be glad no more.
No gracious cloud the sweet rain will bring,
No blade of grass from the ground will spring.
No joy will the wealth of the rich supply,
And the poor and needy will hunger and die.
On the table of Time is no food, and Bread!
Is the cry of thousands who die unfed."
The noble listened, and straight returned
To the court of the king and the lore he had learned.
To his master the words of Yusuf he told,
And made his glad heart like a bud unfold.
"Bring Yusuf to me," said the monarch, "that I

On the truth of these words may more surely rely.
'Tis sweetest to hear a dear friend repeat
With his own lips the words which, reported, are sweet;
And who is content from another to hear
The words he may draw from the lips that are dear?"
    Again to the prison his steps he bent,
And gave Yusuf the message the king had sent:
"Fair cypress, come from thy still retreat,
In the monarch's garden to set thy feet.
O come, and the court of his house will shine
More fair with the rose of that cheek of thine."
"Shall I visit," cried Yusuf, "the court of a king
Who has cast me aside like a guilty thing—
Who has left me in prison long years, nor bent
One pitying glance on the innocent?
Let him first command, if he will that I go
Forth to his court from this house of woe,
That they whom, at sight of me, wonder led
To wound with the knife their own hands till they bled,
Like the Pleiades gathered before his face,
Uplift the veil and make clear my case;
And let them declare for what fault or crime
I have lain in the prison this dreary time.
Then will the secret come forth to light,
And my skirt will be proved to be pure and white.
The path of sin have I never pursued,
But traitorous thought in my heart eschewed.
To my lord I was faithful in deed and in thought,
No perfidy planned, no dishonesty wrought.
Ere thus with my master I stooped to deal,
Like a midnight thief I would plunder and steal."
    The message was given; the monarch heard;
To the women of Memphis he sent his word,
And, called from their homes by the summons, they came
To the light of his presence like moths to the flame.
When their company entered the court of their lord,
He loosened his tongue as a flaming sword:
"How did that pure light offend, that you
The sword of dishonor against him drew?
How could you send to a prison the boy
Whose face was your garden and spring of joy?

Bind chains on the neck of an idol for whom
The weight of a rose were too heavy a doom?
No chains but the links of the dew should be borne
By the rose that is bowed by the breath of the morn."
"O King," they answered, "whose splendor has lent
To the crown and the throne a new ornament,
Purity only in Yusuf we saw,
Honor and love of each holiest law.
No pearl ever lay 'neath the depth of the sea
More pure in the shell that enfolds it than he."

There too Zulaikha sat with the rest,
With no lie on her lip and no guile in her breast.
The schooling of love and his sweet control
Had chastened her spirit and softened her soul.
The splendor of truth from her bosom broke,
And like the true dawning of day she spoke.
The veil of her folly was flung aside,
And, "The light of the truth is revealed," she cried.
"To the charge of Yusuf no sin is laid;
I in my love for him erred and strayed.
With the spells of my love I would draw him near,
And I drove him afar when he would not hear.
To the house of woe for my woes was he sent,
And my sufferings caused his imprisonment.
When the love-grief I felt was too heavy to bear,
Of the load of my sorrows I gave him a share.
I was the tyrant, and, oh! that he
Were repaid for the woes he has suffered through me!
Each grace, each honor and bounty—all
That the king may give—were a gift too small."

He heard Zulaikha the secret disclose;
He smiled like a rosebud, and bloomed like a rose.
He gave command to his servants to speed,
And back from the prison bring Yusuf freed.
"In the loveliest garden the rose should bloom,
And not lie immured in a dungeon's gloom.
In the realm of love he is lord supreme,
And no seat but a throne may that king beseem."
In this ancient lodge 'tis a well-known tale
That ne'er without bitter may sweet prevail.
When the weary days of the moons have passed,

The mother looks on her babe at last.
In the rock pines the ruby till, one by one,
Its veins are filled full of the light of the sun.
 The night of Yusuf was long and drear,
But it fled at last and the dawn was clear.
Long on his heart lay a mountain of woes,
But bright o'er its summit the sun arose.
To welcome him back with due honor, all
The courtiers who stood in the monarch's hall,
Were straightway commanded to line the way
From the court to the prison in full array.
There youths apparelled in rich brocade
And glittering girdles with gold inlaid;
There skilful riders were fair to see,
On the noblest chargers of Araby;
There, bright as the sun, was a minstrel throng
Skilled in all Hebrew and Syrian song;
And the lords of Egypt on every side
Scattered their silver coin far and wide,
While the poor and needy flocked round to gain
A share of the wealth of the shining rain.
 Forth from the prison came Yusuf, gay
In the pomp and sheen of a king's array.
The stately steed by his hand controlled
Was a mountain covered with pearl and gold.
Bags full of jewels and coin, and trays
Of musk and ambergris strewed the ways,
Thrown from each side at the feet of his steed,
And from want the poor were forever freed.
He passed through the street of the royal town;
At the gate of the palace he lighted down,
And silk and satin and gold brocade
Beneath his feet—yea, and heads—were laid,
And o'er azure carpets his steps he bent
Like a moon sailing on through the firmament.
 Swift as the wind the glad monarch pressed,
Warned of his coming, to meet the guest.
He clasped him close to his bosom: so
A box tree her arms round a cypress might throw.
He made him sit on his royal seat:
He questioned him long, and his words were sweet.

First the drift of his dream would the monarch hear,
And Yusuf's words made the meaning clear.
Then of many an action and place and thing
He plied him with eagerest questioning.
Each answer of Yusuf was clear and true,
And the king's delight with his wonder grew.
"Help me with counsel," at last he said;
"This dream which thy lips have interpreted—
How shall I meet the woe threatened? How drain
The bitter cup of my country's pain?"

    "In the years of abundance," he thus replied,
"When the clouds the blessing of rain provide,
Send out thine orders that all shall till
The fields of the land with one heart and will;
With sharp nails harrow each stony place,
And scatter the seed with the blood of the face.
Let the grain, which the ears, when they ripen, afford
For the food of the future, be gathered and stored.
In the days of famine each laden ear
Rends the heart of thy foe with its pointed spear.
Let the gathered corn in the granaries lie;
Then, when the drought and the dearth are nigh,
From the ample stores thou hast gathered give
Enough to each man that his soul may live.
But o'er every business should one preside
Whose skill and knowledge are proved and tried;
Whose keen-eyed prudence each end foresees,
And his hand performs what his head decrees.
Search through the world for such heart and brain,
A man like me will be sought in vain.
This weighty task to my charge commit,
For none in the land wilt thou find so fit."

    The king was glad at his sage reply;
Mid the lords of Egypt he raised him high.
He bade the soldiers his word obey
And gave him the land for his own to sway.
He was Grand Vizir by the monarch's grace,
And sat on the throne in the ruler's place.
Enthroned he sat in his seat of pride,
And the people bowed prostrate on every side.
The shouts of the heralds, as forth he went

To the plain, rose up to the firmament.
To every place, as his fancy led,
By thousands his coming was heralded;
And near their lord, when he chose to ride,
Was a countless army to guard and guide.
  When thus to Yusuf the Lord Supreme
Gave the highest rank in the King's esteem,
The Grand Vizir saw his sun go down,
And low sank the flag of his old renown.
Crushed was his heart by his loss of state,
And he fell a prey to the dart of Fate.


### 8. ZULAIKHA'S REPENTANCE

  A hapless bird was Zulaikha. She pined
In the narrow cage of the world confined.
Befriended by Fortune, in pride and power,
When a rose-bed bloomed in her secret bower;
With her lord beside her to shade and screen
The tender plant when her bud was green—
With all dainty things, if she cared but to speak;
When no lamp was so bright as her youthful cheek:
Yusuf e'en then her whole heart possessed—
The sweet name on her lips, the dear hope in her breast.
Now, when from her side her protector was reft,
When naught of her rank and her treasures was left,
The sole friend of her heart, who ne'er changed his place,
Was the sweet remembrance of Yusuf's face.
She thought of him ever; her sad house seemed
Her dear fatherland when of him she dreamed.
No food could she eat, and she closed not her eyes;
She wept tears of blood and she said with sighs:—
"Beloved Yusuf, where, where art thou?
Why false and faithless to pledge and vow?
Oh, that again those sweet hours I might see,
When one happy home held my love and me!
When no fear of parting could mar delight,
And I gazed on his beauty from morn till night.
When stern Fate robbed me of this sweet joy,
I sent to prison that innocent boy.

Unseen by night to his presence I stole,
And the sight of his cheek was as balm to my soul:
And a glance at the walls where my darling lay
Rubbed the rust of grief from my heart by day.
No joy is now left me, no solace like these;
My heart and my frame perish of pain and disease.
All I have left is the image which still,
Where'er I may be, this sad bosom must fill.
The soul of this frame is that image, and I,
Bereft of its presence, should languish and die."
    Then her breast and her heart she would fiercely tear,
And engrave the form of her darling there.
She would strike her soft knee with her hand till the blue
Of the lotus supplanted the jasmine's hue.
"I am worthy the love of my love," she would cry,
"For my love is the sun and the lotus am I.
As my love is the lord of the east and the west,
The place of the lotus for me is the best." . . .

    Long years of sorrow, each like the last,
In hopeless yearning alone she passed.
White, white as milk grew each plaited tress,
And dark was the light of her loveliness.

She bowed down her back and she bent her head
As if seeking the treasure which long had fled.
Slowly and sadly the tears came round:
Her foot was unringed and her head uncrowned.
There gleamed on her shoulder no satin's sheen,
No precious gems in her ears were seen.
On her neck was no collar of costly stone;
No gold-wrought veil o'er her cheek was thrown.
On the cold bare earth for a bed she lay,
And the cheek once so dainty was pillowed on clay.
Ah, earth, with his love, was a pleasanter bed
Than a silken couch by a Houri spread!
Yes, a jewelled pillow from Paradise seemed
The brick on her cheek when of him she dreamed.

    In this sorrow, of which but a part is sung
In the vocal pearls which my pen has strung,

His name was all that her lips could speak,
The only comfort her soul might seek.
While yet she had treasures, a wealth untold
Of jewels and silver, of pearl and gold,
Her gold and silver she cast at the feet
Of her whom some tale of her love would repeat,
And her pearls and her jewels she gave to each
Who poured forth those jewels and pearls of speech;
But her gold and silver, her pearls, and her vast
Treasure of jewels were spent at last.
With a woollen gown and a girdle rent
From the bark of the palm she was then content.
Then all on the knee of deep silence fell:
No more of Yusuf she heard them tell.
No longer came the sweet tidings to cheer
Her lonely heart through the path of her ear.
     That this food of her life might be still supplied
She built her a hut by the highway side,
That each ear might catch—and the hope was sweet—
The measured tread of his escort's feet.
Ah, poor, unhappy, deserted soul,
From whose hand has fallen the rein of control!
From the love of her darling by Fate debarred,
The voice of her longing was tuneless and hard.
No breath from her love might be wafted to her,
No tidings be learned from a messenger.
Oft would she question the wind if it knew
Aught of her love, and the bird as it flew.
Whenever a traveller passed the place
With the dust of the road on his weary face,
She would wash that brow, she would bathe those feet,
For they came from his home to her lone retreat.
If her lord and king by her cottage passed,
No look on his face had she power to cast,
Content with the sound of his horse's tread,
And the dust of his path on her happy head.

From her cottage of reeds came Zulaikha out
When she knew of his coming and heard them shout.
In grief and anguish of heart by the side
Of the road he would travel she sat and cried.

When the host that preceded his courser was near
Loud rang the voices of boys with a cheer:
"Look, Yusuf himself, whom the sun in the sky
And the bright moon envy, is nigh, is nigh."
Zulaikha answered: "Mine eyes are blind,
But no trace of Yusuf mid these I find.
Mock me not, darlings! oh, spare me the pain,
No breath from Yusuf has reached my brain.
The musk of Tartary scents the place
That is blest with the light of his lovely face,
And when he sits in his litter, thence
A precious perfume pervades the sense."
　　Nearer and nearer, mid loud acclaim,
Of hearts that were jubilant, Yusuf came.
They called to Zulaikha:—"The guards are nigh,
But no trace of Yusuf has met our eye."
"Strive not to deceive me," Zulaikha replied;
"My darling's coming ye may not hide.
Can the coming of one who was born to wield
The sceptre of sway o'er each soul be concealed?
The breath of his fragrance gives life to the whole
Of this world of ours and each single soul;
And the presence of him who gives life is made known
To the poor thirsty soul that must perish alone."
　　When Zulaikha, long buried in darkness and gloom,
Heard the shout of the escort, "Make room, make room!"
A loud cry she uttered: "Rejected, forlorn,
A long age of absence my spirit has borne.
I can suffer no more: I have had my full share:
Loss of patience is now the sole loss I may bear.
Far better, forever excluded from bliss,
To fly from myself than to linger like this."
　　Thus cried Zulaikha, then sank and lay
Unconscious awhile, all her senses astray.
That cup of unconsciousness still she kept,
As, oblivious of self, to her cottage she crept.
Then rose the shrill wail as her sad heart bled,
And reeds sighed in tune with the strain she led.
Thus passed in her sorrow the time away,
And this was the task of each mournful day.

Never content is the lover; each hour
His longing waxes in strength and power.
Ne'er to one wish for two moments true,
A joy still dearer he holds in view.
He would look on the rose when he breathes her scent,
And pluck the fair flower when the stem is bent.
     Zulaikha had sat by the way, but now
She would lift her eyes to his cheek and brow.
At the foot of the image to which she prayed
From the days of childhood her head she laid:
"O thou, to whom praying I turn me, before
Whose feet I have loved thy dear might to adore;
I have served thee devoutly from youth's early day;
But the gem of my sight has been taken away.
Cast a pitying look on my ruin; restore
The light of mine eyes that I sorrow no more.
Between Yusuf and me must there still be a bar?
Oh, let me but see him—one look from afar.
This prayer—thou art mighty; this one wish fulfil;
Give this, and then deal with me after thy will.
What is life to a wretch who must hopelessly pine?
Far better were death than a life like mine."
Thus cried Zulaikha. She laid down her head,
And wet was the ground with the tears she shed.
     To his throne in the east rose the Lord of Day,
And the steed of Yusuf was heard to neigh.
She came from her cottage in beggar's weed
To the narrowest turn in the way of the steed,
With raised hand acted the mendicant's part,
And made a low moan from the ground of her heart.
Before their master, the horsemen's cry,
"Make room, make room!" went up to the sky;
And the tread and tramp of the mighty throng,
And the neighing of steeds as they moved along,
Smote on each ear, and no eye was turned
To the spot where Zulaikha sat undiscerned.
He looked not on her; she rose forlorn,
In a hundred pieces her heart was torn.
Her broken spirit sent out a cry,
And a flame came forth in each burning sigh.

To her house of woe she returned distraught,
And a hundred flames for each reed she brought.

She placed before her the idol of stone,
And to lighten her sorrow thus made her moan:
"O thou who hast broken mine honor's urn,
Thou stone of offence wheresoever I turn,
I should smite—for thy falsehood has ruined my rest—
With the stone thou art made of, the heart in my breast.
The way of misfortune too surely I trod
When I bowed down before thee and made thee my god;
When I looked up to thee with wet eyes in my woe,
I renounced all the bliss which both worlds can bestow.
From thy stony dominion my soul will I free,
And thus shatter the gem of thy power and thee."
     With a hard flint stone, like the Friend,* as she spoke,
In a thousand pieces the image she broke.
Riven and shattered the idol fell,
And with her from that moment shall all be well.

She made her ablution, mid penitent sighs,
With the blood of her heart and the tears of her eyes.
She bent down her head to the dust; with a moan
She made supplication to God's pure throne:—
"O God, who lovest the humble, Thou
To whom idols, their makers, their servants bow;
'Tis to the light which Thy splendor lends
To the idol's face that its worshipper bends.
Thy love the heart of the sculptor stirs,
And the idol is graven for worshippers.
They bow them down to the image, and think
That they worship Thee as before it they sink.
To myself, O Lord, I have done this wrong,
If mine eyes to an idol have turned so long.
I have erred and strayed; let repentance win
Forgiveness, Good Lord, for my grievous sin.
Because I have wandered, nor heeded Thy right,
From mine eyes Thou hast taken the jewel of sight.
Thou hast washed the dark stain of my sin away:

* Abraham, the Friend of God, broke the images which his father and
his people worshipped.

Now restore the lost blessing for which I pray.
May I feel my heart free from the brand of its woes,
And cull from the garden of Yusuf a rose."
      As Yusuf home to his palace hied,
Again by the way stood Zulaikha and cried:
"Glory to God! to a monarch's state
He has lifted the poor and cast down the great.
He has cast the king from his glory down,
And set on the head of a servant his crown."
      When Yusuf the voice of Zulaikha heard,
His heart in his bosom was strangely stirred.
He cried to a lord: "As I hear her speak
My spirit sinks and my heart grows weak.
Who is the beadswoman? Bid her appear
In my council-chamber that I may hear
From her lips the tale of her life, and know
Her share of fortune, her dole of woe.
For the words of praise which mine ears have caught
On my troubled spirit have strongly wrought.
By some grievous woe is her heart down-weighed.
Or why should my soul be so touched and swayed?" . . .


      When Yusuf, freed from the pomp and din,
Had sought his chamber and entered in,
A chamberlain cried at the door: "O best
Of princes, famous from east to west,
That ancient woman in beggar's weed,
Who laid her hand on the rein of thy steed,
Whom by thine order I bade appear
This day in thy presence, is waiting here."
      "Go, hear her petition," thus Yusuf replied,
"Is she poor and in want, for her need provide."
"She is not," said the chamberlain, "one of those
Who will tell me the tale of her need and woes."
      "Admit her," said Yusuf, "that, face to face,
She may lift the veil of her mournful case."
      Zulaikha came in, when permission was won,
As free as the motes in the light of the sun.
Like a bud she expanded: the lips that were pale
Smiled bright as a rose, and she bade him hail.

He asked her her name and her home, the while
He marvelled much at that joyous smile.
 "I am she who chose thee," she cried; "and thou,
Since that one first glance, hast been loved till now;
To whom, bought with my wealth, I devoted the whole
True love of my heart and my mind and my soul.
I cast for thy sake my young life to the wind,
And age has come o'er me and youth declined.
Thine arms for a consort this realm have embraced,
And I am unpitied, forgotten, disgraced."
 From his eye the big tears of compassion fell
As he heard the tale he remembered so well.
"Zulaikha," he said, "what unhappy fate
Has brought thee down to thy low estate?"
 When she heard her beloved her name express,
Zulaikha fell prostrate, Zulaikhaless.
The wine of unconsciousness boiled in her heart,
And the sense from her body was riven apart.
Then thus began Yusuf, as slowly at length
Zulaikha recovered her senses and strength:
 "Where is thy youth, and thy beauty, and pride?"
"Gone, since I parted from thee," she replied.
"Where is the light of thine eye?" said he,
"Drowned in blood-tears for the loss of thee."
"Why is that cypress tree bowed and bent?"
"By absence from thee and my long lament."
"Where is thy pearl, and thy silver and gold,
And the diadem bright on thy head of old?"
"She who spoke of my loved one," she answered, "shed,
In the praise of thy beauty, rare pearls on my head.
In return for those jewels, a recompense meet,
I scattered my jewels and gold at her feet.
A crown of pure gold on her forehead I set,
And the dust that she trod was my coronet.
The stream of my treasure of gold ran dry;
My heart is love's storehouse, and I am I."
 Again spoke Yusuf: "Zulaikha, say,
What is the wish of thy heart to-day?"
"My prayer," she answered, "wilt thou refuse;
But no help save thine can I wish or choose.
And if with an oath thou wilt pledge thy word,

To utter that prayer shall my tongue be stirred.
If not, in silence my lips I close,
And give my soul back to my life of woes."
  "By the truth of that Father* who reared of yore
The temple of prophecy," thus he swore;
"To whom a tulip bloomed forth in the flame,
And from heaven a robe of high honor came;
Whatever thy will be this day, I vow—
If I have but the power—I will grant it now."
  "First, my beauty," she cried, "and my youth restore
In the pride and splendor thou knewest before;
Then add the gift of new sight to those,
To see thee and cull from thy cheek a rose."
  He moved his lips and his prayer began
While the healing stream from his pure mouth ran.
The beauty returned which was ruined and dead,
And her cheek gained the splendor which long had fled.
Again shone the waters† which sad years had dried,
And the rose-bed of youth bloomed again in its pride.
The musk was restored and the camphor withdrawn,
And the black night followed the gray of the dawn.
The cypress rose stately and tall as of old:
The pure silver was free from all wrinkle and fold.
From each musky tress fled the traces of white:
To the black narcissus came beauty and light.
The halo of youth round her age was seen:
For the forty-years' dame stood a girl of eighteen;
Yes, fairer and brighter in loveliness stood
Than in days of her ripening maidenhood.
  Again said Yusuf: "O thou most fair,
If a wish now be left thee, that wish declare."
  "The one sole wish of my heart," she replied,
"Is still to be near thee, to sit by thy side;
To have thee by day in my happy sight,
And to lay my cheek on thy foot at night;
To lie in the shade of the cypress and sip
The sugar that lies on thy ruby lip;
To my wounded heart this soft balm to lay:

* Abraham.
† *ab*, in Persian, means both water and splendor.

For naught beyond this can I wish or pray.
The streams of thy love will new life bestow
On the dry thirsty field where its sweet waters flow."
　　　When Yusuf the prayer of Zulaikha had heard,
He bowed down his head and he spoke no word,
To the world unseen were his eyes turned away,
And he gave her no answer of Yea or Nay.
Then a sound on his ear, as he doubted, fell,
And he knew 'twas the wing-beat of Gabriel.
Thus spoke the Angel: "To thee, O king,
From the Lord Almighty a message I bring.
'Mine eyes have seen her in humble mood;
I heard her prayer when to thee she sued.
At the sight of her labors, her prayers, and sighs,
The waves of the sea of My pity rise.
Her soul from the sword of despair I free,
And here from My throne I betroth her to thee.'". . .

### EPILOGUE

One night from Yusuf's hand in haste she fled;
And limping to obtain release she sped.
Behind he seized her garment as she flew,
And by his hand her robe was rent in two.
Zulaikha said to him: "In days of yore
"Thy robe from off thy body once I tore.
"Thou hast my garment now from off me torn,
"And I my crime's just punishment have borne.
"Of right and wrong I now no longer fear;
"In tearing robes we both stand equal here."

# 8. "Potiphar's Wife" by Sir Edwin Arnold
## (1832–1904)

(After the versions of the Koran, and the Persian poet Jami.)

### I

In Memphis, underneath the palms of Nile,
    The Lady Asenath a house did build
For love of Hebrew Yusuf; who, erewhile
    With flame unquenchable her breast had filled:
The treasures of Prince Itfir 'stablished it
A summer-palace for her fancies fit.

### II

White, in the blue Egyptian sky, it soared
    With mighty graven stones reared outwardly;
This side the gate—enthroned—sate Horus, Lord,
    Finger to lip; and, on that other, Thmei,
Mother of Truth, holding her asp and wand,
Glared with great granite face across the land.

### III

Inwardly, by an alley of black shade,
    The footstep passed on checkered slabs set square,
Into a walled court; where a colonnade
    Framed a glad garden full of odors rare
From heavy blooms and fruits. Without was seen
Golden Noon flaming, here 'twas Evening green!

### IV

And all the wall was painted movingly
    With high-wrought lore, and solemn-storied things:
Anubis, herding souls, was there to see,
    And Thoth the Judge: and proud-apparelled kings
Driving to wars, and bringing spoil again,
Their chariot wheels rose-red with blood of slain.

221

V

And elsewhere Heaven was shown, with bliss unbroken,
    Whereto those mild immortal sisters lead,
Isis and Nepthys; and, for certain token,
    Scarabs in holy rows. The limner's reed
Had drawn their foreclaws holding emblems three
Of Life, and Changelessness, and Sanctity.

VI

And, elsewhere, frowned Amenti—Hell:—but over
    The silver plumes swayed, teaching how the Dead
Should pass beyond dire Typhon, and discover
    Paths to the happy Light, where Ra's bright head
Rebukes all darkness, Regent of the Sun;
And Phtah, Kneph, Athor—every Sacred One.

VII

Also, that cloistered walk was compassed in
    With pillars wonderful for work and hue:
This one a palm-stem; that papyrus thin;
    Yonder, in stone, lotuses pink and blue.
And from the garden and the colonnade
A roofed way to the inner rooms was laid.

VIII

For inner chambers were there seven:—each fashioned
    With matchless wit to make each goodlier
Than that last seen. So, heart and eye, impassioned
    Unto the inmost passed, devised by her,
High Asenath, for love's deep hiding-place,
Beautiful, marvellous, all peace and grace.

IX

Through latticed loops Nile's cooling ripple came—
    Musical, lulling,—to that dim retreat
Which had for light one silver lamp's faint flame
    Burning with fragrant oils before the feet
Of Pasht, in speckled stone, Pasht with cat's head,
And long arms on her levelled knees outspread.

X

The forty carven columns round about
    Showed each some master-piece of subtle craft:
A musk-deer here, in river-reeds, breathes out
    The very musk-scent from him: there, a waft
Of bulrush-heads to the quick current bend,
And the slow crocodiles to dry land wend,

XI

Sunning wet scales. And, next, a gray fox watched—
    In syenite—doves on a tamarisk-tree
Done out of green rock. Wings and necks were matched
    In lazulite and moonstone—fair to see!
Midway a dais mounted to a bed
Of pearl and ebony, with soft cloths spread.

XII

Upon the alcove there, and all around
    Love tales were pictured: some swart lady wooed
A lover still unwilling; he was bound
    In dark warm arms, refusing: then 'twas viewed
How to her spells he melted: then, again,
How what he scorned he sued for—fond and fain.

XIII

And those who thus Love's luxuries had won
    Asenath seemed, and Yusuf. Limb for limb,
Lips, eyes, and brows, the Hebrew boy was done
    Lifelike. The gemmed Egyptian dame with him
Shone Asenath herself, Asenath fair,
With robes ungirt, no fillet in her hair!

XIV

Into this palace 'twas her mind to bring
    Yusuf the slave, and lead him, room by room,
Through all their passages of pleasuring
    Till eyes' delight should heart's cold doubts consume.
But first herself she 'tired, and lovelier made
That loveliness, too rich before arrayed!

### XV

Her eyebrows' arch with pencilled lines she builded,
    And touched each underlid with jetty dye;
Drew the long lashes separate, and gilded
    Her flesh with palm-flow'r dust, to beautify
The ambered satin of her nape and neck;
And deftly with red henna did she deck

### XVI

Her slender finger-tips; and washed with myrrh
    Her long black tresses, braiding them in strings
Which, from the queenly gleaming crown of her
    Swung to her knees, banded with beads and rings;
And 'thwart her breasts—like lotus-blossoms blown—
A purple, spangled, sindon hath she thrown.

### XVII

Then she bade summon that fair Hebrew boy:
    Who came, with palms across his faint heart folded,
And kissed her feet, and prayed: "What swift employ
    May thy true servant find?" Of manhood moulded
In every part was Yusuf; and her eye
O'er-roamed him with a tender tyranny.

### XVIII

Yet more he shunned th' imperious look of love
    Than if her glance had blaze of wrath displayed:
"But," quoth the Princess, "this night will I prove
    If thou be servant true!" Therewith she bade
Follow:—and, entering that first chamber-door,
Shot the bronze bolt; and from his brown throat tore—

### XIX

With swift impatient hand—the leathern thong
    Marking him thrall; and cried: "My soul's desire!
I, thy hid handmaid, do thee daily wrong
    Playing the mistress. By Ra's morning fire
Freed art thou! Make my gift of freedom sweet
Lifting this love-sick giver from thy feet!"

### XX

With that she poured her black imperial hair
    In waves upon his sandals. But, he said:
"Thou, to whom Egypt's noblest kneel in fear,
    Mock me not thus, on whom the charge is laid
To guard thee for my Lord; or, if set free,
Great lady! grant my soul his liberty!"

### XXI

Silent she rose:—drew him on inwardly
    Behind the second door, locking it hard:
Took from a chest,—cut of the almond-tree—
    A cirque, with gods and scarabs set in sard:
"See now!" she cried: "I crown thee Prince and Lord,
Will not those lips, made royal like mine, afford

### XXII

"The word I pine for, which shall pay for greatness?
    Now may'st thou lift thy face, and answer sweet;
We are as one! Quit shame, forsake sedateness!
    Asenath woos Lord Yusuf:—that is meet!"
"Oh, Itfir's wife!" he said, "meet would it be
I were made vulture's food, hearkening to thee!"

### XXIII

Then, through those chambers third and fourth she passed,
    And to the fifth and sixth she led him on,
Bolting each door behind: 'till at the last,—
    Laden with gifts of jade, and turkis-stone,
And robes, and torques—she brought him to her bower,
Where 'twas her thought to put forth Love's last power.

### XXIV

For all four walls with those light pictures burned,
    Painted to life—lovers at play—and these
Asenath seemed, and Yusuf. If he turned,
    Unyielding, from the Princess at his knees,
On the same Princess gazed he, imaged sweet;
And himself yielded, conquered, at her feet.

### XXV

And more than steadfast soul might well withstand
    It was, to bring his troubled gaze again
To that great suppliant, wasting on his hand
    Woeful caressings; and to mark what pain
Filled with clear tears the bright beseeching eyes;
Heaved the soft breasts, as sea-tides sink and rise.

### XXVI

For, when she linked the last door's chain, and seized
    His hands, and, desperate, her last prayer said,
He had been stone or snow to view, unpleased,
    The lustrous glory of that low-bowed head,
The meekness of such majesty forgot,
The queenly pleading orbs, whose light was shot

### XXVII

Star-wise, through sparkling rain; which more o'erpowered
    By grace, than greatness, to the sweet surrender.
Like a charmed snake Conscience its cold hood lowered,
    While, soft as muted lute, in accents tender
Her rich lips murmured, "Oh, how long, how long
Wilt thou do thee and me this loveless wrong?

### XXVIII

"How long? when I, who may command, implore,
    Being named Mistress of the Mouths of Nile?
Yet, if into the Ocean those did pour
    Silver and gold all day, for one kind smile
From those close-curtained eyes, for one light kiss
I would let sea-born Kneph take all of this!

### XXIX

"Give, then, mine heart its will, mine eyelids sleep;
    My head the pillow that can lull its woe.
Shall Asenath of Memphis vainly weep?
    I cry to thee by Him thou honorest so,
Thy Hebrew Jah—if He hath any ruth—
Show mercy! put to fruit thy blossomed youth!

### XXX

"Yea! by the marks thy God hath set on thee
  To make thee most desirable,—thy hair
Glossed like an ibis' wing,—thy brows which be
  Black rainbows to thy sunlike eyes,—the fair
Wonderful rounding of thy temples twain,
And that flower mouth,—which, when it opes again

### XXXI

"Cannot, and shall not say me 'nay'—by these,
  And all thy goodly strength, for Love's use given,
By my salt tears, and by my soul's disease,
  Shut me no longer from the wished-for Heaven;
Its gate is there! there—in those arms tight-locked—
Open them—open! for my heart hath knocked!

### XXXII

"What gives thee fear, when I am none afeard?
  Where is thy shame, if I am naught ashamed?
What whisper of our comforts shall be heard
  From these still walls? How should thy blood be blamed
Mingling with mine, who come of Pharaoh's race?
With mine, that have these brows, this breast, this face?"

### XXXIII

"Ah, thou most high and most beguiling one!"
  Trembling he answered: "tempt me not to this!
Easy it were to do, but ill, being done,
  If I should sell white virtue for a kiss,
And break the bright glass of unstained faith
To burn for shame when our Lord Itfir saith,

### XXXIV

"'Yusuf, my Trusted!' By the living Lord,
  Whose lamp the sun is, seeing everywhere,
Too sore I pity thee! Too soon the word
  Of 'yea' would leap, if it were only fear
Which locks it in my lips: oh, let me go
And on some other day this might be so!"

### XXXV

"Nay, nay!" she cries: "for me is no to-morrow!
     Who, dying in a desert, puts aside
The water-skin? Who, holding cure of sorrow,
     Bears on with agony? When could betide
A better time than now, a surer spot?
What's wrought the Gods themselves will witness not!"

### XXXVI

"My God will witness!" quoth he, "and make know
     My Master." "Oh, thy Master!" brake in she,
"I have a herb of Nile, and, when cups flow,
     Crowned at the banquet, there shall some night be
A strange new savor in his wine:—and, then
Sleep on his eye, and ceasing from 'midst men."

### XXXVII

Backward thereat he drew, as when a snake
     From coralled jaws bares sudden fatal fangs;
But she, distempered, from her belt did take
     A knife: and, while with one fond hand she hangs
Hot on his neck, the other the blade kept
So pressed to the skin the scarlet blood outleapt.

### XXXVIII

And with wild eyes she spake: "My soul hath clung
     Too close to thine. Unkind! to cling in vain;
Mine ears have drunk the music of thy tongue
     Too long for life, except Love heals life's pain!
See! the fond dagger for my scorned blood yearns,
And drinks its first drop, where the bright point burns!

### XXXIX

"Deny me, and I drive this shining death
     Straight to the heart which thou contemnest so;
And when last love-sigh comes with latest breath,
     And o'er thy cruel hands the red streams flow,
My murdered body shall Lord Itfir see,
And the dread charge of this will light on thee!"

### XL

With eager grasp he clutched her wrist, and cried:
        "Great Asenath! have pity on us both!
From such mad frenzy turn thy steel aside.
        Too fair—too dear—to die! too—" She, not loath,
Deeming the boy relenting, sheathed her blade,
And with close-winding arms a warm chain made

### XLI

About his beating breast, and drew him down
        Against her mouth, and dragged 'nay! nay!' away
In such a cleaving kiss his sense did swoon,
        His tongue, shut in with honey, naught could say;
His eyes, meeting her eyes, such fierce flame took
They dropped their lids not to be lightning-strook.

### XLII

Then, while he sank back, will-less, on the silk,
        She rose, of triumph sure, and deftly drew
From her smooth shoulders,—brown and smooth as milk
        With palm-wine mixed—that scarf of purple hue
Veiling her bosom's splendors; this she bore,
Quick-tripping, to the niche beside the door,

### XLIII

Where, on tall pedestal, in pride of place,
        Sate Pasht the Cat, with orbs of green and gold;
And over those green eyes, and o'er the face
        That garment hath she draped, so that its fold
Hid the House-Goddess to her porphyry chin.
"Why doest thou this?" asks Yusuf. "If I sin—"

### XLIV

Answers glad Asenath—"it must not be
        That Pasht, whom every morn I straitly serve
With musk, and flowers, and prayers—great Pasht, should see;
        That Pasht, with those sharp eyes should know I swerve
From law:—for she would blab to Lords of Hell,
But what she does not spy she will not tell."

### XLV

Turning, she made to clip him; but he broke,
    Like the sun bursting through a shattered cloud,
Fierce from her arms: and, all alight, he spoke
    Angrily thus: "Take, too, thy skirt, and shroud
Yon stars that gaze upon us from God's sky!
Cover, with fine-wove webs, the angry eye


### XLVI

"Of dread Jehovah, watching everywhere!
    Bind His free winds, and bid them whisper naught!
Lay hand upon His lightnings, flashing clear
    And bribe them not to strike! Let there be brought
His thunders, muzzled, to thy bower; and win
Their awful voices to forgive our sin!


### XLVII

"Fear'st thou those stony eyes thou didst enfold,
    And shall not I my fathers' Lord fear more,
Whose glance none may shut out, Whose eyes behold
    All things in every place? Tempted full sore,
Lady of Egypt! was thy witless slave:
Now breaks he from thee, better faith to save!"


### XLVIII

With that he darted forth. And Asenath
    Reached at his waist-cloth, rending it atwain;
One portion in her wrathful hand she hath,
    One the fast-flying Yusuf doth retain;
While, in his speed, he flings back bolts and bars
Till, 'scaped, he stands under the mindful stars.

## Chapter V

# Buddhist Homily

The oldest Indian writings, the Vedas, and the somewhat later epics contain no true analogue of the Joseph and Potiphar's wife story; the theme first appears at a considerably later time, in Buddhist literature in the Pali dialect. Even if we accept the oldest possible date for the *Jatakas* or Buddhist birth tales—in which the story is first given in clear form—there still remains as much reason for believing that the Buddhist story is an adaptation of a tale imported from the Near East as that it derives from a lost Indian original. It is necessary to reiterate, however, that a historical connection between the Buddhist analogue and any of the older ones—the Egyptian folktale, the Biblical narrative or the classical legend—is quite hypothetical.

It of course resembles its sister stories, but it has distinctive markings traceable to local religious and cultural circumstances. The best-known Buddhist version, here given, forms a portion of the lore that accumulated around the great Indian emperor Asoka, who established Buddhism as a state religion in the third century B.C. It tells of his marriage to Tishya-rakshita, who thus becomes stepmother to Kunala, his son by a previous wife. Kunala's eyes are so beautiful that they light a fire of love in her heart. Thus, it is not his handsome form, as with Joseph, or his manly strength, as with Bata, or his devotion to a goddess at war with love, as with Hippolytus, that catches the step-mother's attention. Nevertheless, he is the object of a sexual passion which may be presumed to be all the more violent because of the fiancee (or wife) with whom he is provided in this story. Like the devoted Aricie introduced into Racine's adaptation of the classical drama, Kunala's fiancee is willing to share his exile; but, unlike Aricie, she is permitted to live in happiness with him when his ordeal is over. Thus, the Buddhist analogue has elements in common with the Biblical and the Moslem stories. A wholly novel element is the punishment of the townspeople along with the queen for their complicity in the blinding of Kunala.

The punishment of the youth—and here too the story differs from its analogues—is not meted out by the father, but rather without his knowledge by the stepmother. Consequently, the harsh later judgment passed on the queen by her husband is unmitigated. Even though the restored son pleads in her behalf, his forgiveness of her is not translated into judicial pardon, and she experiences an excruciating death by fire. Kunala's disposition to forgive his vicious stepmother is not in itself unique in the universal story. Even Yusuf in the *Koran* was inclined to feel some guilt in the matter. Hippolytus, too, was reluctant to accuse Phaedra until she first brought a charge against him. In two later medieval versions, we shall see the son either maintaining a perplexed silence for a time or winning pardon for the erring stepmother.

But Kunala's willingness to forgive is somewhat more central than in the other instances. It is based in the doctrine of *karma,* the Indian belief that one but acts out the destiny which his soul has earned in previous incarnations. As Kunala says:

> . . . in this world is the reward of one's deeds. How therefore can I describe that which I have suffered as the work of another? In time past, O great king, I have committed some sin. . . . In my heart there is nought but benevolence towards my mother, who commanded my eyes to be torn out.

He is nevertheless keenly aware of the moral wickedness of his stepmother's proposal, for the familiar Indian sexual tabu against the mother (a category that includes "the wife of a king, the wife of one's teacher, the wife of one's friend, the mother of one's wife, and one's own mother") is part and parcel of the Buddhist homily.

✙

The story of Kunala traveled eastward with Buddhism, and we find it being related by the famous Chinese traveler Hsuan Tsiang in his seventh-century account of the western countries. He reports passing a great stupa or memorial mound a hundred feet high in Ta-Ch'a-shi-la (the Indian Takshashila), which was erected by the emperor Asoka to commemorate the spot where the eyes of his son Ku-lang-na (Kunala) were put out. The blind who pray at this stupa are said to have their sight restored. Hsuan Tsiang then tells the story of Kunala from the Pali with but minor variations. Here the queen obtains from the sleeping Asoka not an ivory seal to authenticate her document but the emperor's teeth-bite, which serves as a signature. The blinded prince again recovers his vision, but by a slightly different stratagem: a holy man preaches a very moving sermon which causes the congregation to cry freely; their tears, collected first in individual vessels and later poured together in a golden cup, are used to wash out Ku-lang-na's eyes and miraculously bring sight back to them.

Donald Keene has pointed out an earlier and more completely Sinicized variant of the Kunala story in Chinese, but it is Hsuan Tsiang's version that was carried to Japan, where it appeared in the eleventh-century collection of tales, *Konjaku Monogatari*. The king here is apparently suspicious of the queen's complaint against her stepson; when he sends him to a far province in a sort of banishment, his motive seems to be to guarantee his safety from the vengeful queen. It was to be expected, of course, that the prince, instead of playing on the Indian *vina* or viol, would in the Japanese version play a *koto*.

Donald Keene cites various forms of the universal story in the medieval Noh drama and in the bourgeois puppet theater, Joruri, all of them deriving from the Kunala prototype in two main lines of descent. One of these, the story of Shuntokumaru, is given in an adaptation to the puppet theater of the eighteenth century. The somewhat bizarre character of this drama is in part due to the Joruri form. Ghosts, too, which are so prominent in Japanese mythology, play a leading role, as does the feudal code of honor inherited from the Samurai warrior class.

It is interesting to note, as the translator, Faubion Bowers, points out, that the play was banned from the Japanese stage in 1937 because it depicted a mother's unnatural love of her son. On the other hand, since the end of World War II, it has had wide popularity, presumably as a tragic account of an illicit passion, like Racine's *Phèdre,* with which indeed Donald Keene compares it. There is no mistaking the incest motif; Shuntoku's words are unambiguous:

> . . . it is forbidden for a man of virtue to marry a girl
> who even has the same surname as his. It is absurd for
> you to make love to me. You are my stepmother. . . .
> Shame on you, mother!

The play, however, presents some incongruities. If one takes as genuine the stepmother's avowal that she acted only to save the life of her stepson from his conniving half brother, all her previous exhibitions of passion for the boy seem fraudulent. Moreover, if she truly loved Shuntokumaru, her self-sacrifice to save him from death should not have been delayed until her own dying breath. It would seem as though the emotions of the drama have been somewhat compromised by a condition outside of it; namely, the demand of the eighteenth-century bourgeois theater that the evil mother be redeemed even if in death. Nevertheless, it is a significant fact that only this analogue and the classical drama assign a tragic role to the heroine.

Local variations in the details of the plot have their own interest. In the Kunala source story, the hero had a wife. In the Japanese play, as in Racine's *Phèdre,* he has a fiancee who inspires jealousy in the Lady Tamate. The punishment of the youth is not only blindness here, but also leprosy. Both, however, are curable, and the stepmother's salvation lies in the fact that her death will effect the cure. Thus, the motif of repentance which informs the Moslem parable and the motif of a tragic death which dominates the Greek play are brought together. This analogue is unique, however, in that it is Gappo, the father of Lady Tamate, who assumes the Potiphar role rather than her husband.

The subplot of rivalry for power between the half brothers also recalls the classical analogue, and it is to be seen again in the two medieval variants in the following chapter of this book.

# 9. "The Eyes of Kunala" (about fifth century A.D.)

Rendered into English by Winifred Stephens (n.d.–1944)
from the French translation, by Eugene Burnouf (1801–1852),
of the Pali original

[In the interest of focusing on the essential and thematic episode, I have omitted portions of the story as translated into English.
*Ed.*]

After King Asoka had set up the royal edicts, his wife Padma-
vati bore unto him a son. The child was beautiful to look upon
and his eyes shone with a radiant light. When the King heard
of his son's birth he was transported with joy, and he cried:
"Great is my delight, my heart is filled with infinite gladness.
The splendour of the Mauryas is at its zenith. Because I rule
according to the Law therefore is a son born unto me. May he
cause the Law to bud and to blossom." For this reason was the
child called Dharma-vivardhana, which being interpreted is
"expansion of the Law."

Then was the babe brought unto the King, who, gazing
upon him, was filled with rapture and exclaimed: "How pure
are the beautiful eyes of the child! They are like unto a lotus-
bloom in full flower."

Then said the King unto his ministers: "Unto what can
you liken the eyes of this child?"

"We know no man," they replied, "with eyes like his; but
in the Himavat, the King of Mountains, is a bird called kunala,
with eyes which resemble those of your son."

✥

"Let a kunala be brought," said the King. And straightway
a kunala was presented unto him. Having gazed long at the
eyes of the bird to see if there were any difference between
his eyes and those of his son, the King could observe none; and
so he said to his ministers: "The Prince's eyes are like unto the
eyes of the kunala, wherefore let him be called Kunala."

The young child was confided to the care of eight nurses:
two to give him the breast, two to give him milk to drink, two
to wash him, and two to play with him.

One day, when he was adorned with all his ornaments,
the King, holding him in his arms, began to gaze at him fondly.

Then he cried: "No, not one of my sons is so beautiful as
he. . . ."

When the Prince Kunala grew up there was given unto
him for a wife a young girl named Kanchana-mala.

On a day the King with his son went forth to the hermitage of Kukkuta. There Yasas, the Sthavira of the Assembly,
who was acquainted with five secret sciences, beheld Kunala
and saw that ere long he would lose his eyes. This he made
known unto the King.

"Wherefore shall this come to pass?" inquired the King.

"Because Kunala fails to do his duty."

"Kunala," said the King, "take heed to do all that the
Sthavira shall command thee."

Straightway, throwing himself at the feet of the Sthavira,
Kunala said: "My Lord, what commandest thou?"

"Be persuaded, O Kunala, that the eye is a perishable
thing." Then he added these words: "It is the source of a
thousand evils. Because they esteem it too highly many men
commit deeds which cause them unhappiness."

Kunula fell to meditating on this maxim, which was ever
in his mind. Henceforth he cared for nought save peace and
solitude. Seated in the heart of the palace in a lonely place, he
reflected how perishable is the source of sight and the sources
of all the senses.

On a day Tishya-rakshita, the chief wife of Asoka, passed
by and beheld Kunala, who was alone. Charmed by the beauty
of his eyes, she took him in her arms and said: "Beneath thy
ravishing glance, at the sight of thy beautiful form and thy
radiant eyes, my whole body burns like dry straw consumed by
a forest fire."

At these words Kunala, closing his ears with his hands,
replied: "Cease to utter such guilty words in the presence of a
son, for unto me you are as a mother. Renounce so perverse a
passion; such a love will lead you to Hell."

But Tishya-rakshita, finding that she could not seduce
him, said in wrath: "Since thou turnest away from me when,
transported with love, I offer myself unto thee, then know,
O foolish Prince, that not long hence thou shalt cease to live."

"O mother," replied Kunala, "liefer would I die while
persisting in my duty and remaining pure. I would not live

a life which should deserve the censure of honest folk and the scorn and condemnation of the wise, a life which, by closing against me the path to Heaven, would lead to death."

Henceforth Tishya-rakshita thought of nothing but how to injure Kunala.

It came to pass that the town of Takshasila, situated in the north and under the dominion of King Asoka, revolted. When he heard of the rebellion the King wished to go himself; but his ministers said unto him: "O King, send the Prince; he will bring back the town to its allegiance."

Wherefore the King, having summoned Kunala, spake unto him these words: "My beloved son, go thou to Takshasila, and subdue it."

"Yea, sire, I will go," replied Kunala.

✠

Then Asoka, having caused the town and the road to be decorated, and having sent away all the aged, the sick and the poor, went up into his chariot with his son, and departed out of Pataliputtra. Before returning to the city, when Asoka parted from his son in the way, he fell upon Kunala's neck, and, gazing at his eyes, he wept, saying: "Happy are those eyes, and happy is the mortal who may for ever behold the lotus-flower of the Prince's countenance."

But a Brahman, who was an astrologer, had prophesied that ere long Kunala would lose his sight. Wherefore King Asoka, who could never tire of looking upon his son's eyes, cried, when he had gazed upon them: "The eyes of the Prince are perfect; and the King's heart overflows with love for him. This day I contemplate the pure radiance of those eyes which shed happiness, and of those eyes which are destined to perish. The town whither thou goest shall be happy as Heaven itself when it beholdeth the Prince; but when he shall have lost his eyes, all hearts in that town shall be plunged in grief."

Soon the young Prince reached the neighbourhood of Takshasila. At the news of his approach, the inhabitants, having adorned the town and the highway as far out as two yojanas and a half, went forth to meet him, bearing in their hands vessels filled with precious stones. When they had arrived before him, with hands clasped as a sign of respect, they said: "It is not against the Prince or against King Asoka that

we have rebelled; but because wicked ministers came to op-
press us." Then Kunala in great pomp entered into the town
of Takshasila.

Meanwhile King Asoka had fallen a prey to a terrible
disease. Believing it to be incurable, he commanded that
Kunala should be brought unto him, for he was determined
to place him upon the throne. But Tishya-rakshita, having
heard the King's command, reflected: "If Kunala become king,
I shall be ruined." Wherefore she said to King Asoka: "I will
undertake to cure thee, but thou must forbid any doctor to
enter thy palace." The King did as Tishya-rakshita requested,
and she restored him to health.

When the King was cured of his malady he was full of
joy; and he asked Tishya-rakshita what he should do for her.
"What gift shall I give unto you?" he inquired.

"Let the King," she replied, "grant unto me royal power
for one week."

"And what shall become of me?" inquired the King.

"At the end of one week the King shall resume his power."

So Asoka gave unto Tishya-rakshita royal power for one
week.

The first thought of the Queen was to satisfy her hatred of
Kunala. In the King's name she wrote a letter commanding
the inhabitants of Takshasila to tear out Kunala's eyes. And
she added these words: "For Asoka, a king who is strong and
violent, hath commanded the inhabitants of Takshasila to tear
out the eyes of this enemy who is a disgrace to the house of
the Mauryas."

Whenever King Asoka issued an order which was to be
executed promptly he sealed it with an ivory seal. Tishya-
rakshita said: "I will seal this letter with the ivory seal while
the King is asleep." So she went to Asoka. But just at that
moment the King awaked in terror.

"What troubleth the King?" asked the Queen.

"I have just dreamed a sad dream," he replied. "I beheld
two vultures about to tear out the eyes of Kunala."

"That means happiness for the Prince," said the Queen.

Then a second time the King awaked in terror. "O Queen,"
he said, "I have just dreamed a sad dream."

"What dream?" inquired the Queen.

"I saw Kunala entering the city with long hair, long nails, and a long beard."

"That means happiness for the Prince," cried the Queen.

At length, the King having again fallen asleep, Tishyarakshita sealed her letter with the ivory seal and despatched it to the town of Takshasila.

Meanwhile the King in a dream beheld his teeth falling from his mouth. As soon as the day dawned, he called the soothsayers and asked them the meaning of his dreams.

"O King," replied the soothsayers, "he who dreams such dreams, he who in his sleep beholdeth his teeth decay and fall from his mouth will behold his son bereft of his eyes and will hear of his death."

At these words King Asoka, rising hastily from his seat, and turning, with hands clasped as a sign of reverence, towards the four quarters of the horizon, began to implore the Divinity, uttering these words: "May the Divinity who is benevolent for the Preceptor, for the Law, and for the Assembly, which is the first among all assemblies, may the Rishis who are the first in the world protect our son Kunala."

Meanwhile the Queen's letter had reached Takshasila. When they read this missive the inhabitants of Takshasila, both of the town and of the outlying country, who were rejoiced at the many virtues of Kunala, dared not to make known unto him the cruel order contained in the letter. But, after having reflected long, they said: "The King is violent; he is passionate by nature. If he pardoneth not his own son, then most certainly will he not spare us. He who is capable of nourishing hatred towards so peaceful a Prince, who lives the life of a solitary, whose only desire is that all creatures may be fed, what will he feel towards us?"

At length they resolved to tell Kunala and to give him the letter. Kunala, having read it, cried: "The order must be obeyed; do what is commanded."

Then were the executioners brought and told to put out Kunala's eyes. But, folding their hands as a sign of respect, they cried: "We dare not. And why? Because only he who is mad enough to rob the moon, the star of night, of its brightness can tear the eyes from your countenance."

Then the Prince took the ornaments from his head and said: "Do your duty as a reward for this gift."

But they refused, saying: "Such a deed would be the cause of great misfortune."

Then there came forth a man who was deformed and covered with eighteen spots of a repulsive colour, who offered to tear out the eyes of the Prince. He was brought to Kunala.

At that moment there came into the young man's mind the words of the Sthaviras, and recalling them he said: "It was because they foresaw this misfortune that the sages who know the truth said: "Behold how fleeting is this world, and how varying is the lot of man." Yea, good friends and virtuous, careful of my advantage and desirous of my happiness were those great-hearted sages, and free from passion were those who taught me that Law. When I think on the frailty of all things, when I reflect on the counsels of my masters, I cease to tremble, my friends, at the thought of this suffering, for I know that my eyes are things which perish."

Then turning to the man, he said: "Come, take out one eye and put it in my hand."

The torturer began to do his work; and at that moment thousands of men lifted up their voices in lamentation, wailing: "Ah! Woe! Misery! Misfortune!"

"Lo! the moon, pure in splendour, falleth from heaven; a beautiful lotus-flower is torn from the cluster of white nymphaeas."

While the people thus lamented, the eye of Kunala was torn from him and he received it in his hand, saying: "Why, coarse sphere of flesh, dost thou no longer behold the forms of earth? How mistaken and how guilty are those who are bound to thee and say, 'this is I.' Those who, seriously reflecting, come to recognise in thee an organ, elusive like a ball, pure but dependent, those alone shall be beyond the reach of misfortune."

While the Prince thus meditated on the instability of all beings he was rewarded by attaining the state of Srota-apatti* in the eyes of the assembled crowd.

Then Kunala, beholding truths, said to the torturer: "Take out the other eye."

The man obeyed and placed the eye in the hand of the Prince.

At that moment, Kunala, who had just lost the eyes of

* This is the first stage in the Buddhist path to Nirvana.

the flesh but in whom the eyes of knowledge were purified, uttered these words: "The eye of the flesh, which eludeth the grasp, hath been taken from me; but I have acquired the perfect and irreproachable eyes of wisdom. If I am forsaken by the King, I become the son of the great-hearted King of the Law, who names me his child.

"If I am fallen from supreme greatness, which brings with it so much vexation and grief, I have acquired the sovereignty of the Law, which destroyeth grief and sorrow."

Not long afterwards Kunala knew that his suffering was the work not of his father Asoka, but of the intrigues of Tishya-rakshita. At this news he said: "May the Queen Tishya-rakshita, who hath been the means of securing me so great an advantage, continue long in happiness, life, and power."

Meanwhile, Kanchana-mala heard that the eyes of her husband, Kunala, had been put out. Straightway, asserting her wifely right, she rushed through the crowd in search of Kunala; and she found him sightless and bleeding. Beholding him thus, she swooned and fell to the ground. In haste the bystanders brought water and endeavoured to restore her. When she began to come to herself, weeping bitterly she cried out: "The gaze of those beautiful eyes, which I so dearly loved, was all my happiness. Now that they are cast on the ground and bereft of sight, I feel that I shall die."

Then Kunala, wishing to console his wife, spoke thus: "Dry thy tears; it behoveth thee not to give way to grief. Every man receiveth the reward of the deeds he hath committed in this world." And he uttered this saying: "Recognising this world to be the fruit of actions, and beholding creatures condemned to misfortune, knowing men to be created in order that their dear ones may be torn from them, my beloved, thou oughtest not to weep."

Thereupon Kunala and his wife went forth from Takshasila. From the moment of his conception the Prince's body had been very delicate. Wherefore he was unable to exercise any trade; he knew only how to sing and how to play the vina.* So he went about begging his bread and sharing with his wife that which he received.

Kanchana-mala and the Prince retraced their steps along the road which led to Pataliputtra. Having arrived in the city,

* The Viol.

they thought it their duty to return to the abode of Asoka. But the porter refused them admittance. They were, however, taken to the shed in which the King kept his chariots. At break of day Kunala touched his vina and began to sing how his eyes had been put out and how the vision of truth had appeared unto him. And he uttered these words:

"The sage, who by the pure flame of knowledge beholdeth the eye and the other senses, is freed from the law of transmigration.

"If thy mind, given up to sin, be tormented by the sorrows of existence, and if thou desirest happiness in this world, hasten to renounce for ever the things of sense."

King Asoka heard the Prince's song; and he said joyfully: "It is for me that Kunala sings and plays on the vina, which I have not heard for so long. The Prince hath returned to my dwelling, but he wishes to see no one."

Then, calling one of his guards, the King said unto him: "Does not this singing sound unto you like the singing of Kunala? It seemeth as if he were in trouble. That voice hath profoundly moved my soul. I am as an elephant, who having lost her young has just heard its voice. Go therefore and bring Kunala unto me."

Straightway the guard went to the place where the chariots were kept. There he found Kunala, eyeless and with his body parched by sun and wind. Failing to recognise him, the guard returned to Asoka and said: "O King, this is not Kunala; it is a blind beggar who with his wife is in the place where are kept the King's chariots."

Then was the King greatly troubled, and he thought: "Behold the realisation of my bad dreams; in sooth, this is Kunala, whose eyes have been torn out." And Asoka uttered these words: "According to the omens which formerly appeared unto me in a dream, there is no longer any doubt that Kunala hath been bereft of his eyes."

Bursting into tears he cried: "Hasten to bring this beggar into my presence; for my heart cannot rest for thinking of the misfortune which may have fallen upon my son."

The guard, having returned to the place of chariots, said to Kunala: "Whose son art thou, and what is thy name?"

"Asoka," replied Kunala, "the king who enhanceth the glory of the Mauryas, beneath whose sway the whole earth doth bow in obedience, that king is my father, and my name is Kunala. But to-day am I the son of the Buddha, that descendant of the sun race, who hath established the Law."

Straightway Kunala was led with his wife into the presence of King Asoka.

Beholding Kunala eyeless, his body parched by sun and wind, clothed in a wretched garment discoloured by the rain during his journey, the King, being ignorant of the crime which had been committed, gazed many times at his son, but failed to recognise him. Seeing before him nought but the form of a man, he said: "Art thou Kunala?"

"Yea," replied the Prince, "I am Kunala."

At these words the King swooned and fell to the ground. Thus saith the sacred word:

"Beholding the countenance of Kunala, from which the eyes had been torn out, King Asoka, distracted with grief, fell upon the ground, consumed with the fire of anguish at the sight of his son's misfortune."

Water was thrown over the King; he was raised and placed upon his throne. When he had come to himself, he clasped his son in his arms. Thus saith the sacred word:

"After a few moments, the King, having regained consciousness, threw his arms around his son's neck; and, ofttimes caressing the countenance of Kunala, he lifted up his voice in complaints mingled with his sobs: 'Formerly, at the sight of those eyes, like unto those of the kunala, I called my son Kunala; to-day, now that those eyes are extinguished, how can I continue to call him by that name?'"

Then he said:

"Tell me, tell me, my beloved son, how this countenance with the beautiful eyes hath been bereft of its light and hath become like unto the heavens robbed of their splendour by the waning of the moon?

"The heart of that man is pitiless, O my son, who, being impelled by the hatred of the unrighteous for the righteous who feel no hatred, hath destroyed the eyes of the best of beings, of the image of the Solitary himself. This is a cruel deed which for me is the source of many evils.

"Speak to me and delay not, O thou of the beautiful countenance. Consumed with grief at the loss of thine eyes, my body perisheth like unto a forest devoured by the lightning of the Nagas."

Then Kunala, having thrown himself at his father's feet, spoke unto him thus:

"O King, thou must not sorrow thus over an event which is past. Hast thou not heard the words of the Solitary, who saith that not even the Jinas themselves, any more than the Pratyeka Buddhas,* may escape from the inevitable influence of deeds?

"Like unto ordinary men they reap the fruit of the actions they have committed here below; in this world is the reward of one's deeds. How therefore can I describe that which I have suffered as the work of another? In time past, O great King, I have committed some sin, and under the influence of this sin have I returned to this world, I whose eyes have been the cause of my misfortune.

"Sword, lightning, fire, poison, birds, nothing can wound the spirit, which is unchangeable by nature; it is on the body, wherein the spirit resides, that the cruel sorrows fall which seem to devour the body as a victim."

But Asoka, with grief-racked heart, continued thus: "Who hath bereft my son of his eyes? Who in order to commit this crime hath risked the loss of so great a treasure as life? Into my heart, consumed by the fire of sorrow, wrath enters. Tell me quickly, O my son, upon whom chastisement must descend."

At length the King learned that the crime was the work of Tishya-rakshita. Straightway he had the Queen summoned; and when she was come he said unto her: "Wherefore, O cruel woman, does the earth not open and engulf thee? Beneath the sword or the axe will I cause thy head to fall. I renounce thee, woman covered with crime. Unjust soul, I renounce thee as the sage renounceth fortune."

Then, gazing upon her with a countenance inflamed with the fire of wrath, he added: "Wherefore should I not break her limbs in pieces after tearing out her eyes with my sharp nails? Wherefore should I not hang her alive from the gallows? Wherefore should I not cut off her nose? Wherefore should I not take out her tongue with a razor or cause her to die by poison?"

* Those who had attained the sixth stage in the path of knowledge, to whom there remained only one more stage, that of the perfect Buddha.

Such were the tortures with which Tishya-rakshita was threatened by the King of Men.

Hearing these words, Kunala the magnanimous, filled with compassion, said to his father: "It would be dishonourable for thee to put to death Tishya-rakshita. Respect and honour, but do not slay a woman. There is indeed no reward greater than that of magnanimity. Patience, my Lord, hath been celebrated by the Sugata."*

Then, throwing himself again at the feet of the King, the Prince addressed to his father these words of truth:

"O King, I feel no pain; and despite the cruelty I have suffered, the fire of wrath burneth not within me. In my heart there is nought but benevolence towards my mother, who commanded my eyes to be torn out.

"In order to prove the truth of these words, may my eyes now become as they were formerly."

Hardly had he uttered these words when in the countenance of Kunala his eyes appeared with all their former brilliance.

Nevertheless King Asoka, enraged against Tishya-rakshita, caused her to be thrown into the place of torture, where she died by fire; and all the inhabitants of Takshasila Asoka caused to be massacred.

Then doubt arose in the minds of the Religious; and thus did they question the venerable Sthavira Upagupta, who setteth all doubts at rest: "What deed had Kunala done for his eyes to be put out?"

The Sthavira made answer:

"Attend, O venerable monks. Once in times past, at Benares, was there a certain hunter who went up into the Himavat, there to slay wild beasts. One day when he was on the mountain, in the depths of a cavern he came upon five hundred gazelles herding together; and he caught them all in a net. Then he reflected: 'If I kill them, what shall I do with so much meat?' Wherefore he put out the eyes of the gazelles. And the beasts, being unable to see, could not escape. Thus by his hand were the eyes put out of many hundred gazelles.

"What think ye of that, O monks? This hunter was Kunala himself. Because he put out the eyes of many hundred gazelles, as the recompense of this deed, he hath suffered

* "Sugata" and "Tathagata" are synonymous and mean "the Master."

through many hundred thousand years the torments of Hell. Then, in order to complete the expiation of his sin, his eyes have been put out during five hundred human existences. But what deed had he done to deserve rebirth in a royal family, a beautiful form, and the knowledge of the sacred truths? Hearken, O venerable monks:

"Formerly, in times past, when the life of a man was forty-four thousand years, there appeared in the world a perfect Buddha, whose name was Krakuchchhanda. When he had fulfilled all the duties of a Buddha, he entered the domain of Nirvana, wherein remaineth nought of the elements of existence. A king named Asoka* caused to be made for him a Stupa of four kinds of precious stones. But after the death of Asoka his throne was occupied by a sovereign who knew not the Sacred Truth. The precious stones of the Stupa were stolen by thieves, who left nothing but the wood and earth. The people, having assembled in this place, beheld the ruins of the Stupa and wept. Now among the people was the son of a master craftsman. This young man asked: 'Wherefore do the people weep?' Then the people answered: 'The Stupa of Krakuchchhanda the Buddha was made of four kinds of precious stones; now behold, it is destroyed.'—The young man rebuilt it.

"There had been formerly in this place a statue of the perfect Buddha Krakuchchhanda, which was life size. It also had been destroyed. The young man restored the statue likewise and offered up this prayer: 'May my gift be acceptable in the eyes of such a master as Krakuchchhanda! May I not be displeasing unto him!'

"What think ye of that, O venerable monks? The son of the master craftsman was Kunala himself. He it was who in those days restored the Stupa of Krakuchchhanda, and as a reward for this deed was he born in an illustrious family. Because he restored the statue of the Buddha, therefore was he born beautiful. Because he uttered the prayer we have repeated unto you, therefore was it granted unto him to please so great a master as Sakya-muni, the perfect Buddha, to whom Kunala was acceptable, therefore unto Kunala was it given to know the sacred truth.

* An earlier king, not the father of Kunala. This Asoka is said to have lived one hundred years after the Buddha.

# 10. *Gappo and His Daughter Tsuji (1773)*
## by Suga Sensuke

Translated by Faubion Bowers (1917–  )

[The chanter (or MUSIC) helps to carry forward the action by alternately narrating in the third person and speaking lines of the puppets. *Ed.*]

### CHARACTERS

GAPPO
O-TSUJI (TAMATE GOZEN), *his daughter*
O-TOKU, *his wife*
SHUNTOKUMARU, *Tamate Gozen's stepson*
PRINCESS ASAKA, *Shuntokumaru's fiancée*
IRIHEI, *Tamate Gozen's footman*
MUSIC

Gappo ga Tsuji *tells the story of Gappo who renounced his samurai life, became a priest, and retired to the country with his wife, O-Toku. Their only daughter, O-Tsuji, married one of the ruling lords of the country, and her name became Tamate Gozen, Her Ladyship Tamate. As she was only nineteen, she apparently fell in love with the younger of her two handsome stepsons—partly due to her youth, and partly due to her lack of attraction towards her aged husband. In feudal Japan, the difference between a stepson and a true son was not recognized; thus Tamate's love was technically incestuous.*

*Jiromaru (the older stepson) wished to usurp the power of the house by killing his brother, Shuntokumaru (Tamate's beloved). To save him from death, Tamate gave him a strange potion made from a poisonous abalone. Disfigured and leprous, he flees the house with his sweetheart, the Princess Asaka, and goes to Gappo's retreat in the country.*

*As the play opens, Gappo and his wife are seen offering services for their daughter, who after the scandal of making love to her stepson is considered dead.*

MUSIC: "O-Toku offers a cup of water before the family altar. She prays for their daughter's repose in the other world. She keeps back her tears. The toll of the evening bell comes within hearing.

"Lady Tamate easily finds her way along the road in the night and in the path of love. She seeks Shuntokumaru. Disguised, with her face hidden, she stands at the familiar gate of her parents' home.
"A small voice is heard from outside the gate."

TAMATE: Mother! Mother!

MUSIC: "Gappo is certain he has heard his daughter's voice."

GAPPO: Is my daughter not dead? Has she not yet been killed for her sin?

MUSIC: "Chanting, 'Save us, merciful Buddha,' he rises to his feet; but remembering his wife, he looks back. She has not heard their daughter's voice. He then feigns ignorance."

TAMATE: Open the gate, please. Mother! Mother!

[She kneels at the gate and waits.]

MUSIC: "O-Toku at last hears the voice."

TOKU: Gappo, did you speak?

GAPPO: No, I have said nothing.

TOKU: But I was certain. . . .

GAPPO: You are mistaken!

TOKU: I may have misheard, but I thought I heard our daughter's voice.

MUSIC: "Tamate wonders and rises as she hears her mother's voice."

TAMATE: If that is my mother's voice, then please open the gate. Mother, Tsuji, your daughter, has come home.

TOKU: Our daughter has come back! Could I be dreaming? I am coming—wait a moment.

MUSIC: "She rushes to the gate when Gappo takes her by the sleeve and holds her."

GAPPO: Don't speak of our daughter. I don't know whether she actually gave herself to her stepson or not, but at best she misconducted herself and left her husband's house. Takayasu, her husband, ought to have killed such an evil woman. I wonder how she has lived out until today. Why has she come here? Although we prohibited our daughter from telling her husband of our straitened circumstances, he has helped us in every way. For that reason we have been able to survive up to now. We two owe him a great debt. However, our daughter deceived him and made illicit love to his son. Even if she has returned, I'll not let her cross our threshold nor let her touch the gate. She must be dead! Surely she has been killed! Do you think it's our real daughter that has spoken now? It is a fox or a badger in human form. Were it our daughter, then it must be her ghost. The dead having a close tie with one is a fearsome thing. You must not unbolt the gate. I say now, you must not.

Toku: Even were it a fox, a badger or a ghost, I should like to see our daughter's face once again. Even if it is a terrible thing and I were to swoon in fright, I will be happy only if I see her face once more.

music: "The mother would rather see her daughter again than live."

toku: I should like to glance at her, for one moment, please.

music: "She thrusts Gappo away and goes toward the door, but he again stops her."

gappo: You heard me. Don't you understand? If it were really our daughter, I should have to kill her. Out of my paternal love and my obligation to Takayasu, I should have to punish her for her sin. Although I am now a priest, I cannot permit so vile a creature to live.

toku: Oh, for God's mercy.

gappo: Now, I must stop you. I hate doing so, but you must not open the gate.

music: "Gappo does not shed tears, but his daughter and wife understand his mind. Unable to see her parents, Tamate weeps. She brushes her tears away and puts her mouth to the gate."

TAMATE: It is natural for you to be angry, Father. I have a reason for it, but I must not let others hear my explanation. Open the gate, please.

MUSIC: "She asks them to open the gate in a tearful voice when her mother speaks."

TOKU: Have you heard, Gappo? She has a reason. Please listen to her. If you regard her as a ghost, not as our daughter, we can let her in without reservation. Please do as I say.

MUSIC: "As she speaks, Gappo relents."

GAPPO: Very well. Since it is merely her departed soul, we need not hesitate because of a code.

TOKU: Shall we call it in?

GAPPO: Call the ghost in and offer it rice and tea.—I mean—place the food upon the altar for the dead.

TOKU: I am glad you are persuaded. I will open the gate.

MUSIC: "She loses no time in going to the gate."

TAMATE: Mother.

TOKU: My precious daughter.

MUSIC: "She touches her daughter to make sure that she is really alive."

TOKU: I can hardly believe my eyes. It is neither a fox, badger, nor a ghost. How fortunate that you are alive. Not knowing, I have spent my days and nights in tears. How strange that you returned this very night, while we were offering a million prayers to you. I wonder if it is all a dream. If it is, I hope I will never be awakened.

MUSIC: "The mother embraces her daughter repeatedly and sheds tears of joy. Gappo wants to see his daughter, but from his deep sense of obligation he faces the other way."

TOKU: I have so much to say and hear. Rumor has it that you fell in love with Shuntokumaru and fled from the mansion. People speak ill of you, as if you had committed adultery.

However, I, your mother, am certain that you have not done such a thing. I know it is a false report. It is a lie, isn't it? Isn't it a lie?

MUSIC: "Touched by her mother's kindness in regarding it as false report, Lady Tamate is embarrassed."

TAMATE: Thank you for your kind words, Mother, but as fate would have it, I have such a feeling for him.

MUSIC: "Even when I am asleep, Shuntoku does not leave my mind. I long for him so strongly that I am forced to confess my heart openly. The colder his answer to me, the more do I love him. I hope you will aid me in finding him. Let me marry as man and wife legally. Think of your mother's love for me. I place my hands together and plead with you to comply with my request.

"She places her hands together as if in prayer and urges her mother to comply.

"Her mother is revolted by her words, and can only stare at her. Meanwhile, her father angrily brings a sword from the inner room."

GAPPO: You insect! Fie on you. Now listen. I will tell you of my father, Aoto Saemon Fujitsuna, who was a favorite with Lord Saimyoji Tokiyori at Kamakura, and called the model of men. Thanks to him, I rose high in the world. I was admitted to the rank of lord and worked assiduously. But when the present Lord Saganyudo succeeded his father, I was slandered by his sycophants. I renounced his service and became without employment. More than twenty years have passed since I retired from the world and became a priest. However, I have kept my integrity just as my father would have done. How could I have had such an immoral and beastly woman as you for a child? Think of your indebtedness to Takayasu. You were a lady's maid, but after the death of his wife, he kindly took interest in you and allowed you to become his second wife. Although he must have wanted to kill you, he has suppressed his emotion and intentionally saved your life because of his feeling towards us, your parents. If you appreciate his kindness and have even a spark of shame, you should be able to give up your love—no matter how deeply you may desire. I heard you say you want to become Shuntoku's wife and asked your mother's permission. How could you dare say such a thing? Your husband has spared your life because of his obligations, but I shall have to kill you out of my obligation to him. Be prepared for death! I will kill you!

MUSIC: "He loosens his sword but his wife clings to him."

TOKU: Here, here, Gappo! Wait, you are mistaken.

GAPPO: Why am I mistaken?

TOKU: He has spared our daughter for mercy's sake. Even if you kill her, you will not repay your obligation to him, will you?

GAPPO: Yes and no.

TOKU: Well, now our duty is to dissuade her from becoming Shuntokumaru's wife and let her become a nun instead. Thus, she will be exonerated, no matter how grave her crime may have been.

GAPPO: But . . .

TOKU: If she retires from the worldly life, she'll be as good as dead; and we will have fulfilled our duty towards her husband, our benefactor.

MUSIC: "She soothes her husband, and draws near to her daughter."

TOKU: My dear daughter, as you heard just now, your love will never succeed. Resign yourself and become a nun.

MUSIC: "You are beautiful and young. It is hard for me as your mother to urge you to cut your hair and take the vows, but I only want to save your life.

"She clings to her daughter and weeps that things have come to such a pass. Her daughter jumps back and changes color."

TAMATE: Oh, don't talk nonsense, mother. I hate the thought of becoming a nun. Why should I cut such fine black hair and renounce the world?

MUSIC: "Now I'll change my coiffure into the style worn in the gay quarters. When I meet Shuntokumaru again, then he'll love me. Hearing this, her father loses patience."

GAPPO: You see, there is no good in her. Now, I can restrain myself no longer.

MUSIC: "The father holds himself ready to kill her. Her mother frantically looks to find a way to save her."

TOKU: It is no wonder that you are angry with her. Let me talk to her for a while. I will make her change her mind and give him up.

GAPPO: Well, then, are you going to persuade her?

TAMATE: Oh, no. I can't be persuaded. I won't give him up.

GAPPO: What a thing you say, you fool!

TOKU: Gappo, we've long been in matrimonial harmony and this is my earnest request of you.

GAPPO: I don't want to save her life, but since you are her mother, I shall have to comply.

MUSIC: "At his wife's insistence, he goes to the inner room without casting a backward glance at them. The mother pulls her stubborn daughter's hand and forcibly takes her daughter to the dressing-room."

[Irihei, the footman, loyal to his young mistress Tamate, appears looking for her. He finds her sandal outside the door and she is inside. He hides himself and waits to see if he will be needed.]

"The blind Shuntokumaru, with Princess Asaka holding his hand is led into the room."

SHUNTOKU: Asaka, if my stepmother sees me in this condition, blind and disfigured, then she will lose her love for me. Lead me to her.

MUSIC: "Just then Lady Tamate rushes out of the dressing-room."

TAMATE: Oh, it has been so long since I saw you last, dear Shuntoku. I am happy you are here.

SHUNTOKU: I recognize your voice, Mother. Why have you come here?

TAMATE: I have taken so much trouble to see you again.

MUSIC: "She clings to him. He disengages himself from her grasp."

SHUNTOKU: Don't, Mother. As I told you in the mansion, it is forbidden for a man of virtue to marry a girl who even has the same surname as his. It is absurd for you to make love to me. You are my stepmother. To make matters worse, I have lost my eyesight and have become disfigured by leprosy. Don't you see my miserable condition? Are you not revolted by my face? Shame on you, Mother!

MUSIC: "He sheds tears and reproaches his stepmother."

TAMATE: Don't say such a silly thing. I could never feel other than love for you. It is because of me you are suffering from such a dreadful disease.

MUSIC: "She wants him to love her. How desperate is her love for him. From the Bay of Ashi as far as Naniwa she has pursued him. 'Please love me.'

"She clings to his sleeve, but Shuntokumaru again thrusts her away."

SHUNTOKU: Tell me, mother! Why was my accursed disease caused by you?

MUSIC: "He wants to hear the reason."

TAMATE: Last November I secretly gave you poisoned rice-wine.

ALL: What?

TAMATE: It had the miraculous power of causing a leprous disfiguration. There were two bottles, I drank the ordinary, but poured the poisoned one into your cup. I wanted to disfigure your face so that Princess Asaka would no longer love you. To that extent I have tried to succeed in my love for you.

SHUNTOKU: I am sorry to hear such a terrible thing.

TAMATE: You thought it was caused by some sin in a previous existence; so you left the mansion. Since then I have sought everywhere for you.

MUSIC: "She always keeps the abalone shell from which he drank the poison."

TAMATE: I love you from the bottom of my heart, though I'm afraid I am not worthy of being your stepmother. Please give in to me!

MUSIC: "She prostrates herself beside him and asks for his sympathy. Shuntokumaru is horrified, but since she is his stepmother, he endures the mortification. Asaka loses her temper."

ASAKA: How cruel you are! Why have you disfigured his noble face? It's horrible that you should fall in love with your stepson. Now you must restore him to health. How cruel you are!

[Irihei rushes in.]

IRIHEI: Don't be silly, madam! How can you do such a thing? Even if you did not give birth to Shuntokumaru, you are still his stepmother. It is against the laws of nature to make love to one's son. Such a thing could be done only by animals. He has a fiancée, named Asaka. You have driven him from the house by your advances. Fie, for shame! I beg you to give up this insane love.

MUSIC: "Paying no attention to his warning, Tamate rises to her feet."

TAMATE: Now that I am so deeply in love with him, no one can reason with me. Now I will take Shuntoku with me anywhere. I will succeed in my love for him, even if I die. If anyone interferes he will regret it.

MUSIC: "She leaps on Shuntoku and takes him by the hand. Gappo overhearing this is beside himself in rage. He rushes and stabs his daughter."

GAPPO: I who have not even killed a fly in twenty years, have killed my own flesh and blood, vile daughter! Now die!

TOKU: Merciful heaven! Oh, my beloved daughter!

TAMATE: It is no wonder you are angry with me and hate me, but I've a deep reason behind my actions. Before I die, let me tell you the story.

MUSIC: "Her breathing is painful to her."

TAMATE: Jiromaru, my husband's son by his concubine, did not want to let the legitimate but younger son, Shuntoku, succeed to the family fortune, so he plotted with Tsuboi Heima and attempted to kill the rightful heir. Knowing Shuntoku would be killed, I made love to him and poisoned him to drive him away from the mansion. All only to save his life.

ALL: Truthfully?

TAMATE: I have this abalone cup, which will prove my innocence. I am afraid my husband regards me as an immoral woman and an adulteress. I regret that he will not know the truth before I die.

MUSIC: "She laments, but her father still questions her closely."

GAPPO: If you knew so much about Jiromaru's evil doings, why didn't you tell Takayasu? If you had done so, Shuntoku would not have suffered from the accursed disease and you would not have needed to make illicit love to him. Even if you reply cleverly, I will not be fooled by a trumped-up excuse.

TAMATE: If I had told such to him, he would have forced Jiromaru to commit harakiri, or would have killed him by his own hand even. Though he is a wicked man, he too is still my stepson.

MUSIC: "I have wanted to save both my stepsons at the risk of my life. I am their mother."

GAPPO: If you truly accepted your responsibilities as a mother, why did you run after Shuntoku after he fled from the mansion?

TAMATE: If I had not seen him again, throughout all his life he could not be cured of his affliction.

MUSIC: "Hearing her words, Irihei comes forward."

IRIHEI: Do you mean to say that he cannot be restored to health unless you are with him?

TAMATE: I confessed the circumstances to the druggist when I asked him to make the poisoned rice-wine. I also asked him to tell me in detail of the antidotes. Hereditary leprosy is hopeless, but the disease caused by poison can be cured if the afflicted drinks the life-blood of the liver of a woman who has been born at the hour, on the day and in the month of the year of the Tiger. But it must be drunk from the vessel in which the poison has been put. So I have carried this abalone shell about looking for him. Now I have spoken my mind. Are your doubts about me dispelled?

MUSIC: "Gappo draws close to her."

TAMATE: Are your doubts dispelled, Father?

GAPPO: Yes, yes, yes! Oh, my daughter, forgive me. Not only have I cursed you but have taken your life by my own hand. This done by your very father. Pardon me! Forgive me!

MUSIC: "Asking for her forgiveness, he prostrates himself and sheds tears of regret. Shuntokumaru blindly gropes his way towards her."

SHUNTOKU: I cannot thank you enough for your kindness.

MUSIC: "He bows low to her. Asaka approaches her."

ASAKA: I have not up to now understood you. I have looked down on you and hated you. Please forgive me.

IRIHEI: Although you ought to be called the model of womanhood, I'm sorry you've been falsely charged and now have to die.

ALL: Poor Tamate!

TAMATE: Now, now, Father, take the life-blood of my liver and give it to him with this shell. Act quickly, before I die.

GAPPO: At first I hated her so I could stab her, but now I feel such pity for her that I cannot touch the sword to her. Irihei, you are young, please take my place.

IRIHEI: I cannot take the blood of one who has so cared for my master. Please excuse me. I will do anything but this.

TAMATE: Then I will do it myself.

MUSIC: "She grasps her dagger with the point downward."

GAPPO: Wait a moment, my dear daughter. This is your last moment. I will offer prayers a million times and surround you with the protection of a rosary. Then you will breathe your last peacefully. Let me say a service for you.

MUSIC: "So saying, he counts his beads. Tamate holds herself ready to die. She draws Shuntokumaru near to her and with the dagger in her right hand and the cup in her left hand draws blood from her liver. Thereupon her father frantically beats the bells of salvation. Her mother bursts into tears. Shuntokumaru respectfully drinks the blood. He drains his cup. Suddenly his eyes open and the disfiguration disappears. He looks at them. All are overjoyed that he has been restored."

ASAKA: Oh, at last he has recovered from the disease.

IRIHEI: The remedy worked.

ALL: Yes, indeed!

MUSIC: "They are filled with wonderment."

TAMATE: I am glad I have cleared myself of the dishonor. Now I can die without regret.

MUSIC: "Tamate is a model of womanhood and her mind is as clear as the moon reflected on the inlet. Indeed she is pure."

TAMATE: Tomorrow, I shall see the moon from the lotus flowers of heaven.

[She dies and all are weeping as the curtain is slowly drawn.]

## ✠ Chapter VI ✠
### Medieval Epic and Fabliau

The Moslem and the Buddhist variants of the story of Joseph and Potiphar's wife have brought us chronologically down to the Middle Ages. It was in that perod of history that the story had probably its widest circulation. Except for the Egyptian folktale, which had not yet been discovered, all of the analogues composed up to that time were somewhere or other being read or performed. Some not included in this book, such as the Irish legend preserved in The Book of Leinster, must be presumed to have been known at least in the British Isles. Many of these variants have since moved from the public forum into the scholar's study. John R. Reinhard, inquiring into medieval and Celtic popular literature, has come up in a single footnote with over a dozen analogues of the Joseph and Potiphar's wife story. Not all of the medieval variants are relatable to the several major categories that form the classification system of this book, but two which are, and which have a special interest, must be dealt with.

If indeed Firdausi is the author of the eleventh-century *Yusuf and Zulaikha* attributed to him, he is in the interesting position of having composed two different forms of the story of the Chaste Youth and the Lustful Stepmother. His great epic, the *Shahnama* or *Book of Kings,* in a portion of its sixty thousand couplets, gives one of the most carefully narrated accounts of the universal story. It occurs as an episode in the history of the reign of the great monarch Kai Kaus, for whom the famous hero Rustem fought the fatal combat with his son Sohrab. Siyawush, the "Joseph" character in the episode, has been brought up by Rustem. When he returns to the court of Kai Kaus, his father has taken a new wife, Sudaba. Her slowly ripening passion for the young knight gives us our story.

Siyawush had been mentioned in the old Zoroastrian scriptures upon which Firdausi drew in his proud recollection of the pre-Moslem history of Iran, but the precise source of this episode is not known. The possibility of a connection in the remote past to the Egyptian folktale cannot be entirely discounted. Firdausi could also have known any of the other variants we have been examining—the Biblical, the classical, the Buddhist—and certainly he knew the Koranic. (Despite his sentiment for the Zoroastrian past, he was at least nominally a Moslem, alternately using the Iranian word for God, *Khoda*, and the Semitic *Allah*.) In any case, the poet's homeland was a perfect milieu for the incestuous meeting of many of the analogues of the thematic story, including even the Sindibad cycle to be discussed.

An Indian scholar, C. J. Coyajee, has discovered an unusual parallel between a Chinese legend and the present episode from the *Shahnama*. The motif of the monstrous births in "Siyawush and Sudaba," which is not in any of the other analogues, also appears in Chinese popular literature. While there are various forms of magic in the other variants—from the Egyptian folktale to Thomas Mann's novels—there is nothing quite of the sort described in Firdausi's epic. Coyajee is not certain whether the motif of the monstrous births was carried from Iran to China or from China to Iran. The transmission, he believes, would have been effected in either case by the Saka race of the province of Seistan, a border people that figure prominently in the *Shahnama* stories about Rustem. Thus, we are finally left in doubt about the relation between this and the other analogues of the story here collected.

In Firdausi, as in several other variants, the dynastic struggle is a major factor—even though it does not exclude the factor of the queen's lust for her stepson. Indeed, even after the hero has been vindicated and has won forgiveness for the stepmother (as Kunala sought unsuccessfully to do), Subada, we learn, resumes her plotting against the prince. Like Hippolytus, Siyawush is averse to courts and harems, but unlike his Greek counterpart, he is not ascetically sworn to chastity. As a matter of fact, he later marries twice. The tabu against the mother, however, is rigidly maintained by the hero, who is fearful of offending the Zoroastrian god of light, Ahur-Mazda. The queen's stratagems, on the other hand, are associated with the malign influence of Ahriman, the god of darkness. Thus the dualistic world view of the ancient Persians is clearly projected. There is a more significant correspondence between this story and the Greek legend in the large role assigned to the nurse attendant upon the queen. Notice should also be taken of the striking resemblance between Firdausi's story and the *Book of Sindibad* frame story (below) in the opposition set up between the queen and the sages. In both, the young prince and the king incline towards the antifeminist view of the councilors despite the king's strong devotion to his harem favorite. Although the psychology of the queen's passion for the stepson is carefully defined, she does not manage to win as much of the reader's sympathy as either her classical or her Moslem counterpart. The ordeal through which the youth must pass to prove his innocence is here formal and actual. It is not merely a physical punishment or a spiritual ordeal, as with Bata, Joseph, and Kunala. In this respect, the *Shahnama* episode more closely resembles the other medieval variant with which it is here grouped.

✠

Perhaps the most popular version of the Joseph and Potiphar's wife narrative—certainly the most frequently related during the Middle Ages—is the frame story of the collection generally called *The Book of Sindibad*. Scholarship has not fixed the origin of this collection, but the name Sindibad (of course not to be confused with the Sinbad of Arabian Nights fame) is believed to be a corruption of the Indian name Sendebar, the sage in what has been hypothesized as the original tale. The characters generally appear to move in an Indian setting (although in this version Alcos is called King of Judea); this may prove, of course, only that the story was given its present shape in India. Some still incline to the view that *The Book of Sindibad* is merely an adaptation of the Kunala legend. If it be further accepted that the latter was itself an adaptation of the Egyptian folktale of Anpu and Bata, then the appearance of the Sindibad story in the Near East in the Middle Ages must be regarded as a return rather than an arrival. Needless to say, all this is conjecture.

The numerous forms of the story of Sindibad fall into what are called the "Eastern" and the "Western" categories, although these do not strictly correspond to "Asian" and "European." Obviously, both came into Europe out of Asia, and even the Eastern form was eventually translated into European languages. The story included here, from the Spanish *Book of the*

*Wiles of Women,* is a translation from a lost Arabic Eastern original. An eleventh-century Greek version called *Syntipas* (another corruption of the name Sendebar) is also derived from the Eastern branch of the family. The Western is represented by a twelfth-century Latin text called *Dolopathos* and, more popularly, by *The Seven Sages of Rome,* which exists in both Old French and Middle English. There the hero, named Florentine, is the son of the emperor Diocletian and is brought up under the tutelage of not only the one sage Sendebar but of seven wise men; hence, the name of the story. In some of the Eastern versions too (e.g., the present Spanish one), there is more than one sage, though Sindibad is also present.

The outstanding characteristic of this variant of the story of the Chaste Youth and the Lustful Stepmother is that the role of the youth is minimized and that of his advisors and advocates enlarged. Indeed, the sages play so important a part that one imagines the story to be a form of propaganda in their behalf. The issue really is whether the king is to be advised by them or by his queen. Not only is the Joseph and Potiphar's wife theme confined to the frame story, but the tales told in between concentrate on the sages' attempt to prove the perfidy of women, as in *The Arabian Nights* (into which the Sindibad cycle has therefore naturally been incorporated), and on the queen's counterattempt to prove the untrustworthiness of sages.

Whether this justifies the conclusion of an English medievalist that "in an age dedicated by the West to the worship of women we have here represented the unflattering estimate of womankind held by the East" is another matter. Sir Richard Burton roundly disagrees with this opinion and with the similar view of H. H. Wilson that these stories "originate in the feeling which has always pervaded the East unfavorable to the dignity of women." Burton believes rather that "they belong to a certain stage of civilization when the sexes are at war with each other; and they characterize chivalrous Europe as well as misogynous Asia; witness Jankins, clerk of Oxenforde; . . ." To be sure, the queen is a wicked and unregenerate creature who deserves the summary, if delayed, punishment that comes to her. But it is interesting to observe that in only three Eastern versions is she executed.

More to the point, the moral implications of the cycle of stories that make up the whole *Book of the Wiles of Women* have come to play a secondary role to their entertainment value. A good deal of the vulgarity of the medieval fabliau form had seeped into this story by the time it had made its way from India to Europe, and there is some moral confusion in it. Yet the Youth is still Chaste and loyal and, though he manifests a curious stupidity, his silence is at least explained, unlike that of Hippolytus. The queen, although a Lustful Stepmother, seems to be more concerned with her rights to the throne; politics and sex go hand in hand, as in the lost *Hippolytus* of Euripides and in Racine's *Phèdre,* as well as in the Japanese puppet play. The king plays his traditionally passive role, dispensing justice in a somewhat whimsical manner, as befits an Eastern potentate viewed from the West.

## 11. "Siyawush and Sudaba," *Shahnama*
## by Firdausi (932–1020?)
### Volume II paragraphs 6–14
### Translated (1906) by Arthur G. and Edmond Warner

[The subtitles are those of the translators. I have also retained one of their footnotes. All other footnotes are my own and are so marked. *Ed.*]

1. How Sudaba Fell In Love With Siyawush
2. How Siyawush Visited Sudaba
3. How Siyawush Visited the Bower the Second Time
4. How Siyawush Visited the Bower the Third Time
5. How Sudaba Beguiled Kaus
6. How Sudaba and a Sorceress Devised a Scheme
7. How Kaus Inquired Into the Matter of the Babes
8. How Siyawush Passed Through the Fire
9. How Siyawush Begged Sudaba's Life of His Father

### *1. How Sudaba Fell In Love With Siyawush*

Time passed, the Shah still joyed in Siyawush,
Till as they sat one day Sudaba entered,
Beheld the prince's face, and grew distraught.
Her heart throbbed, "she is wasted to a thread,"
Thou wouldst have said, "or ice before the fire."
She bade one go by stealth to him and say:—
"'Twould cause no wonder if thou shouldest visit
The royal bower anon."
                                    The envoy went,
But noble Siyawush was wroth and said:—
"Entice me not. I am no chamberer,
Or given to romances and intrigues."
        Another day at dawn Sudaba sought
The Shah and said: "O ruler of the host!
The sun and moon have never seen thy peer,
Or any like thy son. Let all the world
Rejoice in him; so send him to thy bower
To see his sisters and thy favourites.
Tell him: 'Go visit oft thy sisters there,
Whose hearts are full, whose cheeks are wet, with yearning.'

264

Then will we pay him worship, give him gifts,
And bring the tree of service into fruit."
    The Shah replied: "Thou sayest right; thou hast
A hundred mothers' love for him."
                           He called
For Siyawush and said: "The blood within
Our veins, and love, will show themselves; moreover
God hath so made thee that thou art beloved
Of all beholders, given thee pure birth;
None e'er was mother-born as pure as thou;
But what availeth blood relationship
To those who see thee only from afar?
Thy sisters and Sudaba, in affection
A mother to thee, are within the bower.
Go now and visit those secluded ones,
And stay awhile that they may do thee honour."
    The prince beheld his father with amazement,
Then mused awhile and strove to clear himself,
Suspecting that his father sought to prove him;
For Kai Kaus was knowing and smooth-tongued,
Wise, shrewd of heart, and ready to distrust.
The prince was troubled, communed with himself,
And in the end determined.
                    "If," he thought,
"I go Sudaba will talk much with me,"
Then said: "The Shah hath given me a patent,
A throne, and crown. From where the lofty sun
Arising maketh dust a thing of price
No king resembling thee in goodness, knowledge,
Demeanour, and pursuits, e'er donned the crown.
Point me the way to sages, men of leading,
And chiefs approved; or show me how to handle
Spear, mace, or bow and arrow, midst the foe;
Or be it king-craft and court-usages,
Or feast and harp, or wine and revellers;
But in the women's quarters of the Shah
What shall I learn? Shall women point the way
To knowledge? Yet if so the Shah commandeth
My custom henceforth is to visit them."
    The Shah replied: "Be happy, O my son!
May wisdom rest upon thee! I have heard

But seldom such fair words. Thy brain will grow
Since thou art thus amenable. Dismiss
All ill surmises from thy heart, away
With trouble, and enjoy thyself. Look in
Upon the children just for once: perchance
It will divert them somewhat."

                           "I will go,"
Said Siyawush, "to-morrow and perform
The Shah's command. Behold I stand before thee
Devoted, heart and soul, to do thy bidding.
As thou requirest so will I behave,
Thou art the world-lord; I am but a slave."

### 2. *How Siyawush Visited Sudaba*

One named Hirbad, purged heart and brain and soul
From evil, never left the Idol-house,*
And kept the key. The Shah commanded him:—
"What time the sun shall draw the sword of day
Seek Siyawush and further his commands.
Instruct Sudaba to present to him
A gift of gems and musk, and let withal
His sisters and the slaves pour emeralds
And saffron over him."

                    When Sol o'ertopped
The mountains Siyawush approached the Shah
And did obeisance. When they had conversed
Awhile in private Kai Kaus instructed
Hirbad, then said to Siyawush: "Go with him
And be prepared to look on something new."

    The twain went off together merrily
Without a thought of care; but when Hirbad
Held up the veil that hung before the door
The mind of Siyawush foreboded ill.
The women came before him one and all
In festival attire to gaze at him;
The house was full of musk, dinars, and saffron,
And at his feet they strewed drachms, gold, and gems:
The floor was covered with brocade of Chin†

* The harem. [*Ed.*]
† Chin is China [*Ed.*]

Enriched with lustrous pearls. Wine, scent, and voice
Of minstrelsy were there, all heads were crowned
With jewels; 'twas like Paradise, replete
With lovely forms and sumptuous furniture.
Now Siyawush on entering the bower
Beheld a brightly shining, golden throne,
With patterns wrought in turquoise, royally
Draped with brocade. There sat moon-faced Sudaba,
Like Paradise itself in hue and perfume,
Sat like the bright Canopus of Yaman,*
Her head adorned with ringlets, curl on curl.
Surmounted by a lofty crown her hair
Descended to her feet in musky lassos.
A slave stood humbly by with golden slippers.
When Siyawush appeared within the veil
Sudaba hastened to descend the throne,
Advanced with graceful gait, saluted him,
Embraced him long, long kissed his eyes and face,
And wearied not to look at him. She said:—
"I offer praise to God a hundred ways
All day and three whole watches of the night,
For no one hath a son resembling thee:
The Shah himself hath not another such."
  Now Siyawush knew well what that love meant,
And that such fondness was not in the way
Of God, and since it was unseemly there,
Went quickly to his sisters, who enthroned him
With many a blessing on a golden seat.
He stayed awhile, then went back to the Shah.
The bower was full of talk: the women said:—
"Behold the head and crown of courtesy!
'He is not,' thou hadst said, 'like other men:
His soul diffuseth wisdom.'"
       Siyawush
Came to his father's presence and spake thus:—
"I have beheld the veil and what it hid.
All good things in the world are thine, no need
For thee to vindicate the ways of God
Who dost in treasure, scimitars, and troops

* i.e., the bright star of the constellation Argo [*Ed.*]

Surpass Hushang, Jamshid, and Faridun."*
    The Shah joyed at the words. He decked his palace
Like jocund spring, had wine and harp and things
Prepared, and banned the future from the heart.
    That night he went among his dames and talked
Thus with Sudaba: "Hide not what thou thinkest
About the judgment and the courtesy
Of Siyawush, his stature, looks, and speech.
Dost thou approve of him and is he wise?
Deserveth he what others say of him?"
    Sudaba answered: "Shah and people never
Saw thy like on the throne, and who is there
To match thy son? Why speak with bated breath?"
    The Shah said: "If he is to live till manhood
We must protect him from the evil eye."†
    She said: "If my words please, and if thy son
And I minded that I should bestow
A wife upon him out of his own kindred,
Not from the great ones that are round about—
A consort who shall bear to him a son
Such as he is himself among the mighty—
Then I myself have daughters like to thee,
Begotten of thy seed, of thy pure stock;
Or should he take a child of Kai Arash,
Or Kai Pashin, she would give thanks with joy."
    He said to her: "It is my wish. My name
And greatness are dependent on the issue."
    Next morning Siyawush approached the Shah,
And called down blessings on the crown and throne.
The monarch caused all strangers to depart
And, speaking with his son in privacy,
Said thus: "I have in me a secret longing,
Inspired by God, the Maker of the world,
That thou shouldst leave a memory of thy name,
And that a king should issue from thy loins,
That as my face refreshed at seeing thee,
Thy heart should be enlarged at sight of him.
I had thy horoscope to this effect
From archimages that can read the stars,

* Earlier mythical kings of Iran [Ed.]
† Open praise, especially of the young, was regarded as unlucky.

That from thy loins a king shall come and be
Thy monument. Now choose thyself a wife
Among the great from those within the veil
Of Kai Pashin or bower of Kai Arash;
Make all things ready and bestow thy hand."
    He said: "I am the Shah's slave and I bow
My head before his counsel and behest.
His choice for me is good, whoe'er she be;
The world-lord is a monarch o'er his slaves.
Would that Sudaba heard it not! her words
Are otherwise, she hath no mind thereto;
I cannot talk to her of this affair,
And have no business in that bower of hers."
    The Shah smiled at the words of Siyawush,
Not witting of the quag beneath the straw,
And said to him: "Thy wife must be thy choice.
Sudaba least of all need be considered,
Her words are full of loving-kindliness;
She tendereth thy welfare."
                            Siyawush
Was gladdened by the words, and reassured
Began to speak the world-king's praise and pay
Him reverence, falling down before the throne,
Yet privily Sudaba with her schemes
Still vexed and troubled him, for well he knew,
And his skin burst: "This is her notion too!"

### 3. *How Siyawush Visited the Bower the Second Time*

Another night thus passed and starry heaven
Turned o'er dark earth. Sudaba radiant
Sat on her throne and donned a diadem
Of rubies. Then she summoned all her daughters,
Arrayed, and seated them on golden thrones.
Before her stood young Idols:* thou hadst said:—
"It is a paradise." The moon-faced lady
Said to Hirbad: "Go say to Siyawush:—
'Afflict thy feet and show thyself to me.'"
    Hirbad made speed to give that lover's message
To Siyawush who, hearing, stood distraught,

* Beauties deserving of worship. [*Ed.*]

And oft invoked the Maker of the world.
He sought in various ways but found no help;
He trembled, and his legs shook under him;
Then went to visit her and saw her state,
Her face, and diadem. She with her head
And tresses decked with gems rose at his coming,
Gave up the throne of gold to him and, standing
Slavelike, displayed her Idols—gems uncut.
"Behold this throne-room," thus she said, "and all
These handmaids with their golden coronets!
They all are youthful Idols of Taraz,
Whom God hath formed of modesty and charms.
If any one of them delighteth thee,
Survey her looks and form from head to foot."
        While Siyawush was glancing lightly round
There was not one who dared to catch his eye,
And as they talked they said: "The moon itself
Would not presume to gaze upon this prince."
        When each, in speculation on her chance,
Had gone back to her seat, Sudaba said:—
"Why dost thou keep thy purpose to thyself?
Wilt thou not tell me what is thy desire,
O thou whose looks are fairy-like with Grace!
For all are struck who catch a glimpse of thee,
Preferring thee to any? Ponder well
Which of these beauties is the worthiest."
        But Siyawush was moved and answered not,
For thoughts like these arose in his pure heart:—
"Far better hold my pure heart's funeral rites
Than take a consort from among my foes.
I have been told by famous warriors
Of all the doings of Hamavaran,
How he entreated the Iranian king,
And how he raised dust from the Iranian chiefs.
This treacherous Sudaba is his daughter,
And will not leave our kindred skin or marrow."
        He opened not his lips to make reply.
The fairy-faced one raised her veil and said:—
"If one should see the new moon and the sun
Here upon this new throne, it would not be
A marvel if the moon should be despised,

And thou shouldst press the sun in thine embrace.
No wonder if the man that seeth me
Upon the ivory throne, with rubies crowned
And turquoise, should not look upon the moon,
But think all other Beauties beautiless.
If thou wilt make a compact with me now,
Turn not away but set my heart at rest,
One of my youthful daughters present here
Will I make stand before thee like a slave.
So make a compact with me now by oath,
And disregard no jot of what I say,
That, when the Shah departeth from the world,
Thou wilt be his memorial with me,
Wilt never suffer me to come to harm,
But hold me dear as life. And now behold!
I stand before thee and I give to thee
Myself and my sweet life. I will fulfil
Whate'er thou asketh me—thy whole desire—
And let my head be taken in thy toils."
        She hung upon his neck, gave him a kiss,
And of a truth forgot her modesty.
He blushed; the very lashes of his eyes
Were red with shame. He thought: "From this div's work
Now may the Lord of Saturn keep me far!
I will not treat my sire disloyally,
Nor will I make a league with Ahriman.
If I speak coldly to this wanton dame
Her heart will seethe; she will grow hot with rage,
Make practice of some secret sorcery,
And cause the world-lord to believe in her.
'Tis best to speak her fair and keep her full
Of tenderness and longing."
                    Then he said:—
"Thou hast not any equal in the world,
And art the rival of the moon itself
In beauty: thou art for the Shah alone.
As for myself thy daughter will suffice;
None other must be mine. Consent to this,
Propose it to the monarch of Iran,
And mark the answer that thou wilt receive.
I will demand her and will covenant,

And give a pledge before thee with my tongue,
That till her stature equalleth mine own
I will not think of any one besides.
For what thou askest further—since my face
Inspireth in thy soul a love for me—
God's Grace hath made me thus, O thou most fair!
Conceal thy secret; speak of it to none:
For me too silence is the only course.
Thou art the chief of ladies and a queen,
And I will think of thee as mother only."

He spake these words and rose to go, but love
Still filled her wicked soul. When next Kaus,
The monarch, visited the women's bower,
Sudaba looked and saw him. She appeared
Before the Shah with news of what had passed,
And spake thus of the case of Siyawush:—
"He came and looked all round the hall. I made
A bevy of the black-eyed Idols there.
The hall was such with all the fair-faced girls
That thou hadst said: 'Love raineth from the moon!'
But, save my daughter, he approved of none:
No other fair was precious in his eyes."

The Shah was so rejoiced that thou hadst said:—
"The moon itself hath come to his embrace!"
He oped his treasury's door: a wealth of gems,
Brocade of cloth of gold, and golden girdles,
As well as bracelets, crowns, and signet-rings,
With thrones and torques such as the noble wear,
And divers kinds of treasures were displayed,
So that the world was filled with things of price.
The Shah then bade Sudaba: "Keep all these
For Siyawush. When he hath need of them,
Give them to him and say: 'This gift is small;
Thou shouldest have two hundred times as much.'"

Sudaba looked in wonder. Full of guile
She thought: "If Siyawush complieth not,
Then he may take my life and welcome too.
Each practice good and evil, which they use
By stealth or openly throughout the world,
Will I employ; and, should he slight me, bring
A charge accusing him before the king."

## 4. How Siyawush Visited the Bower the Third Time

Sudaba sat enthroned, adorned with earrings
And chaplet of wrought gold upon her head.
She called the prince and said, as they conversed:—
"The Shah hath set these treasures forth, and none
Hath seen such crowns and thrones. The sum of gifts
Is past all reckoning: to carry them
Thou wouldst require two hundred elephants,
And I will give to thee my daughter too.
Now look upon my face and head and crown:
What pretext hast thou to reject my love,
And slight my face and person? I am dead
Not seeing thee; I cry out, toss, and suffer:
The light of day is hidden by mine anguish,
My sun is turned to lapis-lazuli.
And now for seven years this love of mine
Hath made my face to run with tears of blood.
Make me a happy woman—none shall know—
Vouchsafe to me a day of youth again.
More than the great king hath bestowed on thee
Will I prepare thee—thrones, crowns, diadems;
But if thou turn aside from my behest,
And if thy heart come not to my relief,
I will destroy thy hope of ever reigning
And make both sun and moon turn black before thee."

　　"Now God forbid," he said, "that I should give
Religion to the winds for passion's sake,
That I should treat my sire disloyally,
And be a coward and a fool at once!
Thou art his wife—the sunlight of his throne—
And shouldst not perpetrate a crime like this."

　　She rose in wrath and hate, clutched him and cried:—
"I told thee my heart's secret, but thine own
Was hidden! In thy folly thou dost aim
To ruin me and show the wise my shame."

## 5. How Sudaba Beguiled Kaus

She rent her robes and tore her cheeks. A cry
Rose from her bower, her clamour reached the street.

The palace was all hubbub; thou hadst said:—
"'Tis Resurrection-night!" News reached the Shah,
Who hurried from the imperial golden throne
Toward the bower in his solicitude,
And when he found Sudaba with rent cheeks,
And all the palace full of babblement,
He questioned every one in deep concern,
Not knowing what that heart of stone had done.
Sudaba wailed and wept before him, tore
Her hair, and told him: "Siyawush approached
My throne. He caught me in his arms and cried:—
'My soul and body brim with love for thee.
Oh! why art thou so cold to me, my fair!
For thou art all I long for, thou alone?'
This is the truth—I am constrained to tell thee:—
'Twas he that threw the crown from my black locks,
And rent the robe upon my bosom thus!"

    The Shah was troubled, asked her many questions,
And thought: "If she saith sooth, and if she hath
No evil end in view, I must cut off
The head of Siyawush: that will unlock
These bonds of villainy."

                What saith the sage?
"Not lust but blood our thoughts must now engage."

    The inmates of the bower, those well advised
And noble servants faithful to their lord,
He bade withdraw and, sitting on the throne
Alone, called for Sudaba and his son,
And wisely said to him: "I needs must know
This secret. 'Twas not thou but I that wrought
The ill. I suffer for my thoughtless words:
Why did I call thee to the women's house?
Now I am grieved that thou art thus involved.
Let me have all the truth, show me its face,
And say what passed."

             The prince related all,
And how he had been wrought on by Sudaba.
She cried: "It is a lie. Of all the Idols
It was my person only that he sought;
I told him what the king of earth proposed
To give him publicly and privily,

Told him about my daughter and the crown,
The precious things, brocade, and treasure-hoards.
I told him: 'I will add as much again,
And give my daughter all that I possess.'
He said to me: 'I do not want the goods,
And do not mean to see thy child. Of all
The world,' he said, 'I need but thee—no more.
No wealth or personage availeth aught
Without thine own self.' Then he tried to force me,
And handled me with hands as hard as stones.
I would not grant his wishes. All my hair
He tore and caused these scratches on my face.
I am with child, O monarch of the world!
By thee, but he was near to killing it
With all his struggles, and the world was strait
And dark before me."

                    Then the great king thought:—
The testimony of them both is worthless,
And this is not a case for instancy,
Because a heart in straits perverteth wisdom.
I needs must first investigate the matter,
And when my heart is calm it will bear witness;
I shall discover which is in the wrong,
And which of them deserveth punishment."

    He sought all means of finding out the truth,
And first he smelt the hands of Siyawush,
His breast, his arms, his head, and all his person.
A scent of wine, rose-water, and fine musk
Was on Sudaba, but on Siyawush
Was none, nor any sign that he had touched her.
The Shah was troubled, he disgraced Sudaba,
And sorely vexed said to himself: "No course
Remaineth but to put her to the sword."
    Then he bethought him of Hamavaran,
How tumult, strife, and battle would ensue;
Next, how, when he was lying there in bonds
And none of all his kin and friends was near,
Sudaba was his handmaid day and night,
And faced the trouble uncomplainingly.
His next thought was: "She loved me wholly once:
I must forgive her everything," and then

That he had children by her, and he counted
The anguish of the children no light thing.
But Siyawush was blameless in the case,
The monarch recognised his probity,
And said to him: "Be not concerned hereat;
Be prudent and consider well thy going.
Talk not about this thing, tell it to none;
The matter must be kept from every one."

### 6. How Sudaba and a Sorceress Devised a Scheme

Sudaba, conscious that she was disgraced
And that the Shah's heart was estranged from her,
Sought in her evil case some remedy,
And set anew the tree of her revenge.
She had a woman in the bower, adept
In charms and spells, deceit and artifice,
And one moreover who was great with child,
Near to the time of her delivery.
Sudaba told her all and sought her aid,
But said: "First give a pledge of thy good faith."
    Sudaba took her pledge, gave her much gold,
And said: "Make mention of this thing to none.
Prepare a drug that thou mayest make abortion,
Remain concealed, and keep my secret close.
It may be that my coil of many lies
May gain some credit through this babe of thine,
For I will tell Kaus: 'This is my child,
Thus murdered by the hand of Ahriman!'
This, it may be, will baffle Siyawush;
So seek a way to compass it. If thou
Refuseth, then my lustre with the Shah
Is dimmed: I shall no more approach the throne."
    The woman said to her: "I am thy slave,
And bow my head to thy command and will."
    When it was night the woman took the drug
And gave birth to a brood of Ahrimans—
Two children as they had been div-begotten:*
What should a sorceess and a div produce?
Then, saying nothing to her servitors,

* i.e., by evil powers [Ed.]

Sudaba had a golden salver brought
Whereon she laid those brats of Ahriman,
And shrieked and flung herself upon a couch.
She hid the woman and retired to bed:
Her wailing reached the palace from her chamber.
Then all the slaves within the palace came
In haste before Sudaba, they beheld
Two infants lying dead upon the salver,
And cries rose o'er the palace and o'er Saturn.
The sound of wailing reached and woke Kaus
Who listened trembling, asked, and heard how fortune
Had dealt with his fair spouse. Sleepless and anxious
He rose at dawn, went in and saw Sudaba
Prostrate, the women frantic, and two babes
In evil plight, flung on a golden salver!
Sudaba rained the water from her eyes,
And said: "Behold this bright sun—Siyawush!
I often told thee of his evil deeds,
But thou didst foolishly believe his words."

    The heart of Shah Kaus was filled with doubt,
He went his way, remained a while in thought,
Then said: "What remedy shall I apply?
I must not treat the case with levity."

### 7. *How Kaus Inquired Into the Matter of the Babes*

Kaus then summoned all the astrologers
Before him, welcomed them, assigning each
A golden throne, and spake about Sudaba,
And of the warfare with Hamavaran,
That they might have a knowledge of her case,
And understand her conduct thoroughly;
He also spake at large about the children,
But kept his own suspicions to himself.
They then took planispheres and astrolabes,
And having spent a sennight on the business
Said: "How can wine be in a cup which thou
Hast filled with poison? These are spurious children,
Not from this mother and the monarch's loins:
We should have found them on the planisphere
With ease if they had been of royal race,

But know that heaven revealeth not their secret,
Nor is this wonder of the earth."
                              They told
The Shah and court of that foul, wicked woman.
Sudaba wailed and cried aloud for justice,
She called upon the world-lord for redress,
And said: "I was the comrade of the Shah
When he had suffered and had lost the throne.
My heart is tortured for my murdered babes,
And ever and anon I swoon away."
        The Shah replied: "O woman! hold thy peace!
Why dost thou utter such offensive words?"
        He gave commandment that the troops on guard
Should search the city and the neighbouring parts,
And bring the wicked woman to the court.
The experienced searchers soon discovered her,
Haled the unhappy woman through the streets,
And carried her in shame before the Shah,
Who questioned her with kindness, held out hopes,
And made her promises for many days,
Howbeit she confessed not anything.
        The noble Shah was still dissatisfied,
And gave command to bear her forth and use
All means and work by spells, and in the end
To cut her down the middle with a saw
If she persisted, as is common justice.
They bore her from the palace of the Shah,
And threatened her with sword and stake and pit.
The sorceress answered: "I am innocent.
What can I say before this noble court?"
        They told the monarch of the woman's words,
And added: "God alone doth know the truth."
        The great king bade Sudaba come to him;
The readers of the stars re-said their say:—
"Both babes are clearly children of the witch,
Begotten from the loins of Ahriman."
        Sudaba said: "They know a different tale,
But dare not speak for fear of Siyawush,
Who privily hath tied them down to silence.
The lions quake in troops for fear of him,
This chieftain of the elephantine form,
Who hath the strength of eighty elephants,

And stayeth at his will the river Nile!
A noble host, a hundred thousand strong,
Take flight before him in the ranks of war!
How shall I stand against him? In good sooth
Mine eyes will evermore weep tears of blood.
What have the readers of the stars to do
Save his command and seek his approbation?
While as for thee—thou mournest not thy babes,
Albeit they are thine as much as mine.
If thou believest such a foolish charge
I leave the question to the other world."
    The sun withdraweth from the river Nile
Less water than Sudaba shed in tears.
The Shah was sorely troubled at her speech;
He joined with her in weeping bitterly,
And then, and with a broken heart, dismissed her.
He brooded constantly upon the matter,
And said: "I will investigate it throughly,
And find out what the bottom of it is."
    He summoned all the archmages of the realm,
And spake about Sudaba. One replied:—
"The monarch's grief will not remain a secret.
If thou wouldst clear up what hath been alleged
On each side, throw a stone and break the pitcher,
Because, however dear his son may be,
The Shah's heart will be still disturbed by thoughts,
While this king's daughter of Hamavaran
Hath made thee doubtful on the other side.
Such being then the statements of the pair
Let one of them be made to pass through fire,
Because high heaven ordaineth that no harm
Shall in this way befall the innocent."
    The world-lord called Sudaba, seated her
With Siyawush to parley on the case,
And said at last: "My heart and my shrewd mind
Trust neither of you; fire will show the truth,
And quickly make the guilty infamous."
    Sudaba answered: "What I said is true;
I showed the Shah two babes untimely born:
What greater outrage can there be than mine?
'Tis Siyawush that ought to right himself:
He sought to ruin me and did the wrong."

The king of earth then asked his youthful son:—
"What seemeth good to thee as touching this?"
    He answered: "Such a charge is worse than Hell!
I would pass o'er a mountain all aflame,
'Twere baseness not to rid me of this shame."


### 8. How Siyawush Passed Through the Fire

The thoughts of Kai Kaus ran on them both;
He said: "If either prove a profligate
Will any henceforth call me Shah? Moreover
My son and wife are blood and brain to me;
Whom then will this perplexing business profit?
Still it is best to purify my heart
From foul surmise and take this dreadful course.
How well the moralizing monarch said:—
'If thou art faint of heart play not the king!'"
    He gave instructions to his minister
To have a hundred caravans of camels
Brought from the plain. These went to gather firewood,
While all the people of Iran looked on,
Till two huge mountains rose that might be seen
Two leagues away; so should a key be found
To loose the bonds of bale, so much he yearned
To learn the truth amid this fraud and wrong.
    When thou hast heard the story thou wilt find
Thyself disposed to shun all womankind;
Seek none of them except the virtuous; she
That worketh ill will bring disgrace on thee.
    They piled two mounts of firewood on the plain
While all the folk looked on. A path was left
Such that a horseman armed might hardly pass
Between the piles. This done, the glorious Shah
Bade pour black naphtha over all the wood.
Came ten score men to light and blow the fire,
And thou hadst said: 'The day is turned to night.'
When first they blew there was a mass of smoke,
But presently the tongues of fire rose fast;
The earth became more radiant than the sky,
The people shouted and the flames ascended.
All that were on the plain were scorched and wept
To see the cheery face of Siyawush,

Who came before his sire with golden helmet,
And raiment all of white. His mien was tranquil,
His face all smiles, his heart all hopefulness;
His black steed's hoofs sent dust up to the moon.
The prince then sprinkled camphor o'er himself,
So bodies are prepared for burial,
And lighting from his charger did obeisance.
The Shah was shame-faced and his words were kind.
"Be not discomfited," said Siyawush,
"That fortune taketh such a turn as this.
I am dishonoured: such a state is ruin.
If I am innocent I shall escape,
While if in fault the Maker will not heed me;
But by the power of God who giveth good
I shall not feel the heat."
                              As he drew near
The flames he prayed the Judge that hath no needs:—
"Grant me a passage through this mount of fire,
And free me from my sire's misprision."
                                          Thus
He testified the anguish of his soul,
Then urged his black steed on like smoke. A wail
Ascended from the city and the waste,
For all the people grieved at what was done.
Sudaba heard the wailing on the plain,
Went to the palace roof, descried the blaze,
Wished ill to him, and babbled feverishly.
The people fixed their eyes upon Kaus;
Their tongues wagged freely and their hearts were wroth.
Meanwhile the prince so handled his black charger
That thou hadst said: "His steed took to the fire."
From every side the flames closed o'er his head,
And none could see his helmet or his horse,
While all the plain wept tears of blood and asked:—
"How will he ever issue from the flames?"
      The noble hero nathless reappeared,
With rosy cheeks and smiles upon his lips.
A roar went up as men caught sight of him:
They cried: "The young Shah cometh from the fire!"
      He came with horse and raiment such that thou
Hadst said: "He beareth jasmine in his breast."
Had flame been water he had not been wetted,

His garments would have holden none of it;
For when all-holy God doth so vouchsafe
The breath of fire is even as the wind.
The horsemen of the host urged on their steeds,
While all the people on the plain threw drachms
Before him; there was universal joy
Among the mighty and the mean alike
As each to other gave the gladsome tidings:—
"God hath shown mercy to the innocent."
    Meanwhile Sudaba in her frenzy plucked
Her hair, wept bitterly, and tore her cheeks.
When all unsmirched, unsinged, unstained, unsoiled,
The guiltless Siyawush approached, his sire
And all the warriors of the host alighted;
But Siyawush with cheek upon the ground
Gave thanks to God that he had been delivered
Out of that burning mount, and had confounded
His foes' device. Then said the Shah: "Brave youth,
Of stainless lineage and ardent soul!
None but a holy mother bringeth forth
A son like thee, and such should rule the world."
    Then clasped he Siyawush against his breast,
Excused his own ill conduct, and in state
Moved palace-ward. He took his seat rejoicing,
And placed the royal crown upon his head.
He had wine brought, the minstrels called, and granted
The prince whate'er he would. The Shah prolonged
Those revels for three days: till they were o'er
No lock or key was at the treasury-door.

### 9. How Siyawush Begged Sudaba's Life of His Father

Kaus the fourth day sat upon the throne
Of kings; an ox-head mace was in his hand.
Fierce in his wrath he had Sudaba summoned
Before him, told her what had passed, and said:—
"Thou art a shameless woman! Thou hast wrought
Enough of ill and grieved me to the heart.
What part is this that thou hast played throughout
In treacherously seeking my son's life,
In causing him to be exposed to fire,
And practising such witchcraft? No excuses

Will now avail thee; go and get thee ready;
Thou are not fit to live. The punishment
For such a crime as this is to be hanged."
          She said: "O Shah! forbear to heap up fire
Upon my head. If I perforce must lose it
In vengeance for the wrong which I have . . . suffered,
Command . . . I am resigned. Yet put revenge
Away. Let Siyawush declare the truth,
And quench the fires within thee. He hath used
All Zal's own sorceries herein, and therefore
The fierce flames harmed him not."*
                              She said withal
To Siyawush: "Thou usest witchcraft still!
Shall not thy back of impudence be bent?"
          The great Shah asked the Iranians: "For the evil
That she hath done by stealth, what shall I do?
How shall I punish her?"
                    All did obeisance,
And said: "The punishment for her is death:
She ought to suffer for her evil deeds."
          He bade the deathsman: "Hang her in the street
Upon the gibbet and be pitiless."
          At her abandonment the woman wailed,
And Shah Kaus was sorrowful of heart;
He strove to hide it but his cheeks were pale.
"Let not thy heart," said Siyawush, "be troubled,
But pardon for my sake Sudaba's fault;
She may be warned and walk advisedly."
"For if," he thought, "she perish by his hand
He will be sorry for it in the end,
And see in me the author of his grief."
          The Shah, who had been seeking some excuse
For mercy, answered him: "I grant thee this
Because I see that right was on thy side."
          When Siyawush had kissed his father's throne
He rose upon his feet, went to the door,
Brought back Sudaba, and escorted her
Home to the palace by the Shah's command,
Where all the women ran to her again,
And did obeisance.

* Zal—the hero Rustem's father, exposed to die at birth but brought up
by the mythical bird, the Symurgh. [Ed.]

## 12. From *The Book of the Wiles of Women*
## (1253 A.D.)

Translated from the Spanish by John E. Keller (1917–     )

[Chiefly the frame story is reprinted here, although it has not
been possible to make a perfectly clean surgical cut between
frame and content. Of Mr. Keller's approximately thirty-six pages,
I have used only about one quarter. From his first seven pages I
have omitted only the first paragraph, which merely tells of how
the story came to be translated from Arabic into Spanish. His next
twenty pages are omitted for they mainly constitute the back and
forth storytelling that takes place between the queen (who has
accused the youth) and the sages (who are defending him). Following the boy's decision to speak out in his own behalf, there is
another omission of eight pages in which the parrying is resumed
between the two principals. The final two short paragraphs of this
abstract provide an equally abrupt ending for the full translation.
*Ed.*]

There was once a king of Judea whose name was Alcos. He
was a mighty monarch and he greatly loved the people of his
kingdom, ruling them ever with justice. He had ninety wives,
and although he had known them all in accordance with his
faith, in none could he beget an heir. As he lay one night with
one of them, he began to worry about who was to inherit the
realm after his death. Pondering this, he grew sad and tossed
in his bed in extreme despondency.

At this time one of his wives, she whom he loved the most,
came to him. She was prudent and wise, and he had tested her
in certain matters. She came to him because she saw that he
was unhappy and she told him that he was honored and loved
by his people throughout the land.

"Why are you so sad and despondent?" she asked. "If you
are afraid of something, or if I have grieved you, let me know
in what way, and I will mourn with you. If it is something
else, you shouldn't worry so much, for thank the Lord, you
are loved by your subjects and all speak well of you and with
affection. May God never sadden you and may you have His
blessing!"

"Pious and beloved one," said the king to his wife, "you
have never failed to comfort me and to lighten my care when

I was sad; but neither I with all my power nor all the people of my kingdom can assuage this sadness that besets me. I should like to leave an heir who would inherit the realm when I die. That is why I am sad."

"I shall give you a good piece of advice," said his wife. "Pray to the Lord, who is all-virtuous, for He is powerful enough to create a son for you and to send him to you. He has never tired of bestowing grace, and you have never asked for anything that He didn't give it to you. When He understands that you pray in earnest, He will give you a son. I think it proper, if it is in accord with your wishes, that we arise and pray with all our hearts that He give us a son in whom we may rejoice and who may become our heir. I believe firmly that He, in his kindness, will grant it to us if we beseech Him. If he sends us a son, we must be happy and must obey His will, be satisfied with His justice, and appreciate His grace, because God is omnipotent and everything rests in His hand. He takes unto Him whomever He will and He smites whom-ever He wishes."

After she had told him this, the king was pleased, for he realized that all she said was true. They both arose and prayed as she had suggested; and after they returned to bed, Alcos lay with her and filled her with child.

As soon as they knew positively, they praised God for the kindness He had done them. Nine months later she gave birth to a healthy son, and the king rejoiced exceedingly and was greatly pleased with him. And the woman praised God for it.

Then the king summoned all the sages that were in his kingdom to come before him to study the horoscope of his son. When they arrived, he was glad to see them and he caused them to come into his presence.

"Welcome!" he said.

And he was with them for a long time, rejoicing and mak-ing merry.

"I declare to you, Sages," he said, "that God, whose name be praised, has favored me with the gift of a son, whom He bestowed upon me to strengthen my arm and to make me happy. Let thanks be given to Him forever! Examine my son's star and learn what his fate will be."

They studied it and informed him that his son's life would be long and that he would be very powerful; but that at the end of his twentieth year something would happen to him, in dealing with his father, through which he would be in mortal peril.

When the king heard this, he was frightened and filled with grief, but he grew happy again and said, "Everything is in God's power. Let Him do what He thinks meet."

Now the prince matured and grew tall and handsome, and God endowed him with great intelligence. In that entire age no other was born his equal. When he was nine years old, the king sent him to learn to write, and he studied until he was fifteen; but he learned nothing, and when the King heard this, he was quite concerned.

He sent for all the wise men of the kingdom. When they all had arrived, he addressed them. "What do you think of the case of my son? Isn't there one of you who can teach him? I will give that one anything he asks, and he will have my everlasting affection."

Then four of the wise men present—nine hundred were there—stood up, and one of these said, "I shall teach him so that no one will be wiser than he."

"Why didn't you teach him?" the king asked a wise man whose name was Sindibad.

At this they all spoke, and afterwards Sindibad said, "Is that all you know? Well, I know all that and consider it little, for nobody is wiser than I. I will teach him. Grant me what I ask, O King, and I shall teach him in six months so much that no one will be wiser than he."*

"He who speaks and does not accomplish," replied one of the four, "is like a flash of lightning with no rain. Why didn't you teach him anything in the years you had him with you, while the king was supporting you?"

"Because of the great pity I felt for him I could not drive him," answered Sindibad, "and because I was trying to find someone wiser than I. Now I realize that no one knows better than I how to teach him."

"There are four things," retorted the second sage, coming to his feet, "which a wise man should not praise before he sees their final outcome: the first is food, until we see what becomes of it after it has been digested by the stomach; the man

* The chronology is odd here: the prophecy spoke of trouble at the age of twenty; it begins, apparently, at fifteen. [*Ed.*]

who goes forth to battle, until he returns from the army; the crop until it is harvested; and the woman until she is pregnant. Therefore, we ought not to praise you until we see why we should. Let us see your hands accomplish something and let us hear your mouth say something that will make known your wisdom and your intent."

"He who has his hands and his feet under control," said Sindibad, "and his hearing, and his sight, and his whole body, is like that wisdom which rules the mind. Just as musk permeates water and fills it with sweet savor, so wisdom in the heart makes the whole body sound."

"One who doesn't learn in infancy," asserted the third sage, "places in his mouth what his stomach will cast up. A woman can never be good when she has no fear of her husband. A man who speaks wisdom, if he doesn't understand and know what it is, never imparts any meaning to the one who hears him, nor does he himself comprehend it. And you, Sindibad, since you were unable to instruct the boy in his infancy, how can you teach him when he is of age?"

"You will see," replied Sindibad, "if God wills and if I live, that I shall teach him in six months what no one else can teach him in seventy years."

"Let me inform you," said the fourth sage, "that when wise men assemble, they meet one another, they debate with one another, and yet they do not understand the wise things they say to each other. Will you do what you say? I want you to prove how you can do so."

"I shall show you," answered Sindibad. "I shall teach him in six months what no one else can teach him in sixty years, in such a way that no one will know more than he, and I shall not delay an hour, because they have convinced me of these things: that in a country where the royal authority is also the judicial and does not dismiss men legally after trial, where it is known that there is no law to correct what the king has done when under the temptation of wealth, that the situation is similar to that of the physician who is so fond of his holidays that he doesn't call upon the sick as they believe he should. If such a state of affairs prevails in a kingdom, one ought not to live in it. Now that I have revealed all this to you, I shall also inform you that kings are like fire; if you go too near, you will be burned, and if you stand apart, you will be chilled. I request,

Sire, that if I teach your son, you will give me what I desire."

"Demand what you will," replied the king, "and if you will not ask, I shall act for you, for there is nothing worse in kings than deceit. Tell me what you want."

"That you will not do to anyone what you do not want anyone to do to you," answered Sindibad.

"I promise," said the king.

They made a contract, and both agreed upon a month and upon the hour of the day that it was to terminate. They wrote in a formal agreement all that was necessary for that day.

During the second hour of the day Sindibad took the boy by the hand and led him to his house where he had prepared a great hall, marvelously beautiful. He wrote upon the wall all the sciences the boy was to learn, all the stars, all the formulae, and all the other things.

"This is my chair," he told the boy, "and this is yours until you learn all the knowledge that I learned in this room. Cheer up! Sharpen your wits and your ears and your eyes!"

He sat down to teach him, and what they had to eat was brought there to them; they did not go out and no one visited them there. Now the boy was keen and intelligent, and before the appointed time arrived he had learned all the facts that his master, Sindibad, had written about the wisdom of mankind.

The king inquired about his son two days before the day designated. When his messenger arrived at Sindibad's house, he said, "The king wants you to come to him immediately."

"Sindibad," demanded the king, "what have you accomplished? What news do you have?"

"Sire," answered Sindibad, "I have news that will please you, for your son will be with you tomorrow two hours after dawn."

"Sindibad," cried the king, "a man like your never broke his promise. Consider yourself in high honor, for you deserve to have a reward from us!"

Sindibad returned to the boy and said, "I shall cast your horoscope."

He cast it and saw that the boy would be in mortal danger if he spoke before the passage of seven days. In great distress he said to him, "I am greatly disturbed on account of the contract I signed with the king!"

"Why are you distressed?" inquired the boy. "For if you

ordered me never to speak, I would never speak. Tell me what you want, for I will do it."

"I made a promise to your father," said Sindibad, "that you would return to him tomorrow, and I must not fail in the agreement that I made with him. When two hours of the day have passed, go to your father, but do not speak until seven days have gone by. In the meantime, I shall hide."

When the next day dawned, the king had the people of his kingdom regaled with food and he had platforms erected to seat the minstrels who were to play before him. Then the son came to his father. The king went to him and greeted him, but the boy did not reply. This the king considered strange.

"Where is your master?" he asked the boy.

Then the king ordered a search made for Sindibad, and heralds went forth to look for him. They searched far and wide but could not find him.

"Perhaps," remarked the king to those who were with him, "the boy is an awe of me and is afraid of me and does not dare to speak."

The king's counselors all spoke to the boy, but he made no reply. Then the king said to those who were with him, "What do you think is the matter with my son?"

"It seems to us," they replied, "that Sindibad, his teacher, has given him something, some drug to make him learn, and the drug has rendered him mute."

And the king considered this of great import and he grieved exceedingly.

The Story of the Wife and How She Took the Prince Aside in Her Apartment, and How, Because of What She Said to Him, He Forgot What His Teacher Had Told Him

The king had a wife whom he loved and honored above all the wives he possessed. When they told her what had happened to the boy, she went to the king and said, "Sire, they have told me what has happened to your son. Perhaps through embarrassment in your presence he doesn't dare to speak. If you agree, let me take him aside, and perchance he will tell me what is the matter, for he used to tell me his secrets, a thing he never did with any of your other wives."

"Take him to your apartment and talk to him," said the king.

She did so, but the prince did not answer anything she asked him. Then she pressed him further, saying, "Don't be a fool, for I know well that you won't oppose my will. Let's kill your father. You will be king and I shall be your wife, for your father is quite old and weak. You are a young man and your life is just beginning and you ought to expect a great deal more than he."

As soon as she had said this, the boy was furious and he forgot what his teacher had told him, all that he had commanded him.

"Ah, Enemy of God, if the seven days were but passed I would give an answer to what you say!" he cried.

He had no sooner said this than she realized she was in danger. Screaming and calling for help, she began to tear her hair, so that the king, hearing her, wanted to know what was the matter.

"This one," she lied, "who you say cannot speak, tried to violate me utterly, and I would never have thought it of him!"

On hearing this, the king flew into a great rage and cruelly ordered the boy executed. Now the king had seven privy-counselors without whose advice he never acted. When they saw that the king had ordered his son put to death without having consulted them, they understood that he did so in wrath because he believed what his wife had told him. They took counsel together and said, "if he kills his son, later he will be sorry, and will blame nobody but us; hence we must give some reason for the sparing of the prince."

"I will excuse you all from the embarrassment of speaking with the king," said one of them.

This counselor went straight to the king, fell upon his knees before him, and said, "Sire, man should never do anything until he is certain. If you do so, you will commit a wrong."

✠

And the king ordered them not to execute his son.

### Of How on the Eighth Day the Prince Spoke
### and Went Before His Father

When the eighth day came, early in the morning before the sun rose, the prince called the woman who was serving him during those days when he was not speaking.

"Go and call So-and-So, who is privy-counselor to the king," he ordered her, "and tell him to come as fast as he can."

As soon as she saw that the prince was speaking, the woman went running and called the privy-counselor, who arose and came quickly to the prince. He wept with him and told him why he had not spoken and what had happened to him with his stepmother.

"And I did not escape death except through you and your companions, who strove to help me out of justice and loyalty. May God reward you for it, and I shall give you a reward if I live and learn what you desire. Now I want you to hasten to my father and tell him my tidings before that false whore, my stepmother, goes to him, for well do I know that she is an early riser!"

As soon as the prince had spoken, the privy-counselor went with all speed to the king.

"Sire!" he cried. "Reward me for the news I bring about the good and the mercy that God has done you because you didn't kill your son. He now speaks, and has sent me to you."

He did not tell the king all that the prince had said.

"Go quickly and tell the prince to come to me immediately," commanded the king.

He came and made obeisance, and the king asked him, "What was the matter with you that you didn't speak to me in the face of death?"

"I shall tell you," said the prince.

He told it all to him, how it had befallen him and how his master, Sindibad, had forbidden him to speak for seven days.

"But I tell you that the woman took me aside and tried to instruct me. When she learned that I couldn't answer for seven days, she had no other plan than to make you put me to death before I could speak. Therefore, Sire, I beg you, that if you consider it a good thing, you have all the wise men of the realm and of your peoples assemble, for I should like to speak before them all."

When the prince had spoken, the king was very happy.

"God be praised," he cried, "for all the good He has done me! He did not permit me to commit such a great error as to put my son to death."

The king had his people summoned to court. When they had arrived, Sindibad came in to the king and said, "Sire, I bow before you."

"What became of you, wicked Sindibad, during all these days?" asked the king. "I was on the point of killing my son because of what you told him to do!"

"God shed so much grace upon you," answered Sindibad, "and so much prudence and understanding, that you had to act as you did when you knew the truth. You kings, above all men, ought to be most certain of the truth. The prince did not fail to do what I commanded him to do. You, Sire, should not have ordered him slain on the word of a woman!"

"Praised be God that I did not put my son to death," cried the king, "for I would have lost this world and the next! Now, you Sages, who would have been to blame had I executed my son? Would the blame have been mine? My son's? My wife's? The teacher's?"

Four sages stood up, and one of them said, "When Sindibad examined the boy's star and what his fate was to be, he should not have gone into hiding."

"It is not as you say," said another sage, "for Sindibad was not at fault, because he had made a contract with the king which he could not break. The fault must be the king's, because he ordered his son put to death on the word of a woman, when he did not know if her story was true or false."

"It is not as you say," said the third sage, "for the king was not to blame, because in all the world there is no wood colder than sandalwood, nor anything colder than the clovepink, yet when they are rubbed together, they will generate so much heat that fire will come forth. Now, if the king had been wise in his judgment, he would not have been swayed by the will of a woman; but since she was the woman the king loved, he could not help listening to her. The fault lay with the woman, because she deceived him with her words and caused him to order his son slain."

The fourth sage said that the blame was not the woman's,

but the prince's, because he refused to keep secret what his master had commanded him to.

"For the woman," he said, "after she realized how handsome and well-made the prince was, desired him all the more when she had him alone with her.

"Now when she understood what the prince was saying, she knew that she would be discovered at the end of the seven days by what the prince would say. She was afraid that they would execute her, and therefore she took pains to have him put away before he could speak."

"It is not as you say," stated Sindibad, "for the greatest of all wisdom lies in speaking."

"I shall speak, if you command me," the prince said.

The king told him to say what he wished.

"Praise be to You, O God," exclaimed the prince, getting up, "Who caused me to see this day and this hour! Who permitted me to make known my story and my mind! It is necessary that I reveal my thoughts, for I wish to demonstrate my wisdom and to tell you a tale about it."

✠

And "Sire, I gave you this tale for the sole reason that you might distrust women, who are evil; for the sage says that if the earth should change into paper, and the sea into ink, and its fish into pens, they would not be able to set down the wickedness of women."

And the king commanded her to be roasted in a dry cauldron.

## CHAPTER VII

# Epilogue in Twentieth-Century Europe:
## Thomas Mann's "Joseph" Novels

The foregoing selections demonstrate that the universal story of Joseph and Potiphar's wife has in the past engaged the attention of some of the world's greatest authors. It is quite appropriate, therefore, that one of the giants of the literature of the twentieth century should also have turned to it for the crowning achievement of his distinguished career. The fictional tetralogy which Thomas Mann wrote on the theme of Joseph and his brothers was admittedly a sort of Midrash or commentary on the Bible account. At the same time, it was also a new telling of the story. Inevitably, the novels drew upon the lore that had accumulated about the story in over three millennia—particularly that portion of it here surveyed.

The third part of the tetralogy, *Joseph in Egypt,* published in two volumes, provides the substance of the Potiphar's wife episode; indeed, its second volume is given over entirely to an exegesis of the few verses of Genesis 39. Portions of the narrative spill over into the fourth and concluding installment, *Joseph the Provider.* In a sense, however, the whole massive undertaking, from the *Tales of Jacob* on, is steeped in the various traditions that have nourished the selections in the present volume.

As will be shown in greater detail, Mann was acquainted with, and made use of, not only the Bible story that formed his text, as it were, but also its older Egyptian analogue and possible source. He absorbed much of the spirit of the Greek variant and makes allusion to it. He rifled the Moslem accounts for scenes and insights, picking and choosing according to his taste. There is a good possibility that he knew, in German translation, the story of "Siyawush and Sudaba," and we have no reason to suppose that so scholarly an author as Mann did not have at least a passing acquaintance with some of the medieval European variants, here represented by the Spanish *Book of the Wiles of Women.* Finally, it is not a very large assumption that he was familiar with the Kunala legend, since

while he was composing the Joseph tetralogy he took time out
to retell an old Indian story in *The Transposed Heads*.

✠

What gives Mann's retelling of the Joseph and Potiphar's
wife episode its unique character is precisely the self-consciousness with which it is retold. When Joseph or Osarsiph is being
hard pressed by his mistress to betray his master and lie with
her, he urges that she should not allow to come to pass what
the Bible story tells us did in fact come to pass:

> Hearken, Eni, and in God's name recall your understand-
> ing for that which I would say, for my words will stand,
> and when our story comes into the mouths of the people,
> so will it sound. For all that happens can become history
> and literature, and it may easily be that we are the stuff
> of history. Therefore have a care for yourself and take
> pity upon your story, that you do not become a warning
> in it and the mother of sin. Much could I say and give
> words to many involved matters, to resist your desire and
> mine own; but for the people's mouth, should it come to
> be put into it, will I say the simplest and most pertinent
> thing, which every child can understand, thus: . . .

There follow verbatim the familiar words of the eighth and
ninth verses of Genesis 39:

> My master hath committed all that he hath to my hand;
> there is none greater in this house than I; neither hath he
> kept back anything from me but thee, because thou art
> his wife. How then can I do this great wickedness, and
> sin against God?

A certain degree of self-consciousness has no doubt been
present in every reiteration of this story in its long history, but
it is perhaps most prominent in this version from our own self-
conscious age. Mann's belief that the past is a bottomless well
which is never fathomed, and that every supposed source has
in turn its source, leads him to push the present story back
even beyond the historical evidences of it. He takes it back to
the oldest myths of the human race, in which are already to

be found dim adumbrations of that fatal confrontation between the Chaste Youth and the Lustful Stepmother. Mann strikes these anthropological chords frequently in his account of Osarsiph's resistance of Mut-em-enet or Eni (as he variously calls the wife of Potiphar). When the youth rejects the woman's loaded offer to make feast garments for him to wear if he will but lie with her, Mann is recalling not only the charmingly simple offer of Anpu's wife, or the self-deluding mother-feelings of Jami's Zulaikha, but something analogous to both, which happened a long time before even the telling of the Egyptian folktale. Mann says that present in Osarsiph's mind was the identity of his case with that of the Babylonian hero Gilgamesh when "Ishtar made assault on his beauty and said: 'Come, then, Gilgamesh, thou shalt mate with me and give me thy fruit,' and promised many splendid presents in return for his compliance." Osarsiph simply says: ". . . in him [i.e., Gilgamesh] I see myself, as through myself I understand him," to which the author elsewhere adds: ". . . he had moments when he understood Gilgamesh, who in furious impatience one day tore out the phallus of the sacred bull and flung it in Ishtar's face."

The incest phobia that has been noted in several of the variants has likewise its mythic counterpart, as Mann points out. When Joseph raises the moral question of his yielding to, as it were, a surrogate mother, his mistress does not assert that he is not the true son of Potiphar (which she truthfully could have done). Rather, she boldly proclaims that in the mythic archetypal pattern of life, "with his mother each man sleeps—the woman is the mother of the world, her son is her husband, and every man begets upon his mother. . . ." She then equates herself to Isis, who was both sister and wife to Osiris, the mangled and resurrected god whose career is conceived of as a prototype of Joseph's. In this Jungian-Frazerian world, the incest phobia is in the heart of the son and not the mother, as it also was in the classical and the Buddhist variants of the story.

On the purely naturalistic levels, too, Mann attributes to his Biblical hero an awareness of the literary antecedents of his situation. Osarsiph knows the Egyptian tale of Anpu and Bata and does not hesitate to use it for his own instruction in a moment of crisis. Taunted by the wife of Potiphar with the innuendo that he is rejecting her because of his impotence, he bitterly replies:

> "Do you think so? . . . then be quiet. For if it were with me as you pretend to think, then were it easy, and my temptation were not like a dragon and a roaring lion. Believe me, woman, I have had the thought of putting an end to your agony and mine by making of myself what you impute to me, like the youth in one of your legends, who took a sharp leaf of the sword plant and cut himself and threw the offending member into the river for fish to devour, to witness his innocence."

This is obviously intended to recall both Bata's desperate measure and Gilgamesh's violence with the phallus of the sacred bull. The symbolistically disposed reader may wish to connect it further with Kunala's willing sacrifice of his offending fleshly eyes.

It is perhaps not too farfetched to assume that the wife of Potiphar in Mann's novel also was familiar with the tale of Anpu and Bata. When Joseph betrays his readiness for her despite the words that come out of his mouth—when, as Mann says, his flesh rose up against his spirit—her triumphal cry is "I have seen his strength!"—words very likely suggested by the admiration which Anpu's wife showed for Bata's physical prowess. It is certainly Mann's intention to imply that the Egyptian story was widely known in Joseph's day. When, later in prison, Osarsiph is discussing his lot with the warden Mai-Sachme, their discourse turns to the Egyptian tale which Joseph has recently re-enacted. The passage gives so much evidence of the formative influence of that tale on Mann's account (although there are slighting references to the portions of it omitted in this anthology) that it ought to be quoted at length. Mai-Sachme is counseling Joseph:

> "When I hear of a woman being led astray by a man, I chuckle to myself, for it sounds like a joke and I think: By the great Triad! Because, after all, we know whose business seduction has been since the time of the gods and it was not the business of us stupid men. Do you know the story of the Two Brothers?" . . .

"I know it well, my lord," answered Joseph. "For I had often to read it aloud to my master, Pharaoh's friend, and I also had to copy it out fair for him, with black and red ink."

"It will continue to be copied," said the commandant; "it is a capital invention not only in its style, which carries conviction even though the episodes are really almost incredible when one thinks them over calmly, for instance where the queen conceives through a splinter which flies into her mouth from the wood of the persea tree, which is too contradictory to medical experience to be taken literally. But despite that the story is likelife, as when the wife of Anup leans against the youth Bata, finding him great in strength, and says to him: 'Come, let us have joy in each other for a little and I will make thee two feast-garments,' and when Bata cries to his brother: 'Woe is me, she has turned all to ill!' and before his eyes cuts off his manhood with the blade of the sword-reed and gives it to the fishes to eat—that is thrilling. Later on, the narrative degenerates and becomes unbelievable; yet it is edifying too when Bata turns himself into a Hapi-bull and speaks: 'I shall be a wonder of a Hapi and the whole land will exult in me,' and makes himself known and says: 'I am Bata, lo, I live still and am the sacred bull of God.' These are, of course, fantastic inventions; but yet how plastically life does sometimes pour itself into the most extraordinary forms of the creative fancy!"

✠

During the composition of the "Joseph" novels, Mann was engaged in a lengthy correspondence with the Hungarian classical scholar Karol Kerenyi. When *Joseph in Egypt* appeared, Kerenyi enthusiastically applauded Mann's creation of the character of Mut-em-enet, in whom he immediately recognized a newborn sister of Phaedra. There cannot be much doubt that, despite his commitment to the Biblical text for his basic story line, Mann was desirous of imparting some human attractiveness to the unlovely figure of the female in the story. And so his Potiphar's wife, like her counterpart in the Greek analogue, is made to struggle against her passion, to bite her tongue lest it utter forbidden thoughts. In her behalf the author asks: "Shall we not concede that the lot of Potiphar's wife, lewd wanton as she was in the popular legend, was a tragic one?" Mut-em-enet, though she does not meet a tragic end in Mann's comedy, is certainly his greatest contribution to the universal story of the Chaste Youth and the Lustful Stepmother, as it was the greatest contribution of Euripides. And yet nowhere in the Joseph novels does he mention Phaedra explicitly.

He does allude to Hippolytus. In his characteristically far-ranging thoughts that constantly move the story back and forth in time, he allows Joseph to speculate that:

> . . . some day the virgins of the world may mourn for me before they wed, bringing me their maiden tresses and singing a melancholy ditty in which they lament my youth and recount the tale of one who withstood the hot solicitation of a female and so doing lost his life and his repute.

This, of course, is sheer plagiarism by Joseph of the words to be spoken by the goddess Artemis about his counterpart in Euripides' drama:

> To ease you a little of your pain, know this:
> Dead, you shall have honor in Trozen,
> And girls before their wedding day shall clip
> The bright tracts of their hair,
> And there in the shades you shall reap the shadowy harvest,
> The bitter fragrance of tears . . .
>                      as elegy
> Always the musical sorrow of young girls
> And they will talk together
> Of Phaedra's love and of your death
> Remembered always. . . .

✠

We come next to possibly the most important of the sources, aside from the Bible, of Mann's account of the Potiphar's wife episode. In several places Mann acknowledges the Moslem

stories of Yusuf and Zulaikha, even though he does not particularly care for the name that they give to Potiphar's wife.
He mentions specifically the *Koran*, Firdausi's and Jami's poetic
versions, and "seventeen Persian songs . . . as well as countless
renderings by pencil and brush." The number seventeen is a
bit perplexing. He has probably misremembered the eighteen
Persian versions of the Yusuf and Zulaikha (including, however, Firdausi's and Jami's) mentioned by the Orientalist Hermann Ethe in his scholarly article on the subject. The same
article was accompanied by an abstract, in German verse, of
the poem attributed to Firdausi. Mann's reference to "Dsch-
ami's [the German spelling of Jami, retained in the English
translation] late and subtle version" indicates he had read that
also, probably in a poetic German translation. Certainly there
is ample evidence that he knew it well and made use of it.
May the allusion to "countless renderings by pencil and brush"
not be reasonably taken to include, besides such famous paint-
ings as Rembrandt's of the robe-snatching, the many Persian
miniatures illustrating one of the story's most famous scenes—
the ladies' party given by Zulaikha to spite her envious friends?

This is the scene which Edith Hamilton, in a review of
Mann's novel, unhappily singled out as an example of the farfetched character of Mann's imagination, saying:

> The court ladies who at a garden party are so thrown off
> their base by the appearance of the beautiful Joseph that
> they "cut themselves, one and all, frightfully" with their
> fruit knives—"a fearful sight, their little hands drenched
> with the red liquid"—are not like any court ladies we
> have ever known or read about.

This is, indeed, perhaps the point at which the Hellenic and
the Islamic imaginations are at their greatest polarity; yet we
have by now several times read about just such court ladies.
And it is to the credit of Thomas Mann, as an advocate of
Goethe's concept of a *Weltliteratur,* that he made this ultimate
effort to fuse into a single unity the diverse traditions that have
formed this world story.

Mann's Mut-em-enet is made to anticipate the events of
this notable party in a dream which she has very early in her
relationship with the slave Osarsiph, whom her husband has

purchased in the market. She dreams that she has cut her hand and is bleeding profusely. No one in her household helps her until the Canaanitish slave Osarsiph, seeing her plight, walks to where she is sitting, takes her hand to his mouth, and stanches the flow of blood. When she awakes from this dream, it is with a keen sense of pleasure at the thought of him. But how had she cut her hand? She was peeling a pomegranate with a sharp knife, and this reminds us of the famous later scene in the Moslem versions which Mann also in good time appropriates. His comment at that point is interesting:

> We who know the revelatory dream dreamed by Mut-em-enet at the beginning of the three years of her love can easily understand the connection between it and the ingenious, pathetic device she adopted to open the eyes of her friends.

The connection is simply that it was the dream which had first opened her own eyes to the presence of Joseph in her household. There is no doubt also a far-off recall here of the visions which made the youthful Zulaikha fall inescapably in love with Yusuf.

The somewhat roguish Osarsiph and the melancholy Potiphar (or, as he is called, Petepre) are typical Mann characters, and they owe more to his invention than to the sources which he used for the incidents of his fiction. Petepre's being emasculated, which Mann takes from Jami, well suits the type of person who has been set apart from life, and he the better represents spirit against body in Mann's familiar dichotomy. His sympathy is therefore naturally with Joseph, whose last-moment resistance of the temptress is due to the vision of the face of his father: "an image of memory and admonition, the father's in a broad and general sense." Now there is nothing to this effect in Genesis, but the *Koran*, as we have seen, speaks obscurely of "the demonstration of his Lord" and Jami reports that Yusuf's recognition of the pagan idol worshipped by Zulaikha awakened him from his lax moral state and recalled him to his spiritual mission.

Lest, however, the impression be left that Mann's story follows the Moslem versions with any greater fidelity than it does the Egyptian or the Biblical, it is perhaps best to quote in full Mann's final word on the matter. Just as he disposes of the story of Anpu and Bata with an ironic mixture of admiration and impatience, so he assigns to Jami's symbolical romance its subordinate place in the formulation of his own story:

> The people, and to please them the poets, an all too easy-going breed, have spun out in a variety of ways this tale of Joseph and Potiphar's wife, which was only an episode, if an important one, in the life of Jacob's son. Any possibility of more to follow was, of course, completely excluded by the final catastrophe. But they have written sentimental continuations and give it a predominant place within the Joseph story. In their hands it becomes a sugary romance with a proper happy ending. According to these poetasters, the temptress—who goes by the name of Zuleika, a fact at which we can only shrug our shoulders—after she had got Joseph into prison, withdrew full of remorse into a "hut" and there lived only for the expiation of her sins. Meanwhile, through the death of her husband she became a widow. But when Yusuf (meaning Joseph) was about to be freed out of the prison, he had refused to have his "chains" removed until the female aristocracy of the country had come before Pharaoh's throne and borne witness to his innocence. Accordingly the entire nobility of the sex had come before the king and with one voice the whole lovely bevy had announced that Joseph was the prince and pattern of purity, the very freshest ornament in her crown. After which Zuleika took the floor and made public confession that she alone had been the offender, and he an angel. The shameful crime was hers, she frankly avowed it; but now she was purified and gladly bore the shame and disgrace. Even after Joseph's elevation she continued to do penance, growing old and grey in the process. Only on the festal day when Father Jacob made his alleged triumphal entry into Egypt—and thus at a time when Joseph was actually the father of two sons—did the pair meet again. Joseph had forgiven the old woman, and as a reward heaven had restored all her former seductive beauty; whereupon Joseph had most romantically married her, and thus, after all these tribulations, her old wish came true, and they "put their heads and feet together."

"All that," Mann adds in a postscript, "is just Persian musk and attar of roses. It has nothing whatever to do with the facts." If he had not so emphatically insisted that the ladies' party scene—which is not in the Bible—was an authentic part of the whole story, the irony of the above passage might escape us.

✠

One last touch was needed to make this old, old story new, which it is in the nature of myth to do. This Mann imparts to it by an allusion to events contemporary with the composition of the novel although suggested by a verse in Genesis. The words of Potiphar's wife after her false accusation were: "See, he hath brought an Hebrew unto us to mock us." Mann's Mut-em-enet speaks at much greater length to the feast-drunken Egyptian mob that has gathered in response to her outcry. The author alludes angrily to "that well-known speech which at all times has been counted against her by all men; which even I, despite all I have done for Mut-em-enet's saga and cause, cannot fail to condemn." Employing the demagogic techniques of the National Socialists who had driven Mann from his native land (he had to leave behind the manuscript of this very novel!), Mut exploits the racial prejudices of the mob by referring to them as "Egyptian brothers" and by depicting Joseph as "this Hebrew youth who came down out of his wretched country to Egypt, Osiris's beautiful garden, the throne of Re, the horizon of the good spirit."

Her success in this undertaking is the measure of her movement out of the sphere of the sympathetic yet tragic Phaedra (a "foreigner" among Athenians), and the sympathetic because contrite Zulaikha. She now moves back into the sphere of the unattractive hussy of the Bible. Only the exigencies of the European political situation in which the character was conceived and brought into being by Mann can excuse his ultimate betrayal of her in this way. Yet, perhaps the character of the Lustful Stepmother has always been subject to such a movement back and forth between what have been referred to as the Hebraistic and the Hellenistic polarities. The dualism was certainly inherent in all of Mann's work; the wisdom of the moment would have to decide which pole was to feel the sharper edge of his irony. Meanwhile, his Joseph novels remind us how inextricably this familiar story is interwoven with both the history and the literature of the whole human race.

# Bibliographical Notes

## Chapter I
### Prologue in the Ancient Near East: The Archetypal Folktale

The discussion of the origin and dissemination of folktales is drawn from Stith Thompson's *The Folktale* (Dryden Press, New York, 1946) and from Andrew Lang's *Myth, Religion and Ritual* (Longmans Green, 1913), the quotation being taken from Volume II, page 318. Sir Richard Burton's observation is made in a footnote on page 127 of Volume VI of his *The Book of the Thousand Nights and One Night*, 10 vols. (Burton Club, n.p., n.d.). The story of Crispus and Fausta is told in Chapter XVIII of Gibbon's *Decline and Fall of the Roman Empire*.

✠

Maurice Bloomfield's article was published in *Transactions and Proceedings of the American Philological Association*, edited by Clarence P. Hill (Western Reserve University, Cleveland, 1923), Volume I, pages 141ff. Donald Keene's article is to be found in *The Yearbook of Comparative and General Literature*, No. 11, Supplement (University of Indiana, 1962), pages 162–71. I have relied heavily upon it for my later discussion of the Buddhist variants. Stith Thompson's *Motif-Index of Folk-Literature* (1955) was published by Indiana University Press in a revised and enlarged edition in six volumes. The two listings are under K2111 and T418. His *Tales of the North American Indian* (Harvard University Press, Cambridge, 1929) tells the story of "The Jealous Father" on page 116. Eugene O'Neill's *Desire under the Elms* has been included as an analogue in *Phaedra and Hippolytus: Myth and Dramatic Form*, edited by James L. Sanderson and Irwin Gopnik (Houghton-Mifflin, Boston, 1966). N. M. Penzer's notation is in *The Ocean of Story, Being C. H. Tawney's Translation of Somadeva's Katha Sarit Sagara (or Ocean of Streams of Story)*, 10 vols. (C. J. Sawyer, London, 1924–28), Volume II, page 120, note 2.

✠

For a full analysis of the story of "Anpu and Bata" the reader is referred to Mr. Petrie's "Remarks" following his edition of the tale and to Andrew Lang's *Myth, Ritual and Religion* (cited above). Henry H. Halley in *Bible Handbook* (Zondervan Publishing House, Minneapolis, 1962), page 66, suggests the Biblical incident as the source of the Egyptian folktale. Donald Keene (cited above), among others, considers the reverse possibility.

## CHAPTER II
### Biblical Narrative

For the Rabbinical commentaries on the Genesis account, I have used *Midrash Rabbah*, the Genesis volume (II), translated by Rabbi Dr. H. Freedman (London, 1939), pages 802–11. Mark Twain's words I owe to Louis J. Budd's "Mark Twain on Joseph the Patriarch," *American Quarterly*, XVI (Winter, 1964), pages 577*ff.*

✠

The Hellenistic background is given by Moses Hadas in his *Hellenistic Culture: Fusion and Diffusion* (Columbia University Press, New York, 1959) and by Martin Braun in his *History and Romance in Graeco-Oriental Literature* (Basil Blackwell, Oxford, 1938). *The Testament of Joseph* is to be found in R. H. Charles' *The Apocrypha and Pseudepigrapha of the Old Testament* (University Press, Oxford, 1913), Volume I, pages 346*ff.* Aylett's English versification has been consulted in microfilm at Columbia University Library (FP578), the quotation coming from page 56 of the Folger Library text. The world history of the Hebrew-Christian story of Joseph is traced in Hans Priebatsch's *Die Josephgeschichte in der Weltliteratur, Eine Legendgeschichtliche Studie* (M. und H. Marcus Verlag, Breslau, 1937). The story of its German adaptations is covered in a monograph by Margarete Nabholz-Oberlin, *Der Josephroman in der deutschen Literatur von Grimmelshausen bis Thomas Mann* (Bauer, Marburg, 1950). Thomas Mann's comments on the Joseph film are quoted from John C. Thirlwall's *In Another Language* (Alfred A. Knopf, New York, 1966), pages 144–45. The dramatic presentations in English referred to are discussed by Louis J. Budd in the article cited at the beginning of the notes to this chapter.

## CHAPTER III
### Classical Drama

For Greek legends on the Potiphar's wife theme, see Robert Graves, *Greek Myths*, 2 vols. (Penguin, 1955), Volume I, pages 252 and

356. Euripides' plays on this theme are discussed by P. W. Harsh, *A Handbook of Classical Drama* (Stanford University Press, Stanford, 1944), Chapter 3, "Euripides." A discussion of the Hippolytus myth by Hazel Barnes and a new translation of Euripides' play by Donald Sutherland may be found in *Hippolytus in Drama and Myth* (University of Nebraska Press, Lincoln, 1960). See also *Phaedra and Hippolytus: Myth and Dramatic Form* (cited in Chapter I, above) for the text of five plays on the theme, including Seneca's and Jeffers', as well as critical discussions. Walter Pater's narrative essay "Hippolytus Veiled" is in *Greek Studies* (Macmillan, London, 1910). Moses Hadas treats fully the later Greek variants in *Hellenistic Culture* (cited in notes to Chapter II, above). David Grene's translation of *Hippolytus* is published by the University of Chicago Press, Chicago, 1924 and Rex Warner's by the Bodley Head Ltd. (London, 1949). The comments of Ian Fletcher and D. S. Carne-Ross are taken from the introduction to an earlier version of their translation published in *Adam: International Review* (London, Autumn, 1953) Volume II, Number 4, page 15. *Heliodorus: an Aethopian Romance,* translated by Thomas Underdowne in 1587, may be consulted in a revised edition by F. A. Wright (George Routledge and Sons, London, n.d.).

✠

The quotations from Racine's 1677 Preface to his *Phèdre* are, with permission, by Howard E. Hugo from *World Masterpieces,* edited by Maynard Mack and others (W. W. Norton, New York, 1956), Volume II, pages 1260–62. Robert Lowell's translation of *Phèdre* is in *Phaedra and Figaro* by Robert Lowell and Jacques Barzun (Farrar, Straus and Cudahy, New York, 1961). John Dryden's remarks about Hippolytus are taken from *Types of English Drama, 1660–1780,* edited by David Harrison Stevens (Ginn and Company, Boston and New York, 1923), page 134. The lines from *Aureng-Zebe* may be read in the same book page 110, lines 115*ff.*

✠

Mr. Rexroth's *One Hundred Poems from the Japanese* was published by New Directions in 1955. His knowledge of the Japanese Noh drama is revealed in an article on the plays of William Butler Yeats in the volume called *Bird in the Bush* (New Directions, Norfolk, Conn., 1947). He has admitted to me personally that the Buddhist allusions in his *Phaedra* are not mere accidents.

## CHAPTER IV
### Moslem Parable

For the *Koran,* see Richard Bell, *Introduction to the Qur'an* (Edinburgh University Press, Edinburgh, 1953). Louis Ginzberg's *Legends of the Jews* (Jewish Publications Society of America, Philadelphia, 1910), Volume II, page 44 has a section on "Joseph and Zuleika."

✠

The best discussions of the Moslem variants are by Hermann Ethe in "Firdausi's Yusuf und Zulikha," *Berichte des VII Internationalen Orientalisten-Congresses* (Vienna, 1889), pages 19*ff.;* and E. J. W. Gibb, *A History of Ottoman Poetry,* Volume II, edited by E. G. Browne (Scribner's, London, 1902), pages 142*ff.* For further discussion, including the authorship of the "Yusuf and Zulaikha" attributed to Firdausi, see E. G. Browne's *A Literary History of Persia,* Volume II, pages 146–47, and Volume III, pages 531–33; and Arthur J. Arberry's *Classical Persian Literature* (George Allen and Unwin, London, 1958), pages 44 and 442.

✠

The German adaptations of the Joseph story are covered in Margarete Nabholz-Oberlin's monograph cited in the notes to Chapter II, above. For Josephus' treatment of the story, see *The Complete Works of Josephus,* a new, revised edition based on Havercamp's translation (Bigelow, Brown and Company, New York, n.d.), Volume I, pages 81–86, "Concerning the Signal Chastity of Joseph." Louis N. Parker's *Joseph and His Brethren* was published by John Lane (London, 1913). See notes under Chapter II, for Louis J. Budd's article on dramatic presentations, including Parker's.

## CHAPTER V
### Buddhist Homily

The Indian variants are mentioned in the article by Maurice Bloomfield cited in the notes to Chapter I; to him is also owed the summary of the mother tabu in Indian literature. The *Jataka* version may be read in Edward B. Cowell's edition (Luzac & Co., London, 1957), Volume III, page 116, Number 472.

✠

For the later Buddhist accounts I have relied upon Donald Keene's article cited in the notes to Chapter I. Hsuan Tsiang's version may be found in Samuel Beal's translation, *Chinese Accounts of India*, new edition (Susil Gupta Ltd., Calcutta, 1958), pages 181*ff.*

CHAPTER VI
Medieval Epic and Fabliau

I am grateful to Mr. Jerome Fried, formerly of New Directions, for calling to my attention the Celtic analogue, "The Death of Mael Fothartaig Son of Ronan," *Early Irish Literature* by Myles Dillon (University of Chicago, 1948). John R. Reinhard's article entitled "Florismondo" is in the *Publications of the Modern Language Association*, XXXVIII, No. 3 (September, 1923), pages 472*ff.*; see especially note 102 on page 456. Sir C. J. Coyajee's "Some Shahnameh Legends and Their Chinese Parallels" appeared in *The Journal and Proceedings of the Asiatic Society of Bengal*, N.S. XXIV (Calcutta, 1928), pages 177–202.

✠

The following sources have been tapped for the discussion of *The Book of Sindibad* and its Near Eastern and European progeny:
 1) John E. Keller's introduction to his translation of *The Book of the Wiles of Women*, M.L.A. Translation Series, No. 2, University of North Carolina Press (Chapel Hill, 1956);
 2) Urban T. Holmes' *A History of Old French Literature* (F. S. Crofts, New York, 1937), especially the chapter on "The Fabliau and the Tale";
 3) Killis Campbell's "A Study of *The Seven Sages* with Special Reference to the Middle English Versions," *PMLA*, Volume XIV, Number 1, 1899, pages 1*ff.*;
 4) W. A. Clouston's *Popular Tales and Fictions* (Blackwood and Sons, London, 1887), 2 vols., Volume II, Appendix XI, pages 499*ff.*
The English medievalist referred to is J. W. H. Atkins, "Metrical Romances, 1200–1500," *Cambridge History of English Literature* (Cambridge University Press, Cambridge, 1908), Volume I, Chapter XIV. Sir Richard Burton's remarks are in a footnote of his translation of the Arabian Nights cited in the notes to Chapter I above.

CHAPTER VII

Epilogue in the Twentieth Century:
Thomas Mann's "Joseph" Novels

Kate Hamburger's *Thomas Mann's Roman "Joseph und Seine Brueder"* (Berman-Fischer, Stockholm, 1945) is the only full-length treatment of Mann's tetralogy; Harry Schlochower's *Thomas Mann's Joseph Story* (Knopf, New York, 1938) is slight. Margarete Nabholz-Oberlin's monograph cited in the notes to Chapter II, above, is a useful historical study. Mann's own Library of Congress lecture on "The Joseph Novels," reprinted in *The Stature of Thomas Mann,* edited by Charles Neider (New Directions, Norfolk, Conn., 1948), was delivered before the appearance of the last volume but gives his general view of the myth he was treating.

✠

The correspondence with Karol Kerenyi is published in the latter's *Romandichtung und Mythologie* (Rhein-Verlag, Zurich, 1945).

✠

Translations of excerpts from "Firdausi's" *Yusuf and Zulaikha* by O. M. von Schlechta-Wssehrd accompany the article by Hermann Ethe cited in the notes to Chapter IV, above. The metrical translation of Jami's poems was made by V. E. von Rosenzweig-Schwannau (Schmid, Vienna, 1824).

Edith Hamilton's review of *Joseph in Egypt* appeared in *Saturday Review of Literature,* September 3, 1938, page 11.

✠

An article by Julius Bab in the Neider volume, above, discloses that some of Mut-em-enet's passionate words to Osarsiph were paraphrases of Mann's own youthful love verses. Mark Van Doren's essay *"Joseph and His Brothers:* a Comedy in Four Parts," in *Thomas Mann: a Collection of Critical Essays,* edited by Henry Hatfield (Prentice-Hall, Englewood Cliffs, N.J., 1964), defends Mann's ironic treatment of Mut-em-enet.